D1610292

Digital Death, Digital Assets and Post-Mortem Privacy

Future Law

Series Editors: Burkhard Schafer and Edina Harbinja

Books in the series are critical and topic-led, reflecting the global jurisdiction of technology and culture interacting with law. Each title responds to cutting-edge debates in the field where technology interacts with culture to challenge the ability of law to react to frequently unprecedented scenarios.

Series Editors

Burkhard Schafer is Professor of Computational Legal Theory at the University of Edinburgh

Edina Harbinja is Reader in Media/Privacy Law at Aston University

Available titles

Buying Your Self on the Internet: Wrap Contracts and Personal Genomics
Andelka M Phillips

Digisprudence: Code as Law Rebooted
Laurence E Diver

Future Law: Emerging Technology, Regulation and Ethics
Lilian Edwards, Burkhard Schafer and Edina Harbinja (eds)

Technology, Innovation and Access to Justice: Dialogues on the Future of Law
Siddharth Peter de Souza and Maximilian Spohr (eds)

Digital Death, Digital Assets and Post-Mortem Privacy
Edina Harbinja

edinburghuniversitypress.com/series/fl

Digital Death, Digital Assets and Post-Mortem Privacy

Edina Harbinja

EDINBURGH
University Press

Edinburgh University Press is one of the leading university presses in the UK. We publish academic books and journals in our selected subject areas across the humanities and social sciences, combining cutting-edge scholarship with high editorial and production values to produce academic works of lasting importance. For more information visit our website: edinburghuniversitypress.com

Edinburgh University Press Ltd
The Tun – Holyrood Road
12(2f) Jackson's Entry
Edinburgh EH8 8PJ

Typeset in 11/13pt Adobe Garamond Pro
by Manila Typesetting Company, and
printed and bound in Great Britain

A CIP record for this book is available from the British Library

ISBN 978 1 4744 8536 4 (hardback)
ISBN 978 1 4744 8538 8 (webready PDF)
ISBN 978 1 4744 8539 5 (epub)

Contents

Acknowledgements

I have never been a fan of lengthy acknowledgements that thank all the humans who have been there on a long and, often, exhausting writer's journey. They know who they are, and if I have not expressed my love and gratitude in person, this won't do much.

Just briefly, to my great academic inspiration, more than a friend – Prof. Lilian Edwards – my gratitude, friendship and love. I have been fortunate to have met you and have had you by my side in completing my PhD and starting an incredible academic adventure.

Death Girl

Table of Cases

European Cases (European Court of Human Rights and Court of Justice of the European Union)

Germany

United Kingdom

United States

Table of Legislation

Treaties, Conventions and other Documents

1

Introduction

It has been nearly twenty years since the issue of digital assets and death was first discussed in the media. Nevertheless, there is still little clarity in the law in most places. In 2005, a judgment was handed down in the US, *In re Ellsworth*,[1] where the family of a US Marine, Justin Ellsworth, killed in Iraq, requested access to his emails stored in his Yahoo! account. Yahoo! refused, referring to its terms of service, which banned access to all third parties on death. Yahoo! claimed that the law prohibits it from disclosing deceased users' personal communications without a court order. The family argued that as his heirs, they should be given access to Justin's emails and the account, his sent and received emails, as his last words. Yahoo!, on the other hand, had a non-survivorship policy, and there was a risk that Ellsworth's account could have been deleted for good. The judge allowed Yahoo! to enforce its privacy policy and did not order the transfer of the account credentials. Instead, he made an order requiring Yahoo! to enable access to the deceased's account content by providing the family with a CD containing copies of the emails. The media reported that Yahoo! initially provided the emails received by Justin Ellsworth on a CD and, after the family complained again, allegedly subsequently sent paper copies of the emails.[2]

In a more recent case in Germany, the parents of a fifteen-year-old girl who allegedly committed suicide wanted to access the account and private messages to understand why it happened. Facebook refused to grant access to the deceased girl's Facebook account to her parents, arguing that its duty

[1] No 2005-296, 651-DE (Mich Prob Ct 2005).

[2] A Kulesza, 'What happens to your Facebook account when you die?' *Blog* (3 February 2012) <http://blogs.lawyers.com/2012/02/what-happens-to-facebook-account-when-you-die/>; Associated Press release, *justinellsworth.net* (21 April 2005) <http://www.justinellsworth.net/email/ap-apr05.htm> last accessed 30 January 2022.

of confidentiality was owed to her and her contacts.[3] The Court of Appeal in Berlin upheld Facebook's decision, but the Federal Court of Justice overturned this, applying the law and the principle of universal succession (i.e. that heirs 'step into the deceased's shoes' for all her rights and obligations).[4]

In another US case, *In re Scandalios*,[5] Ric Swezey died unexpectedly in 2017. His will did not explicitly authorise his husband, Nicholas Scandalios, to access his digital assets, including many family photos in his Apple account. Unsurprisingly, Apple iCloud's terms and conditions stated that 'any rights to your Apple ID or content within your account terminate upon your death', unless required by law. However, the New York County Surrogate's Court ordered Apple to give the deceased's husband and the executor of the estate access to the deceased's Apple account. In 2015, Rachel Thompson was denied access to her late husband's phone in a similar UK case, leaving the family photos and videos locked away. Rachel wanted to gain access to her husband's account and share the photos and videos with their daughter. Apple refused this request and said they would only grant her access if she got a court order to that effect. A court order was made in 2019 by the Central London County Court judge.[6] The judge commented that the law should be reformed to provide clarity in future cases, which are likely to be frequent.

We have seen numerous other court cases and media stories that resemble those above. More recently, Western media have reported an increased number of stories involving the creation of deep fakes and chatbots of the deceased, which raised a few eyebrows on Twitter and sparked patchy interest in this area. It also reminded some of the Black Mirror episode 'Be Right Back'[7] and all the ethical, legal and social issues it illustrated so aptly.[8]

[3] BBC News, 'Facebook ruling: German court grants parents rights to dead daughter's account' *BBC News* (12 July 2018) <https://www.bbc.com/news/world-europe-44804599> last accessed 30 January 2022.

[4] Kammergericht, Urteil vom 31. Mai 2017, Aktenzeichen 21 U 9/16 <https://www.berlin.de/gerichte/presse/pressemitteilungen-der-ordentlichen-gerichtsbarkeit/2017/pressemitteilung.596076.php> last accessed 30 January 2022; appealed BGH, 12 July 2018, Docket No III ZR 183/17.

[5] 2017-2976/A NY Surr Ct 2019.

[6] Mark Bridge, 'Widow wins long battle for iPhone family photos' *Times* (19 May 2019) <https://www.thetimes.co.uk/article/widow-wins-long-battle-for-iphone-family-photos-h7mv9bw7t> last accessed 30 January 2022.

[7] Season 2, Episode 1, 11 February 2013. Series currently available on Netflix and More4.

[8] For a commentary, see L Edwards and E Harbinja, '"Be right back": What rights do we have over post-mortem avatars of ourselves?' in L Edwards, B Schafer and E Harbinja (eds), *Future Law: Emerging Technology, Regulation and Ethics* (Edinburgh University Press 2020).

This book tackles key legal and ethical issues illustrated in the scenarios above and elsewhere. It provides the first comprehensive academic account of the transmission of digital assets on death in the UK and more widely.[9] The book also builds on the most relevant research around digital death and dying in the humanities and social sciences.[10]

To achieve this overall aim, in Chapters 2 and 3, I will set out the book's theoretical framework. In Chapter 2, I will consider the theory and doctrine of property, and in Chapter 3, the focus will shift to considerations of autonomy, testamentary freedom and post-mortem privacy. This will enable me to set out an adequate background and underpinnings for case studies in Chapters 4, 5 and 6 and offer suggestions and solutions in Chapter 7.

The first part of the book is thus primarily theoretical, looking at theories and doctrines of property, autonomy, post-mortem privacy, postmortal privacy and digital immortality, which are the key questions to answer before looking at digital legacy and the legal nature of digital assets in more detail.[11] The consideration of property is vital for one fundamental reason. If a digital asset is property, this has to be established clearly at the outset. If an asset can be considered property of the deceased user, it forms a part of an estate and transmits on death in most countries. The same is valid for intellectual property (IP) (primarily copyright), arguably a subset of property. Even if we reject the categorisation of IP as property, copyright protection transmits on death and lasts for seventy years post-mortem in most Western countries. Whereas copyright protection has been harmonised to a great extent within these jurisdictions, the doctrinal and normative conceptions of property vary by jurisdiction, especially regarding common and civil law. This lack of harmonisation is vital since digital assets are typically located in a transnational space, for example on a server physically located in Ireland, owned

[9] E Harbinja, *Legal Aspects of Transmission of Digital Assets on Death* (PhD thesis, University of Strathclyde 2017).

[10] MH Jacobsen (ed.), *Postmortal Society: Towards a Sociology of Immortality* (Routledge 2017); R Kastenbaum, *On Our Way: The Final Passage through Life and Death (Life Passages)* (University of California Press 2004); C Öhman and L Floridi, 'The political economy of death in the age of information: A critical approach to the digital afterlife industry' (2017) 27 *Minds & Machines* 639.

[11] In addition to the above literature on death and dying, the theory part focuses on key justifications of property and incidents of property in the works of Bentham, Locke, Hegel, Radin, Honoré, Hohfeld, Penner, Bridge and Marx. In terms of autonomy and privacy, key authors that the book considers are Mill, Locke, Bentham, Rawls, Hegel, Henkin, Cohen, Nissenbaum, Schwartz, Samuelson, Desai, Edwards, Schafer, Floridi and Bernal. In terms of post-mortem and postmortal privacy, I build on my own work in the area and the work of Birnhack, Desai, Edwards, Buitelaar and Malgieri.

by a US company, and accessed by and created by users from many different jurisdictions.

Conversely, if a digital asset is not an object of property, it would be an aspect of post-mortem privacy, which I started developing earlier in my work, referring to theories of autonomy, privacy and data protection.[12] This concept is then used as a basis for a new concept of postmortal privacy, which includes philosophical conceptions of the informational body, sociological research around digital immortality and technological developments of artificial intelligence (AI).[13]

I will then test these theories and issues of contract law and copyright on chosen case studies of digital assets. Digital assets include a wide variety of different assets, and their number is growing with the development of new technologies (business accounts, emails, social networks, games, personal data, domain names, virtual currencies, etc.). Due to their number and features, it is argued that it would not be viable to look at the legal nature, and consequently the transmission on death, of all these different assets. Therefore, using the theoretical framework set out in the following two chapters, the book analyses the three most typical and widely used types of assets, that is, emails, social networks and virtual worlds and games (virtual realities). It is not argued here that these assets are the most economically valuable or will continue being as significant as technology develops. Instead, the examples are chosen for their current prominence, usage, user base and complexities surrounding their legal nature. These assets are perhaps most intrinsically intertwined in the everyday life of an average user and, since the focus of the book is on the users and not on the businesses, the examples are appropriate. I have already analysed aspects of the transmission of the chosen digital assets in my earlier work.[14] This book will develop this research further, update and consolidate findings and recommendations, and offer novel theoretical and practical considerations under a more coherent legal framework.

[12] In particular, E Harbinja, 'Post-mortem privacy 2.0: Theory, law and technology' (2017) 31 *International Review of Law, Computers & Technology* 26; Harbinja, *Legal Aspects* (n 9).

[13] E Harbinja, 'The "new(ish)" property, informational bodies, and postmortality' in M Savin-Baden and V Mason-Robbie (eds), *Digital Afterlife: Death Matters in a Digital Age* (Taylor & Francis 2020) 89–106.

[14] E Harbinja, 'Virtual worlds – a legal post-mortem account' (2014) 11:3 *SCRIPTed* 273; E Harbinja, 'Virtual worlds players – consumers or citizens?' (2014) 3(4) *Internet Policy Review* 1; E Harbinja, 'Legal nature of emails: A comparative perspective' (2016) 14 *Duke Law and Technology Review* 227; E Harbinja, 'Social media and death' in L Gillies and D Mangan (eds), *The Legal Challenges of Social Media* (Edward Elgar 2017); E Harbinja, 'Emails and death: Legal issues surrounding post-mortem transmission of emails' (2019) 43(7) *Death Studies* 435.

The book will offer theoretical arguments around post-mortem and post-mortal privacy, suggestions for law reforms, technology solutions and developments, and practical advice for users. These arguments and the framework can further be used to test new types of digital assets, their legal nature, and their transmission on death. Criminal law and jurisdiction will be discussed but are not a primary consideration for the book, as these areas deserve a separate in-depth discussion and analysis.

1.1 The Concept and Value of Digital Assets

The notion of digital assets is a relatively new phenomenon, lacking a proper legal definition, with diverse meanings attributed to it. From a lay person's perspective, digital assets could be anything valuable online, any asset (account, file, document, digital footprint) that has a personal, economic or social attachment to an individual. The legal meaning, however, needs a little more precision. Determining the legal definition and nature is essential to enable adequate legal treatment and regulation. So far, there have been a few attempts to define and classify digital assets. Most definitions are inductive and try to theorise starting from the existing assets online, trying to make appropriate generalisations and classifications. Many authors interchangeably use the terms 'virtual assets' and 'digital assets'. In this book, for precision and consistency, the term 'digital assets' will be used as an umbrella term unless otherwise stated. The term 'virtual assets' will be reserved for Chapter 5 and considerations of assets in virtual worlds.

One of the most comprehensive definitions so far has been offered by Cahn. She categorises digital assets into the following: personal assets ('typically stored on a computer or smartphone or uploaded onto a website, including photographs, videos, or even music playlists'[15]), social media assets ('including websites such as Facebook and Twitter, as well as email accounts'[16]), financial assets ('bank accounts, Amazon accounts, Pay-Pal accounts, accounts with other shopping sites, or online bill payment systems'[17], and virtual currency) and business accounts (which 'generally include customer addresses and patient information'[18]). Perrone accepts and uses this categorisation.[19]

[15] N Cahn, 'Postmortem life on-line' (2011) 25 *Probate & Property* 36, 36–7.

[16] Ibid.

[17] Ibid.

[18] Ibid.

[19] M Perrone, 'What happens when we die: Estate planning of digital assets' (2012/13) 21 *CommLaw Conspectus* 185.

Due to their unique features, some assets could be included in all these categories. One example is an eBay or Instagram reputation or following, which is personal, dependent on the social interactions (user's feedback), tied to a business account and brings financial benefits. With the increased integration of online services, many platforms now include all of these categories simultaneously. For instance, Gmail, Google's email platform, might be used for business purposes, for storing photographs and videos (connected to Google Drive, Google's cloud storage service), for social network purposes (as it is connected to Google+, Google's social network site) and as a payment system (with the recent feature of sending money via Gmail, though a user's Google Wallet service in the US and UK). It is, therefore, sometimes difficult to separate and define the categories of digital assets.

Another categorisation places digital assets into the following categories: access information, tangible digital assets, intangible digital assets and metadata.[20] The access information includes account numbers and login information, which, according to Haworth, are not assets in the strict sense as they only enable access to other assets. On the other hand, tangible digital assets are digital property, held in a definable form, which are likely to be transferred and converted into physical assets (photos, documents, emails, online banking account balances, domain names, blog posts).[21] Further, intangible digital assets are those harder to conceptualise, spread over the Internet in volumes and likely needing to be deleted or shut down ('likes' on Facebook, website profiles, comments, reviews). Lastly, according to Haworth, metadata ('data about the data', histories, deleted data, code, location tags, etc.) encounters similar issues to intangible assets, being even harder to find and gain access to.[22] Therefore, in her opinion, only the category of tangible digital assets is assets and digital property *stricto sensu*.

This categorisation is quite problematic. First, most of the assets categorised as tangible for this definition will never really be converted to a physical, offline form. Log files and metadata can hardly be conceived of as digital assets, as these are just properties of an underlying system and not something that has an individual and independent value and existence. Metadata signifies some properties of other data and is derived from them, and login data serves as a tool provided by service providers for users to gain access to their other assets. As a side note, metadata can be valuable to service providers, as it provides critical analytics and indicates users' behaviours. Therefore,

[20] S Haworth, 'Laying your online self to rest: Evaluating the Uniform Fiduciary Access to Digital Assets Act' (2014) 68 *University of Miami Law Review* 535, 538.

[21] Ibid.

[22] Ibid. 539.

Haworth's definition is problematic, just like those of Hopkins and Băbeanu et al., who argue that metadata, a valuable piece of data, can also represent a type of digital asset and help detect and find other digital assets.[23]

A more general definition starts with defining the terms that coin the notion of digital assets. For instance, the *Oxford English Dictionary* defines digital as 'Of signals, information, or data: represented by a series of discrete values (commonly the numbers 0 and 1), typically for electronic storage or processing.'[24] Similarly, 'virtual' is defined as 'occurring or existing primarily online' or 'being simulated on a computer or computer network'. According to this definition, 'virtual assets are the electronic information stored on a computer or through computer-related technology'.[25] Hopkins defines a digital asset as an asset that 'exists only as a numeric encoding expressed in binary form' or 'any electronically stored information'.[26] Importantly, as rightly noted by Haworth, any definition of digital assets needs to be both broad (to encompass innovations online) and still clear enough so that everyone understands what it means.[27]

The US Uniform Law Commission Fiduciary Access to Digital Assets Committee proposed an all-encompassing definition of digital property in its first draft,[28] which includes both digital assets and digital accounts (providing

23 JP Hopkins, 'Aferlife in the cloud: Managing a digital estate' (2013) 5 *Hastings Science and Technology Law Journal* 210, 211; D Băbeanu et al., 'Strategic outlines: Between value and digital assets management' (2009) 11 *Annales Universitatis Apulensis Series Oeconomica* 318, 319.

24 *Oxford English Dictionary* (*OED*) (online edn, Oxford University Press 2016) <http://www.oed.com/> last accessed 1 August 2021.

25 American Law Institute, American Bar Association Continuing Legal Education 'Representing estate and trust beneficiaries and fiduciaries: Virtual assets' *ALI-ABA Course of Study* (14–15 July 2011) 1 <http://www.cobar.org/repository/Inside_Bar/TrustEstate/SRC/Virtual%20Asset%20Subcommittee%20Research%20%231.pdf> last accessed 1 August 2021.

26 Hopkins (n 23) 202. See similarly N Dosch, 'Overview of digital assets: Defining digital assets for the legal community' *Digital Estate Planning* (14 May 2010) <http://www.digitalestateplanning.coml> last accessed 1 August 2021, who defines a digital asset as 'any file on your computer in a storage drive or website and any online account or membership'. Conner accepts and uses this definition. See J Conner, 'Digital life after death: The issue of planning for a person's digital assets after death' (2010–11) 3 *Estate Planning & Community Property Law Journal* 301, 303.

27 Haworth (n 20) 3.

28 National Conference of Commissioners on Uniform State Laws, Drafting Committee on Fiduciary Access to Digital Assets, 'Fiduciary Access to Digital Assets Act' (15–16 February 2013 Drafting Committee Meeting) <http://www.uniformlaws.org/shared/docs/Fiduciary%20Access%20to%20Digital%20Assets/2013feb7_FADA_MtgDraft_Styled.pdf> last accessed 1 August 2021.

access to a digital asset or a digital service).[29] The second draft, from May 2013, retains this definition, clarifying that digital property does not include the content of electronic communication. However, the October 2013 draft seems less ambitious in its definition, discarding the notion of digital property and retaining only the revised concept of digital assets.[30] The July 2014 draft of the Act revised the definition once more, namely:

> 'Digital assets' include products currently in existence and yet to be invented that are available only electronically. Digital assets include electronically stored information, such as: 1) any information stored on a computer and other digital devices; 2) content uploaded onto websites, ranging from photos to documents; and 3) rights in digital property, such as domain names or digital entitlements associated with online games. . . . Both the catalogue and content of an electronic communication are covered by the term 'digital assets'.[31]

Therefore, the definition is quite inclusive and technologically neutral, as it leaves room for assets 'yet to be invented'. In addition, it includes different general types of content, such as information, content uploaded online, rights and catalogues of electronic communications (meaning log files). The definition, however, expressly excludes 'an underlying asset or liability unless the asset or liability is itself an electronic record'.[32] The Uniform Law Commission (ULC) revised the Act in December 2015, narrowing down the definition further, including only electronic records 'in which an individual has a right or interest'. Similarly to the previous draft, the ULC expressly excludes underlying assets or liabilities.[33]

[29] Ibid. '(8) "Digital asset" means information created, generated, sent, communicated, received, or stored by electronic means on a digital service or digital device and includes, without limitation, any usernames, words, characters, codes, or contract rights pursuant to the terms of service agreement that controls access to a digital account.'

[30] National Conference of Commissioners on Uniform State Laws, Drafting Committee on Fiduciary Access to Digital Assets, 'Fiduciary Access to Digital Assets Act' (22 October 2013) <http://www.uniformlaws.org/shared/docs/Fiduciary%20Access%20to%20Digital%20Assets/2013nov_FADA_Mtg_Draft.pdf> last accessed 1 August 2021.

[31] National Conference of Commissioners on Uniform State Laws, Drafting Committee on Fiduciary Access to Digital Assets, 'Fiduciary Access to Digital Assets Act' (July 2014), s 2(8) and p 9 <http://www.uniformlaws.org/shared/docs/Fiduciary%20Access%20to%20Digital%20Assets/2014_UFADAA_Final.pdf> last accessed 1 August 2021.

[32] Ibid. s 2(8).

[33] National Conference of Commissioners on Uniform State Laws, Drafting Committee on Fiduciary Access to Digital Assets, 'Revised Fiduciary Access to Digital Assets Act' (December 2015), s 2(10) <http://www.uniformlaws.org/Act.aspx?title=Fiduciary%20Access%20to%20Digital%20Assets%20Act,%20Revised%20(2015)> last accessed 1 August 2021.

A similar definition has been crafted by Lamm, a US probate attorney, emphasising that the concept includes IP and contractual rights.[34] Lamm also notes that the full access to a standard account 'isn't all that valuable to family members or fiduciaries'. He argues that 'the contents of the online account are where the financial or sentimental value is located'.[35] Conner, conversely, confuses these concepts, claiming that virtual property and digital assets are synonymous.[36] As we shall see later in this chapter, virtual property is usually used to describe a player's property in virtual worlds and games. In discussing property, Conner finds it essential to place digital assets in one of the traditional types of property, tangible or intangible. Thus, he concludes that it is difficult to make a clear distinction here, as digital assets could change their quality and become tangible from their initial intangible state (e.g. printing of photos).[37]

Edwards and Harbinja define digital assets 'widely and not exclusively to include a vast range of intangible information goods associated with the online or "digital world"', giving examples of different digital assets.[38]

To conclude, a digital asset is any asset of personal or economic value available only in an electronic form (capable of post-mortem transmission). Such an asset could have property quality, contractual relation, IP, personality right or personal data.

This book will use the case study method and analyse the legal nature of emails, social network accounts, and virtual world assets to recognise the practical difficulties. Other valuable assets, such as financial accounts (online banking), businesses (domain names, eBay, Amazon accounts), other personal assets (MP3 collections, photograph collections, etc.) are outside the scope of this book.

[34] J Lamm, 'To my son, I leave all my passwords' *Trusts and Estate Magazine* (July 2009) <http://www.gpmlaw.com/portalresource/lookup/wosid/cp-base-4-5968/media.name=/To_My_Son_I_Leave_All_My_Passwords.pdf>; J Lamm, 'What is digital property?' *Digital Passing Blog* (21 June 2010) <http://www.digitalpassing.com/2010/06/; J Lamm, 'Digital property created on the Internet every 60 seconds' *Digital Passing Blog* (20 June 2011) <http://www.digitalpassing.com/2011/06/20/digital-property-created-internet-every-60-seconds/> all last accessed 1 August 2021.

[35] J Lamm, 'Planning ahead for access to contents of a decedent's online accounts' *Digital Passing Blog* (9 February 2012) <http://www.digitalpassing.com/2012/02/09/planning-ahead-access-contents-decedent-online-accounts/> last accessed 1 August 2021.

[36] Conner (n 26) 25.

[37] Ibid.

[38] L Edwards and E Harbinja, '"What happens to my Facebook profile when I die?": Legal issues around transmission of digital assets on death' in C Maciel and V Pereira (eds), *Digital Legacy and Interaction: Post-Mortem Issues* (Springer 2013) 115.

We will, therefore, explore a few typical and currently relevant digital assets as examples and case studies, that is, emails, social networks sites and virtual worlds/games. As technology develops, models of protecting and transmitting these assets proposed herein could probably be more readily applicable to other kinds of emerging communications, social networks, and other virtual technologies and communities. I plan to continue exploring the nature of some other digital assets (business, financial, etc.) in future research.

The questions around the significance of this area often revolve around this critical consideration: are digital assets valuable at all? The value, of course, does not only need to be monetary; personal attachments and memories are also valuables for individuals. These are, however, harder to measure and conceptualise; their place in succession laws is not as prominent as the place of pecuniary interests since it is the primary function of this area of law to enable and facilitate the transfer of wealth.

Let us consider some general statistics first. In the UK, 92 per cent of adults and almost all adults aged sixteen to forty-four years are recent Internet users. The proportion of those aged seventy-five years and over who are recent Internet users grew from 29 per cent in 2013 to 54 per cent in 2020.[39] The vast majority of these users use social media, all of whom will die, leaving behind digital assets, personal data and other digital remains. Research predicts that on Facebook, for instance, the dead will outnumber the living within fifty years.[40] There is clear evidence of an increased online presence during the COVID-19 pandemic, which will result in an even greater value of digital remains. The issues are further exacerbated by the emergence of new forms of digital death industry/death entrepreneurs during the pandemic, which offer inadequate solutions for digital assets management, online mourning and grief, digital funerals, and so on (e.g. LastPass, SocialEmbers, Eternime).

So, how valuable could digital assets be? According to a 2011 survey from McAfee, Intel's security-technology unit, Americans valued their digital assets, on average, at almost $55,000.[41] World Internet users have roughly $37,438 in digital assets across a variety of digital devices and platforms. These assets

[39] Office for National Statistics, 'Internet access – households and individuals, Great Britain: 2020' (7 August 2020) <https://www.ons.gov.uk/peoplepopulationandcommunity/householdcharacteristics/homeinternetandsocialmediausage/bulletins/internetaccesshouseholdsandindividuals/2020> last accessed 1 August 2021.

[40] C Öhman and D Watson, 'Are the dead taking over Facebook? A big data approach to the future of death online' (2019) *Big Data & Society* 1.

[41] Fiduciary Access to Digital Assets Act (n 33) s 4. See also A Dale, 'More estate plans account for "digital assets"' *Wall Street Journal* (13 June 2013) <http://online.wsj.com/article/SB10001424127887323734304578543151391292038.html> last accessed 1 August 2021.

included: entertainment files (e.g. music downloads), personal memories (e.g. photographs), personal communications (e.g. emails, notes), personal records (e.g. health, financial, insurance), career information (e.g. resumes, portfolios, cover letters, email contacts), and hobbies and creative projects. When broken down into categories, the value shown was personal memories at around $19,000, personal records at $7,000, career information at $4,000, hobbies at $3,000, personal communications at $3,000, and entertainment files at $2,000. The result was an average of 2,777 digital files per person.[42]

In the UK, in October 2011, the Centre for Creative and Social Technology (CAST) at Goldsmiths, University of London, released a study of Internet use in the UK entitled 'Generation Cloud'. The study determined that British users have at least £2.3 billion worth of digital assets stored in the cloud. The study shows that 24 per cent of UK adults estimate that they have digital assets worth more than £200 per person in the cloud, which amounts to at least £2.3bn in total.[43] It is also interesting to note the amount of digital content created and posted every sixty seconds online.[44] Notably, not all the assets have value and a considerable amount could be qualified as 'digital trash'.[45]

The volume and value of digital legacy (often dormant) is not the only concern. Deceased individuals' personal data and aspects of their identities are being used to recreate the deceased through chatbots, holograms, deepfakes and other similar technologies.[46] Such a recreation raises many ethical and legal problems related to autonomy, privacy and dignity. At the same time, the deceased's informational body[47] and aspects of their self and identity (digital footprints) are increasingly curated online and remain dormant, justifying an inquiry into the desirability of protection. Interestingly, some early data indicates that users express concern over post-mortem privacy

[42] McAfee, 'McAfee reveals average Internet user has more than $37,000 in underprotected "digital assets"' (27 September 2011) <http://www.mcafee.com/hk/about/news/2011/q3/20110927-01.aspx> last accessed 1 August 2021. See Hopkins (n 23) 221.

[43] Rackspace Hosting, 'Generation cloud: A social study into the impact of cloud-based services on everyday UK life' (16 November 2011) <http://www.rackspace.co.uk/sites/default/files/whitepapers/generation_cloud.pdf> last accessed 1 August 2021.

[44] Digital Passing, 'Digital property created on the Internet every 60 seconds' *Digital Passing Blog* (20 June 2011) <http://www.digitalpassing.com/2011/06/20/digital-property-created-internet-every-60-seconds/> last accessed 1 August 2021.

[45] Hopkins (n 23) 231.

[46] E Harbinja, L Edwards and M McVey, 'Governing ghostbots' (2022) *Computer Law and Security Review* (forthcoming).

[47] L Floridi, *The Fourth Revolution: How the Infosphere Is Reshaping Human Reality* (Oxford University Press 2014) 121.

when specific questions and issues are brought to their attention, but their behaviour pre-mortem does not correspond to these concerns.[48]

This data concerning digital assets, further development and dominance of digital technologies and the information society, where our lives and our wealth will increasingly take on digital forms, all indicate the importance of exploring the legal nature of digital assets. Legal reality should follow the technological, economic and social one. The economic and social importance of the chosen case studies will be further elaborated in chapters that examine these assets individually.

1.2 Stakeholders

We will now identify critical stakeholders involved in any discussion around the transmission of digital assets on death. These stakeholders have different interests in digital assets, and the interests are often conflicting. Sometimes, however, they also converge, depending on the type of asset. The specific relationship between these assets will be analysed in more detail in the case study chapters. These chapters will consider the characteristics of the assets and a myriad of relationships, legal and societal, existing therein.

Users are the most significant stakeholder for this book's purposes. We start from the standpoint that users' interests are not the sole but are the paramount policy consideration in the debates surrounding digital assets. What are the reasons for this?

First, in the offline world, most legal systems already recognise that individuals can dispose of their tangible and intangible property (although this may be limited by other interests, e.g. the rights of spouses or children or society's right to inheritance taxes).

Second, the arguments for rights of testamentary freedom are arguably more robust in the online world than the offline, given the prevalence of personal data in digital assets, for example emails, social network posts, playlists, pictures, chatbots, and so on.

Third, the book draws on normative theories to question the propertisation of digital assets, one of which, personhood theory, is closely linked to the personality and creative acts of the user. This argument is powerful when looking at digital assets that also fit the category of copyright, for example online literary or musical works. If digital assets cannot be perceived as property or protected by copyright, the analysis looks at post-mortem privacy.

48 T Morse and M Birnhack, 'The posthumous privacy paradox: Privacy preferences and behavior regarding digital remains' (2020) *New Media and Society* 1.

This concept, again, focuses on the individual, allowing for a different kind of post-mortem control that we explore in the case study chapters.

Therefore, user interests are at the centre of the argument, underpinning findings in all the chapters, that is, respecting the autonomy and wishes of the deceased, expressed pre-mortem, concerning the transmission of their assets on death.

Another group of stakeholders includes the deceased users' **heirs, next of kin and families**, on the one hand, and the **users' friends**, on the other. As shown in the hypothetical scenario earlier and in court cases analysed later in the book, the heirs and families usually aim to access the accounts/content in a digital asset, treating these as the deceased user's estate. On the other hand, friends are also interested in controlling their online relationship with the deceased, either by preserving the shared and co-constructed content or by discontinuing their relationship online. The analysis in this book does not follow the established succession law principles, where next of kin take priority in the intestate succession (the lack of a will). Instead, I recognise the shift in online and offline cultures, co-constructed and shared profiles, and the increasingly vital interests of users' friends. It is argued that the culture of sharing content online, particularly on social networks, deserves a better policy and legal recognition. Users should be able to decide and leave their assets to friends in the context of a specific digital asset, be it a social network or virtual world. A basis for this can be found in the anthropological and psychological evidence I have explored. This proposition is less applicable to the context of emails, where the feature of sharing and co-construction is not equally prominent.

Service providers and platforms (e.g. Facebook, Google, Twitter, Blizzard) have legitimate interests in preserving and developing their businesses. The providers have created their platforms, investing money and effort in them, and this should be considered. However, conventionally in the West, and especially the US, until recently, countries have tended to take a fairly *laissez-faire* attitude to the regulation of corporations. It is argued that the importance of these platforms and businesses is so significant that it merits a regulatory account. For example, Facebook's user base is enormous, more significant than any state population, and legitimate concerns of users need to be recognised (e.g. privacy concerns). In addition, the very nature of digital assets depends largely upon service providers, their computer code and servers. Borrowing from Lessig's taxonomy of regulation of the Internet,[49] it is worth noting that service providers have the power to modify, destroy and

[49] L Lessig, *Code: Version 2.0* (Basic Books 2006).

create digital assets through 'code', and this control cannot be left out of any considerations of digital assets. As demonstrated later in this book, solutions created by service providers support our main argument, the user's autonomy, as they enable in-service control over a user's content. In addition, service providers support post-mortem privacy arguments, so it is not overly difficult to consider these interests in a book focused on individual users.

Society and public interests are also worth mentioning when discussing the post-mortem treatment of digital assets. These are predominantly interests in keeping accurate historical records, archival interests, but also the potential conflict between free speech and post-mortem privacy. This perspective is not the focus of the book, however. It is argued that certain safeguards and exceptions can be established to account for these interests, but the analysis here will not discuss this in detail.

Finally, an emerging category of stakeholders is **online digital legacy services**, which aim to assist in the disposition of digital assets on death. Examples include digital wills, passwords and/or content depositories, memorial websites, messaging services and chatbots. These services aim to shift the control of digital assets to users by enabling the designation of beneficiaries who will receive the passwords/content of digital asset accounts. However, the services usually conflict with the terms of service of digital asset service providers. Furthermore, the law does not recognise them, they are not valid wills, and conflict with intestacy laws may arise. These issues will be further analysed in the final chapter, where different solutions to the issues identified in the book are assessed. However, it is worth noting here that the issues surrounding these services are significant, and it is not recommended in this book that the services are used in their current form and with the law as it stands now.

1.3 Definitions

For clarity, Table 1.1 presents definitions of the key concepts used in this book.

Table 1.1 Key Concepts Used and Developed in This Book[50]

Concept	Definition	Author
Digital death	Death in the digital realm; death of an individual who leaves fragments of their identity and digital assets in the digital afterlife (e.g. digital biographies, dossiers, autobiographies and archives).	Sofka et al. 2017; Kasket 2019; Harbinja 2020
Digital immortality	Immortality reached in the digital realm as a consequence of a symbolic, a proxy or technology.	Jacobsen 2017
Digital assets	Any electronic asset of personal or economic value.	Harbinja, *Legal Aspects* 2017
	Widely and not exclusively include a huge range of intangible information goods associated with the online or 'digital world'.	Edwards and Harbinja 2013
Informational body	Inorganic body of a human constituted and existing through information related to their identity.	Floridi, 'Distributed morality' 2013; 2014
Postmortem privacy	The right of the deceased to control their personality rights and digital remains post-mortem, broadly, or the right to privacy and data protection post-mortem, narrowly defined.	Harbinja, 'Post-mortem privacy 2.0' 2017
Postmortal privacy	Protects aspects of immortality understood as the survival of the informational body, which is constituted by and exists through personal information, digital remains and memes.	Harbinja 2020

[50] Adapted from E Harbinja, 'The "new(ish)" property, informational bodies, and postmortality' in M Savin-Baden and V Mason-Robbie (eds), *Digital Afterlife: Death Matters in a Digital Age* (Taylor & Francis 2020) 90.

2

Theoretical Underpinnings: Property

This chapter sets out a basic conceptual foundation for this book, which will be used in the case study chapters to determine the fundamental question of the nature of assets exemplified in this book. We will consider whether certain types of digital assets fit within the notion of property and consequently transmit on death like some of the more traditional types of property.

Suppose digital assets analysed in this book are found to be property or protected by IP rights (copyright in particular). In that case, their transmission is clear: property transmits on death, and copyright protection lasts for many years post-mortem (seventy years in the referent jurisdictions, US and UK). To confirm or discard this proposition for each of the case studies, we will explore the meaning of property, its incidents and justifications in this chapter. This discussion will be further applied to examine whether social networks, emails, games and virtual world asserts are property objects.

The analysis sits alongside the discussion in Chapter 3, where autonomy and privacy are examined as further examples of the conceptual underpinning of the book. I, however, do not rely on any claim about the relationship between property, privacy and autonomy. I make no claim, for example, that autonomy underpins property or that the concept of privacy somehow 'mediates' between the concepts of autonomy and property. Instead, property is examined from various angles simply to determine whether virtual assets could (doctrinal question) and should (normative question) be regarded as property. If the answer to either of these questions is 'yes', then these assets can be transmitted on death by testate and intestate succession laws. If the answer is 'no', because some assets are primarily made of information and personal data that cannot constitute property, privacy and autonomy take precedence in this conceptual framework.

This chapter will not discuss copyright from a theoretical perspective. The reason for this is that copyright's transmission on death is clear and settled in law, so if a digital asset meets copyright protection requirements, this right will be passed on to the heirs of a deceased user. Instead, the chapters discussing case studies will assess whether some of their content satisfies copyright requirements from a doctrinal perspective. Although the transmission of property is also evident, property features are not as settled or harmonised in law or theory. Conversely, the requirements for copyright protection have been harmonised (at least from a black letter law perspective, without going into the debate around whether the current copyright regime is desirable or justified). Instead, as will be seen later in this chapter, it is highly contested whether the information or other non-copyrightable content of digital assets is or should be property. Therefore, we will debate property from a theoretical and doctrinal perspective to enable this evaluation in the case study chapters.

Conversely, as another dominant type of digital asset content, information has not been assessed from the perspective of post-mortem transmission. The legal nature of different types of information is often unclear, and one of the most significant considerations is whether information can be considered property. If the answer is affirmative, either from a black letter law or a normative perspective, then the content including predominantly information will transmit or should transmit on death like traditional property. Conversely, if the answer is negative or unclear, each case study in this book will be assessed from the perspective of its specific content, excluding the general transmission of information. The discussion on property in information and personal data is more specific than the general theorising of property set out in this chapter, and it is primarily relevant to the case study analyses in Chapters 4 and 6. Therefore, that specific discussion will utilise findings of the general concept of property explored in this chapter but will be delayed to Chapter 6, where it sits more naturally.

2.1 Defining the Notion of Property

This section will briefly explore the origin, usage and possible definitions of the word 'property'. It will demonstrate that all attempts at a comprehensive and all-encompassing definition, even on a fundamental, abstract level, are fruitless. This discussion is necessary for this book since digital assets are typically located in a transnational space, for example on a server physically located in Ireland, owned by a US company, and accessed by and created by users from many different jurisdictions. Therefore, issues relating to the transmission of digital assets are likely to be even more complex when systems have wildly divergent views on what constitutes property.

George notes that property is 'notoriously difficult to define', and the debate about its definition and nature has been going on for ages and 'seems set to rage for some time yet'.[1] Throughout this chapter, the key features of the property concept will be explored and suggested, even if it does not lead to a precise conclusion about the definition and nature of this critical concept.

The word 'property' comes from the Latin *proprietas*, possibly through French *propriété*, meaning 'the peculiar nature or quality of a thing' and 'ownership'. The word is derived from the adjective *proprius* meaning 'own' or 'peculiar', opposed to *communis* (common) or *alienus* (another's). Furthermore, the word can be rooted in the Greek *πρo* or Sanskrit *pra* meaning 'in front of', 'before', 'close to', 'on behalf of'. Donahue interprets this core meaning as something that represented an idea of 'what distinguishes an individual or a thing from a group or another' even before getting its legal meaning.[2]

The word has been used in different contexts and with various and sometimes contradictory meanings between the different legal systems and within the same ones. For instance, older usage in England referred to a relationship between a persona and resources, while later, after the seventeenth century, the meaning pertained to the object of an ownership interest.[3] Along this line, Gray indicates a blurred distinction between property as a 'relationship' and property as a 'thing', arguing that the former use is correct and quoting Bentham and Macpherson to support his stance.[4] Further, he emphasises the dynamic quality of this relationship, changing in time in both subjects and objects of property.

It would be highly complex and, arguably, impossible to provide a widely accepted definition of property for all legal cultures and systems. This is a fact even in a philosophical, abstract definition, since throughout the history of contemplation on property there has been hardly any agreement on its essence and definition. There have been attempts to offer some common characteristics for the notion. For example, as Honoré puts it, ownership, *dominium*, *propriété* and *Eigentum* 'stand not merely for the greatest interest in a thing in a particular system but for a type of interest with common features transcending particular systems'.[5] Honoré uses the term in 'the "liberal" concept of "full" individual ownership'.[6]

[1] A George, 'The difficulty of defining "property"' (2005) 25(4) *Oxford Journal of Legal Studies* 813, 813.

[2] See J Donahue, 'The future of property predicted from its past' in JR Pennock and JW Chapman (eds), *Property* (New York University Press 1980) 31.

[3] JW Harris, *Property and Justice* (Clarendon Press 1996) 10.

[4] K Gray, *Elements of Land Law* (Butterworths 1987) 8–14.

[5] AM Honoré, 'Ownership' in AG Guest (ed.), *Oxford Essays in Jurisprudence: A Collaborative Work* (Oxford University Press 1961) 108.

[6] Ibid. 107.

Definitions in legal codes, according to Honoré, are not 'a safe guide'. However, even though he notes the similarity between the French Civil Code and Soviet Civil Code definitions, both emphasising the absoluteness in the term, he also warns of the different limits laid down by law.[7] According to this, it could be argued that ownership is the greatest interest in a thing in many modern legal systems, but the argument about the common features is much harder to sustain.

Another notable example in support of the argument put forward by Honoré is Blackstone's view on property, which is similar to that predominantly accepted in the Continental, civil law tradition. Blackstone uses the term 'the right of property', as an equivalent of the ownership right in civilian usage. As will be demonstrated later in this chapter, ownership is only a subset of property, one of many property rights in civil law tradition.

Blackstone's view was later rejected by most common law scholars and the judiciary, who embraced the 'bundle of rights' concept, as discussed later. His position is best reflected in this famous quote:

> There is nothing which so generally strikes the imagination, and engages the affections of mankind, as the right of property; or that sole and despotic dominion which one man claims and exercises over the external things of the world, in total exclusion of the right of any other individual in the universe. And yet there are very few, that will give themselves the trouble to consider the origin and foundation of this right.[8]

While legal scholars have mainly expressed the views mentioned in brief above, the usage of the term and its definition become even more diverse if we look at other disciplines and contexts. Thus, for example, Grey tried to summarise contemporary usages of the term 'property' in law, economics and legal theory.[9] One of the usages amongst teachers and law students in England is 'the whole body of law concerned with the use of land'; another is inherent to lawyers and some economists, who identify it with rights *in rem* (rights against the whole world), as opposed to rights *in personam* (rights against a determinate person).

Economists, such as Posner and Demsetz, use the word to indicate the purpose of property, including all rights with the purpose to advance allocative efficiencies, such as the rights to life, liberty and personal security. Others invoke the 'new property', like Reich, arguing that the traditional purpose of

[7] Ibid. 110.

[8] SW Blackstone, *Commentaries on the Laws of England (1765–1769)* (18th edn, S. Sweet etc. 1829) Book II, chapter 1.

[9] TC Grey, 'The disintegration of property' in Pennock and Chapman (n 2).

property is to ensure independence and security, thus proposing a revision of the concept in terms of welfare and public education law.[10]

Another specialised usage defines property as opposed to the liability according to the remedies available to protect it. Thus, property can be enforced, amongst other options (e.g. vindication, restitution), both by injunction and by criminal law sanctions, whereas obligations are usually followed with damages as a remedy.

In Grey's elaboration of property, the author concludes that 'from a glance at the range of current usages, the specialists who design and manipulate the legal structures of the advanced capitalist economies could easily do it without using the term property'.[11]

From a philosophical point of view, Waldron argues that property is 'a concept of which many different conceptions are possible',[12] and the conceptions are relative to different societies and their respective conception of incidents of ownership.[13] Further, defining the general concept, he states it is 'a system of rules governing access to and control of material resources'.[14] Resource further is 'a material object capable of satisfying some human need or want'.[15]

Now that we have sketched the notion of property and possible viewpoints and stances regarding its definition, the concept itself should become more apparent and familiar after identifying its main features and categories, focusing on the common law conceptions. Also, the definitions and features will reflect the currently predominant capitalist economy conceptions of property in the Western world, notwithstanding different conceptions elsewhere, which reflect cultural, economic and societal characteristics of these societies (e.g. socialist conceptions and rejection of private property, tribal and indigenous conceptions of property). The reason for focusing on the former is that this book is primarily looking for practical and policy solutions in the current socio-economic system in the UK and US. Therefore, property in its Western conception is used as a tool to suggest solutions for the transmission of digital assets on death, in the system 'as is'.

10 C Reich, 'The new property' (1964) 73 *Yale Law Journal* 733, discussing the wealth allocation of property function in relation to 'government largesse', different social benefits and services. For an interesting overview, see Harris (n 3) 149–51.

11 Grey (n 9) 71–3.

12 J Waldron, *The Right to Private Property* (Clarendon Press 1990) 31.

13 Ibid.

14 Ibid.

15 Ibid.

(a) Incidents of Property

We will identify critical incidents of property and use them further in the discussions on whether digital assets include these incidents to constitute property.

Honoré has offered one of the best-known attempts at defining the common elements or features of property or ownership. He identifies eleven exhaustive incidents of ownership that 'are not individually necessary, though they may be together sufficient, conditions for the person of inherence to be designated as "owner" of a particular thing in a given system'.[16] These incidents are the right to possess, the right to use, the right to manage, the right to the income of the thing, the right to the capital, the right to security, the rights of transmissibility and absence of term, the prohibition of harmful use, the liability of execution, and the incident of residuarity.[17]

Interestingly, these incidents do not explicitly include the right to destroy and exclude, though these could arguably fall under the rights to manage or right to use and the prohibition of harmful use. Thus, it looks like the quality of absoluteness discussed below and pertaining to civilian systems has not been considered as primary in this theory. However, since it strives to discover common incidents for different legal regimes, this omission is entirely understandable.

Similarly, building on Honoré's theory of property and his eleven elements of the notion, Becker proposes thirteen elements, namely the right (claim) to possess, the right (liberty) to use, the right (power) to manage, the right (claim) to the income, the right (liberty) to consume and destroy, the right (liberty) to modify, the right (power) to alienate, the right (power) to transmit, the right (claim) to security, the absence of term, the prohibition of harmful use, liability to execution, and residuary rules.[18] He further argues that a person who has any one of the first eight elements plus the right to security then has a property right and there are 4,080 such combinations possible (mathematically calculated). Like Honoré, Becker argues that full ownership consists of all the elements in the same individual.[19]

Conversely, unlike Honoré, Becker considers the right to destroy as one of the incidents of ownership. Furthermore, his theory focuses on property as a relative concept, consisting of different interests, with ownership as an absolute one. This concept of a 'bundle of rights' is a dominant feature of the

[16] Honoré (n 5) 112–13.
[17] Ibid. 113–28.
[18] L Becker, 'The moral basis of property rights' in Pennock and Chapman (n 2) 190–1.
[19] Ibid. 192.

common law tradition and will be used in the case studies chapters as a starting point for analysing the legal nature of specific digital assets.

The bundle of rights theory permeates both American and English legal thought and practice, and it is adopted as a practical and flexible approach in our attempt to conceptualise digital assets. This theory is based on Hohfeld's theory of legal relations as jural opposites (rights–no-rights; privilege–duty; power–disability; immunity–liability) and jural correlatives (right–duty; privilege–no-right; power–liability; immunity–disability), which define legal concepts, including property, as a set of these correlatives and relations.[20]

Penner notes that it is 'clearly dominant in the United States, where even the Restatement of Property begins with a Hohfeldian outline of rights and duties, and where the "bundle of rights" is regularly cited by courts in important property cases',[21] and that it is undoubtedly prevalent in England as well. Lawson and Rudden, for example, refer to the law of property as providing an owner with 'a bag of tools'.[22] For Penner, this indicates that property 'is a concept without a definable "essence"; different combinations of the bundle in different circumstances may all count as "property" and no particular right or set of rights in the bundle is determinative'.[23] In this regard, he refers to Munzer's characterisation:

> The idea of property – or, if you prefer, the sophisticated or legal conception of property – involves a constellation of Hohfeldian elements, correlatives, and opposites; a specification of standard incidents of ownership and other related but less powerful interests; and a catalogue of 'things' (tangible and intangible) that are the subjects of these incidents. Hohfeld's conceptions are normative modalities. In the more specific form of Honoré's incidents, these are the relations that constitute property.[24]

Thus, the bundle of rights theory could be best presented and understood as a Hohfeldian–Honorian bundle of jural correlatives, opposites and incidents. This theory will be referred to in the case study chapters later in this book.

Additionally, discussions on conceiving digital assets as property will also refer to significant economic features of property objects. These qualities,

[20] WN Hohfeld, 'Some fundamental legal conceptions as applied in judicial reasoning' (1913) 23 *Yale Law Journal* 16.

[21] *Moore* v *Regents of the Univ of Cal*, 793 P.2d 479 (Cal 1990); *Keystone Bituminous Coal Assn et al.* v *DeBenedictis, Secretary, Pennsylvania Department of Environmental Resources, et al.*, 480 US 470 (1986).

[22] JE Penner, 'The "bundle of rights" picture of property' (1996) 43 *UCLA Law Review* 43, 713.

[23] Ibid. 724.

[24] Ibid. 724.

arguably, qualify various objects as property. The list presented here is not exhaustive; instead, only the most crucial features will be defined here, namely rivalrousness, excludability, persistence (temporality) and interconnectivity.

Rivalrousness (subtractability) is an economic term primarily relating to consumption and the physical quality of an object. It arises in situations 'where one person's use subtracts from the available benefits for others'.[25] In other words, it means that consumption cannot be common for these resources.[26] Most tangible objects are intrinsically rivalrous (e.g. food, clothing, most private goods), whereas most intangible ones are non-rivalrous (information, objects of IP, but not domain names, radio spectrum). Related to this concept is a notion of excludability, meaning the individual's power to control the use of an object.[27] It usually depends on the property rights granted to enable a person to exclude others from using an object.[28] The two terms should not be confused since, for instance, non-rivalrous objects can be excludable. An obvious example is IP, mainly non-rivalrous but excludable since the law has granted exclusive protection, a monopoly, to it. Here the valid question is the cost of excludability and not the exclusion itself.

Persistence is another quality of property objects, both tangible and intangible. It does not mean permanence *per se*; it only implies a certain degree of stability.[29] On the other hand, theoretically, property rights have an indefinite duration, unlike IP, whose duration is still time-limited, conferring different terms of protection to certain kinds of IP.

Interconnectivity, another characteristic of objects in the real world, means that they can affect each other 'by the laws of physics';[30] they are connected and can be perceived as such by senses, or more than two people can experience the same property at the same time.

2.2 Key Categories of Property in Common and Civil Law Countries

After having shown the possible ways to define property and the primary features of the concept, we will further demonstrate the main differences at conceptual and practical levels of consideration of property in two major law traditions, namely common and civil law. Only the most representative

[25] C Hess and E Ostrom, *Understanding Knowledge as a Commons from Theory to Practice* (MIT Press 2007) 9, 352.

[26] DL Weimer and AR Vining, *Policy Analysis* (5th edn, Longman 2011) 72.

[27] Ibid.

[28] Ibid.

[29] See TJ Westbrook, 'Owned: Finding a place for virtual world property rights' (2006) *Michigan State Law Review* 779, 782, 783.

[30] J Fairfield, 'Virtual property' (2005) 85 *Boston University Law Review* 1047.

examples will be mentioned, in an endeavour to help understand the categorisation presented afterwards, find common themes, and indicate some solutions for defining and categorising virtual assets and property. The chapter thus assesses which legal system would be more susceptible to the inclusion of new objects of property. The analysis of this distinction will be especially helpful in Chapter 5, where a hybrid common–civil law solution will be introduced for the games and virtual worlds case study.

The differences between conceptions of property in the two prominent legal families could be explained through the historically and culturally conditioned viewpoint. Continental legal scholars prefer more clearly and coherently defined concepts and theories, almost a dogmatic approach. Thus, Bouckaert notes, 'continental legal science puts a much stronger emphasis on definitions and general principles than its Anglo-American counterpart. Continental jurists at one time identified this conceptual level of legal science as "legal dogmatic" or "legal theory."'[31] Moreover, as Penner remarks, in the common law, 'The specialist fragments the robust unitary conception of ownership into a more shadowy "bundle of rights".' As a result, he claims, the law and legal theorists in common law systems no longer have one single, coherent concept of property.[32]

Nevertheless, the differences and possible similarities between different property concepts have not been exciting to comparative law scholars. As van Erp notes, comparative law focuses on the law of obligations because of the dominant elements of convergence, while property law has not been an area of great interest for comparative lawyers.[33] Furthermore, he argues that the comparative lawyers have taken for granted fundamental, historically rooted differences between civil and common law, considering that there is no possibility for any convergence.[34] Van Erp calls this approach to property law 'technocratic conservatism', 'a legal mentality that aims at preserving the status quo and that accepts changes only when these are completely unavoidable'.[35] However, he predicts shifts in this mentality due to global market integration. He also notes that property law has never been as static as generally considered, giving examples of influences of case law in Germany and the Netherlands (transfer of ownership for security purposes), on the one

[31] B Bouckaert, 'What is property?' (1990) 13 *Harvard Journal of Law and Public Policy* 775, 775–6.

[32] Penner, '"Bundle of rights"' (n 22) 769.

[33] See S van Erp, 'Comparative property law' in M Reimann and R Zimmermann (eds), *The Oxford Handbook of Comparative Law* (Oxford University Press 2006) 1044.

[34] Ibid. 1044–5.

[35] Ibid. 1048.

hand, and changes in common law affected by statutes (Law of Property Act 1925), on the other.[36] The evidence that this view is sound is the attempts at unifying private law at the EU level (see the discussion below). Concerning van Erp's prediction, it is suggested that the global nature of the Internet and the increasing importance of digital assets will contribute to a change of mentality in the long term.

When discussing the difference in concepts of property between common and civil law systems, it is essential to note that within the EU, property is still subject to the national law of member states.[37] Thus, the distinction between common and civil law conceptions is still in place, even if we disregard the US conception, which inherited and received the common law tradition, and currently mainly stands by the aforementioned bundle of rights theory.

There are significant moves within the EU to harmonise aspects of national property laws, provided that we accept the argument that IP is property.[38] Notably, Article 118 of the Treaty on the Functioning of the European Union (Lisbon Treaty) calls for the 'creation of European intellectual property rights to provide uniform protection of intellectual property rights throughout the Union'.[39] There have been similar global attempts to harmonise IP law, within WIPO, WTO, multilaterally and bilaterally, by different treaties and conventions.[40] Though this aim is currently far from being achieved, it sheds important light on the possible intentions of unifying IP.

[36] Ibid. 1048–9. Here he argues that the Law has introduced the *numerus clausus* principle in common law, limiting the number of estates in s 1.

[37] Article 345 (ex Article 295 TEC) of the Treaty on the Functioning of the European Union OJ C 83/47 30/03/2010.

[38] The debate over whether IP is, in effect, property or a statutory monopoly and privilege is outside the scope of this book. For more on the rich academic debate, see for example J Hughes, 'Copyright and incomplete historiographies: Of piracy, propertisation, and Thomas Jefferson' (2005–6) 79 *Southern California Law Review* 993; M Kretschmer, L Bently and R Deazley, 'The history of copyright history (revisited)' (2013) 5(1) *WIPO Journal* 35; L Lessig, *Free Culture: How Big Media Uses Technology and the Law to Lock Down Culture and Control Creativity* (Penguin 2004); MA Lemley and PJ Weiser, 'Should property or liability rules govern information?' (2007) 85 *Texas Law Review* 783; HL MacQueen, 'The war of the booksellers: Natural law, equity, and literary property in eighteenth-century Scotland' (2014) 35(3) *Journal of Legal History* 231; HL MacQueen, 'Intellectual property and the common law in Scotland c1700–c1850' in CW Ng, L Bently and GD Agostino (eds), *The Common Law of Intellectual Property: Essays in Honour of Professor David Vaver* (Hart 2010). In addition, an interesting view of IP being an example of the Scots law concept of 'exclusive privilege' has been offered by Black. See G Black, *A Right of Publicity in Scots Law* (PhD thesis, University of Edinburgh 2009) 192–4, 205–10.

[39] Treaty on the Functioning of the European Union (n 37).

[40] The most important international IP guidelines involve four treaties: the Paris Convention for the Protection of Industrial Property of 20 March 1883 (as revised); the Madrid Agreement

Furthermore, there are efforts to unify contract law or create some legal core that would foster the Single Market and benefit consumers at the EU level. The proposals range from a non-binding 'toolbox' that would improve consistency and harmonise member states' contract rules to an all-encompassing contract or even civil code for the EU.[41] The process has gone as far as a proposal for a common framework for sales law,[42] which means that in the short to medium term, we may expect a European code of some kind, contract or civil, or even the harmonising of private law in general.

Differences between the legal families are notable if we consider property remedies. In common law, the primary remedy is damages and not the return of the property like in civil law. Thus the law of tort (trespass and conversion) deals with this protection rather than the law of property.[43] Discussing remedies in English law, Reid notes that the remedies for recovering the possession of the thing owned are provided by the law of obligations, based on tort. However, even then, as he interestingly puts it, 'the law of obligations is the servant and not the master' because in order to use the remedy provided by the law of obligations, one must first own the property.[44]

One of the most relevant classifications of property objects for our discussion is that of tangible and intangible property. Digital assets are inherently intangible, so this analysis will be relevant to each of the case studies.

While common law recognises various items and phenomena as things, making them susceptible to the property law concept, the same cannot be said of civil law. The German Civil Code (BGB) restricts property to things, defined therein as tangible and corporeal.[45] Consequently, an incorporeal

Concerning the International Registration of Marks of 14 April 1891 (as revised); the Berne Convention for the Protection of Literary and Artistic Works of 9 September 1886 (as revised); and the Trade-Related Aspects of Intellectual Property Rights (TRIPS). Also relevant are the WIPO Copyright Treaty (WCT) and the WIPO Performance and Phonogram Treaty (WPPT).

41 See European Commission, 'Green paper from the Commission on policy options for progress towards a European Contract Law for consumers and businesses' COM(2010)348 final. For more, see R Zimmermann, 'Comparative law and the Europeanization of private law' in Reimann and Zimmermann (n 33) 540–77.

42 European Commission, 'Proposal for a Regulation of the European Parliament and of the Council on a Common European Sales Law' COM(2011) 635 final 2011/0284(COD).

43 M Bridge, *Personal Property Law* (3rd edn, Oxford University Press 2002) 47.

44 KGC Reid, 'Obligations and property: Exploring the border' (1997) *Acta Juridica* 225, 226.

45 For more, see EJ Cohn, *Manual of German Law* (British Institute of International and Comparative Law; Oceana Publications 1968) 174–80.

thing does not exist in German private law and cannot be subject to the concept of ownership. This aim has been achieved through other legislation.[46]

The protection of property offered by the basic law of the Federal Republic of Germany 1949,[47] Article 14, was extended by the Federal Constitutional Court,[48] expanding the interpretation of this clause beyond the limits of the private law concept, for the meaning and context of the whole Constitution. This created different property concepts in public, constitutional, criminal and private law, as defined in the BGB. Public property law, created administratively and constitutionally, violated some of the principles of the BGB, such as that property must be corporeal. In this way, electricity was recognised as property.[49] Furthermore, the constitutional property concept included IP rights, a claim for unemployment benefits, and bills of exchange.[50] This phenomenon is known as the theory of dualism of private and public property in German law.[51]

In French law, the word *biens* is used to designate both tangible and intangible property. The term is used in the Code Civil instead of *chose* meaning thing, to designate a value rather than a thing itself.[52] Incorporeal things are considered movable property by prescription of law, but this category is not as broad as that of English common law (Article 527 of the French Civil Code).

On the other hand, English common law has been quite flexible when applying the concept of ownership to intangibles, using the same principle as for tangibles. Thus, Maitland argues that 'any right or group of rights that is of a permanent kind can be thought of as a thing . . . mediaeval law is rich with incorporeal things'.[53] As Lawson and Rudden note, this approach is still

[46] Trademarks: Markengesetz of 25.10.1994. BGBI. I S. 1273; Patents: Patentgesetz of 16.12.1980. BGBI. 1981 I S. 1; Copyright: Urheberrechtgesetz of 9.91965. BGBI. I S. 1273. See generally MJ Raff, *Private Property and Environmental Responsibility: A Comparative Study of German Real Property Law* (Kluwer Law International 2003) 191–3; W Ebke and MW Finkin, *Introduction to German Law* (Kluwer Law International 1996) 227.

[47] See AJ van der Walt, *Constitutional Property Clauses: A Comparative Analysis* (Kluwer Law International 1999) 121–63.

[48] BVerfGE 51, 193 (Warenzeichen case) 1979 219 in van der Walt (n 47) 151.

[49] See Raff (n 46) 164–5. See similarly Ebke and Finkin (n 46) 72, 73.

[50] See the leading case describing the constitutional guarantee of property: *Hamburg Dyke Case* (1969) 22 NJW 309 and Raff (n 46) 170–1.

[51] Raff (n 46) 164.

[52] J Bell et al., *Principles of French Law* (2nd edn, Oxford University Press 2008) 270.

[53] Quoted in FH Lawson and B Rudden, *The Law of Property* (Oxford University Press 2002) 82.

being used in the cases of 'owner of patent' or a mortgage.[54] Discussing rights as things, Reid argues that incorporeal assets and rights are already a part of a person's patrimony, and their importance has increased significantly. Thus, he concludes, 'It seems odd to deny them the status of things.'[55] However, as seen in the case of information later in this book, this does not necessarily have to be true. English law is still very reluctant to recognise property in information, as seen in the example of emails in Chapter 6. Some recent developments suggest this may change in the future, especially concerning crypto assets and cryptocurrencies.[56] However, at the time of writing, the law reform is still at a very early stage, and the uncertainty remains.

Prima facie, it seems that intangibility will not represent an obstacle to recognising digital assets as property, especially in English law. However, this proposition does not prove true in the case of information and personal data, where the analysis in Chapter 6 demonstrates that only US law occasionally shows readiness to recognise certain types of information as property. This inconsistency serves as another argument against recognising digital assets as property.

Another peculiarity of common law, when compared with civil law systems, is the category of choses in equity and equitable ownership. This concept will be analysed to show some successful examples of legal transplants and cross-pollination between legal systems, providing support for hybrid solutions offered in Chapter 5 for games and virtual worlds.

Historically, English equity law was created by the Chancellor and the Court of Chancery, and unified by statute at the end of nineteenth century to make it applicable to one system of courts. However, it is unclear whether these two systems fused, and this question for Penner 'remains controversial'.[57]

The most significant contribution of equity is the trust, existing when a fund of property is held by a legal owner, a trustee, with an enforceable legal obligation that it be used for another, the beneficiary.[58] Alternatively, simply put, it is 'a flexible grouping of people and property in which one group of people (trustees), look after assets for another group (beneficiaries)'.[59] Trustees are referred to as 'the legal owners', because the property is in their

[54] Ibid.

[55] Reid (n 44) 231.

[56] Law Commission, 'Digital assets: Call for evidence' (April 2021) <https://www.lawcom.gov.uk/project/digital-assets/> last accessed 1 August 2021.

[57] Penner, '"Bundle of rights"' (n 22) 1332.

[58] For more and a comparison with choses in action see J Penner, *The Idea of Property in Law* (Oxford University Press 1997) 133–8.

[59] J Ball, 'The boundaries of property rights in English law', Report to the XVIIth International Congress of Comparative Law (2006) 10(3) *Electronic Journal of Comparative Law* 8.

name, but they do not enjoy the benefit of the property. They simply manage the trust for the benefit of the real, equitable owners – the beneficiaries. Trust is usually formed by contract, but this is not a rule. In the case of implied or constructive trust in England, no formality is needed to establish a trust,[60] apart from the constructive trust arising when a person deals with property in an 'unconscionable manner'.[61] Another type of constructive trust arises in the sale contracts, from the moment the price is paid, where it is deemed that a property is held in constructive trust for a transferee.[62]

The nature of trust, however, is still to be resolved. While proponents of Scott's view argue that it is a branch of property law, Langbein considers trust a contract, highlighting that the power and duties of the trustee are the default contract terms between the settlor of the trust and the trustee.[63]

Merrill and Smith identify characteristics of both regimes in trust, especially given the complicated position of the trustee who is subject to both property and contractual regimes. They put it succinctly: 'Thus, we can think of a trust as the transfer of in rem rights associated with ownership, subject to a set of in personam duties designed to fulfil the settlor's intentions toward the beneficiary.'[64]

Elements of both regimes, and particularly on the side of beneficiaries, are detected by Ball, too. She notes that while a beneficiary's rights in relation to a trustee are personal, the beneficiary also has real, property-like relations to third persons.[65]

Hansmann and Mattei are amongst those who argue that the principal contributions of trust are those related to property-like aspects. Here they refer to an interesting feature of property, explaining, 'When we say that assets are someone's property, we generally mean (among other things) that those assets are presumed available to satisfy claims of that person's creditors.'[66]

The most important contribution of trust law, in Hansmann and Mattei's opinion, is that of arranging relations between the trust parties and third parties, including creditors, relations that cannot be easily dealt with by the rules of contract and agency law in civil law countries, at least not without significant transaction costs. The critical feature of a trust is 'partition of a

60 See Law of Property Act 1925, s 53(2).

61 See Millet LJ in *Paragon Finance plc* v *DB Thakerar & Co* [1999] 1 All ER 400.

62 See *Chinn* v *Collins* [1981] AC 533.

63 As set out in H Hansmann and U Mattei, 'The functions of trust law: A comparative legal and economic analysis' (1998) 73 *New York University Law Review* 434, 469–70.

64 TW Merrill and HE Smith, 'The property/contract interface' (2001) 101(4) *Columbia Law Review* 773, 844.

65 Ball (n 59) 9.

66 Hansmann and Mattei (n 63) 470.

discrete set of assets', managed separately and capable of being security to creditors, as a distinct entity.[67]

Unlike the Anglo-American tradition, where a dual system of common law and equity arose, the latter creating the concept of trust, property law in civil law countries was predominantly developed by academic lawyers, based on the Roman law tradition. The central concept was the obligation, which framed trust-like arrangements,[68] like the Roman concept of *fiducia*, creating contractual, not property, relationships between parties.[69] However, trust as property, not obligation, would be contrary to the civil law doctrine of the unity of property, the *numerus clausus* principle mentioned later. This doctrine was developed after the French Revolution, regarding the division of property rights as a relic of feudalism.[70]

Nevertheless, an institution resembling trust can now be found in French law. That is *fiducie*, a trust-like institution, introduced in the French Civil Code by the Law of 19 February 2007, amending former Articles 2011 to 2031 of the Civil Code. Although the definition from Article 2011 is similar to the common law concept,[71] it is only applied to relations *inter vivos*, which is not the case in common law. Furthermore, it must be made clear, it is a formal contract and there is nothing like the implied or constructive trust in England discussed earlier in this section. Also, *fiducie* is not open to individuals but only to institutions. As discussed above, its nature is contractual, whereas English trust has a mixed nature, involving both contractual and property elements. Finally, and importantly, the most innovative aspect of this institute is that it is separate from the fiduciary's personal assets, which breaks the unitary conception of *patrimoine* (estate, all rights *in rem* and *in personam*)[72] in French law.[73]

This institute is an example of a legal transplant between common and civilian legal systems.[74] It shows once more that a useful legal concept, effective in a legal and economic milieu, can be exported and recognised in a different legal system that, at first glance, would not be susceptible to its reception. One of the reasons for introducing this concept is related to globalisation and the fact that companies were moving their assets to jurisdictions with

67 Ibid. 466.
68 Ibid. 441.
69 Ibid. 443.
70 Ibid. 442.
71 Article 2011 du Code Civil (loi du 19 février 2007).
72 E Steiner, *French Law: A Comparative Approach* (Oxford University Press 2010) 379.
73 For more, see ibid. 387–9.
74 A Watson, *Legal Transplants: An Approach to Comparative Law* (Scottish Academic Press 1974) 20.

more flexible and competitive legal instruments.[75] It confirms Watson's argument that transplanting is the most fertile source of development. Changes in many legal systems are the results of borrowing. According to Watson, the law is similar to technology, it is 'the fruit of human experience', and when a rule is invented by one nation, it can be appreciated and used for the needs of many other people.[76] However, since *fiducie* is not an exact or close replica of trust, with essential features missing (e.g. post-mortem features), it cannot be seen as a very representative example either, at least not yet.[77] Nevertheless, these law reforms have introduced a previously unimaginable concept into a civil law legal system, demonstrating the potential for cross-pollination between legal systems and providing an argument for reform proposals suggested in this book.

(a) Some Consideration of Categories of Property in Common Law

The historical development of the property concept in common law systems is characterised by the progressive relativisation of this, initially, absolutely defined concept and the dephysicalisation of the notion. This development has been soundly described and discussed by Vandevelde.[78] He describes the shift from Sir William Blackstone's eighteenth-century conception to the nineteenth century.[79] The exceptions to the physicalist and the absolutist elements of Blackstone's conception were incorporated into the law by courts, which sought to protect beneficial interests as property 'even though no thing was involved'. Vandevelde sees the rationale for that in a theory of natural law and in the instrumentalist public policy of the state. Vandevelde calls this phenomenon, the protection of value rather than things, 'the dephysicalisation of property'.[80]

Further developments led to the complete abandonment of the Blackstonian conception of property by the beginning of the twentieth century. The most outstanding contribution to the establishment and formulation of a new conception was made by Hohfeld, in his theory discussed earlier.[81] Property rights were no longer seen as absolute but limited, without

[75] Steiner (n 72) 388. See also Watson (n 74) 97.

[76] Watson (n 74) 95, 100.

[77] See for example D Baudouin, 'Fiducie in French law' (2007) 2 *International Business Law Journal* 276, 276–81; P Matthews, 'The French fiducie: And now for something completely different?' (2007) 21(1) *Trust Law International* 17, 17–42.

[78] KJ Vandevelde, 'The new property of the nineteenth century: The development of the modern concept of property' (1980) *Buffalo Law Review* 29, 325.

[79] Ibid. 330. See also Section 1.1.

[80] Vandevelde (n 78) 329.

[81] Hohfeld (n 20).

favouring any set of rights over others. As Vandevelde usefully summarises, 'the particular combination of rights that comprised property in a given case would be decided according to the circumstances'.[82]

These developments have not been followed in the civil law family, where the concept of absolute ownership and the *numerus clausus* principle (finite number of property rights, prescribed in statutes or codes) are predominant, both in legal literature and statutory rules.[83] The principle of *numerus clausus* in German law means that the BGB limits the number, kind and content of rights *in rem*. The reason underpinning this principle is to enable third parties to assess risks arising from absolute rights.[84]

In England, as McKendrick describes, property rights are predominantly made by judges and have not yet been incorporated into statutes (apart from the Law of Property Act 1925), unlike in civil law countries where property law forms a significant part of civil codes or statutes. However, it is uncertain whether such a practice will continue.[85] However, as he notes, quoting Lord Wilberforce in *National Provincial Bank Ltd* v *Ainsworth*,[86] there is a 'continuing creative ability of the courts' to recognise the right or interest in the category of property if it is 'definable, identifiable by third parties, capable in its nature of assumption by third parties, and have some degree of permanence or stability'.[87] As far as England is concerned, Lawson and Rudden note that 'the English legislator – perhaps wisely – gives merely inclusive definition covering both objects and interests in them'.[88]

Further, property in England historically developed from relations involving land and tangible assets within the framework of common law (except a few statutes like the Law of Property Act).[89] Therefore, it had to evolve from

[82] Vandevelde (n 78) 336.

[83] N Horn et al., *German Private and Commercial Law: An Introduction* (Clarendon Press 1982).

[84] Ebke and Finkin (n 46) 230.

[85] See E McKendrick in N Palmer and E McKendrick (eds), *Interests in Goods* (Lloyd's of London Press 1993) 41.

[86] [1965] AC 1175, 1247–8.

[87] Lord Wilberforce in McKendrick (n 85) 40.

[88] Lawson and Rudden (n 53) 10; Theft Act 1968, c 60; Law of Property Act 1925, c 20; Trustee Act 1925, c 19 (the most comprehensive definition, including real and personal property, estate shares and interests in property, debt, anything in action, any other right and interest whether in possession or not; see s 68(11). However, the Trustee Act 2000, c 29, in s 39(1) completely abandoned the notion of property referring to assets as including 'any right or interest').

[89] 'The logic of property law is bound up with tangibility.' See A Hudson, 'The unbearable lightness of property' in A Hudson (ed.), *New Perspectives on Property Law, Obligations and Restitution* (Cavendish 2004) 9.

precedents developed concerning land, primarily to deal with complex chattels and intangible assets. The consequence of this was that the concept and the logic behind it 'was likely to be stretched too far'.[90] In addition, even the existing legislation did not help shed much light on the concept of property in England since the Law of Property Act 1925 classifies property instead of defining it. Therefore, Ball rightly notes that 'The nature of property rights frequently has to be deduced from a piecemeal collection of *ad hoc* definitions, usually in case law, borrowing from various sources.'[91]

There is a general preference in English law to focus on remedies rather than principles, in that, 'in English law, the legal question tends to be not necessarily based on the definition of the property but whether something can be protected by the law or handled by the law, perhaps on death, by a transfer or in the law of theft'.[92] Thus in common law, there is 'a predominance of procedural law as means for the delivery of justice', whereas, in France, codification from the early 1800s separated procedural law from the legal principles and substantive law. Therefore, if the French case can be brought within the definitions, then the procedural aspect of the case and, disputably, justice would follow.[93] English law, especially the law of equity, prefers procedural principles.[94] As Samuel argues, French law starts from a subjective right (*le droit subjectif*), and if there is a right, a remedy will be found, whereas English law starts from actions, and there has to be an action and a remedy in order to have an enforceable right.[95] The case law confirms this argument.[96]

In English law, property is divided into personal and real property. Real property refers to land, while personal is everything else. Personal property is residual, and, as Bridge argues, the 'somewhat formless nature of the subject' makes it capable of extension, 'both in respect of recognition of novel kinds of property and of its quantity'.[97] Until the mid-nineteenth century, personal property could not be recovered *in rem* (i.e. the property could not be

[90] Ibid.
[91] Ball (n 59) 4.
[92] Ibid. 8.
[93] This is according to the famous principle, accepted in French legal tradition, 'ubi ius, ibi remedium' (when there is a right, there is a remedy, too). See ibid. 8.
[94] Ibid.
[95] G Samuel, '"Le droit subjectif" and English law' (1987) 46(2) *Cambridge Law Journal* 264, 264–86; Bell et al. (n 52) 7.
[96] See for example Sir Nicolas Browne – Wilkinson VC in *Kingdom of Spain* v *Christie, Manson & Woods Ltd* [1986] 1 WLR 1120, 1129; *F* v *Wirral MBC* [1991] 2 WLR 1132 (CA).
[97] Bridge (n 43) 1.

retrieved as such), as was the case for real property and actions *in rem*.[98] Only a claim for monetary damages was allowed until the Common Law Procedure Act 1854 (s 78),[99] which enabled the return of the chattels detained as a primary remedy.[100]

The personal property further comprises chattels real (leasehold interests in land) and chattels personal. Chattels personal are divided into choses in action and choses in possession.[101]

Choses in possession are tangible, movable things (when they are a subject of sale, they are considered goods), and are more regularly referred to as chattels.[102]

Choses in action are a different type of intangible (incorporeal) property, residual as well. As Bridge argues, they pertain to what remains after eliminating the choses in possession (i.e. debts, goodwill, rights under an insurance policy, shares, bills of exchange and IP).[103] The main characteristic of choses in action is that they can only be claimed by action, legal procedure, and not *in rem*, reclaiming possession.[104] Scholars like Hudson label choses in action 'quasi property', a purely personal claim, recognised as property due to its transferability (the transfer pertains only to the right to receive something) and 'separability' (established by Penner and discussed earlier).[105]

Choses in action further divide into pure intangibles (e.g. debt, goodwill, copyright) and documentary intangibles (bill of lading, bill of exchange, promissory note, shares, insurance policy).[106] These categories fall under the group of common law property. In addition, there exists equitable property (i.e. trust), discussed earlier.

[98] Note the possible confusion between the real and personal property and rights *in rem* and *in personam*. While the former are concerned only with property and thus defined only in common law systems, the latter concern division of rights, differentiating between the rights against the whole world (*in rem*, property rights) and only against a particular person (*in personam*, contractual rights etc.).

[99] Bridge (n 43) 2.

[100] Specific Delivery of Chattels, Common Law Procedure Act 1854, c 125, s 78.

[101] 'All personal things are either in possession or in action, the law knows no tertium quid between the two.' The famous dictum of Fry LJ in *Colonial Bank* v *Whinney* (1885) 30 Ch D 261, a view shared by the House of Lords on appeal: (1886) 11 AC 426.

[102] Bridge (n 43) 3.

[103] Ibid. 4.

[104] *Choses in action* are 'personal rights of property which can only be claimed or enforced by action and not by taking physical possession' or 'a thing which you cannot take, but must go to law to secure'. See *Torkington* v *Magee* [1902] 2 KB 427, 430; TC Williams, 'Property, things in action and copyright' (1895) 11 *Law Quarterly Review* 223, 232.

[105] Hudson, 'Unbearable lightness of property' (n 89) 23–30.

[106] Bridge (n 43) 6–9.

The example of the California Civil Code illustrates similarities with the English categories of property. The general division has been slightly altered and refers to real or immovable and personal or movable property.[107] The general divisions and effects are still very similar, and the property law regimes share vocabulary and principles.[108] Some differences and exceptions will be emphasised in examples relevant to this book, such as property in information.

Choses in action are an exciting peculiarity of common law, for some authors representing 'compromised forms of property'.[109] As Penner explains, the proprietary character of choses in action shows when 'things go badly wrong'. Penner interestingly explains their 'thinghood': 'It is not because they are alienable that they are "things" of this kind. Rather, they are alienable because they are things.' This means they do not have a quality of thinghood, namely alienability, that would naturally qualify them as things. Instead, they have been recognised by law as things, arguably quite artificially, and the law has attributed alienability to them. The classic example is debt, recognised as property in common law and assigned a feature of alienability, unlike in civilian law. Another example is IP, which does not intrinsically have all the classical property features (e.g. exclusivity, rivalrousness, corporality), but has been recognised as property and, arguably, put into this category.

The importance of finding the common elements and themes in civil and common law conceptions of property will be demonstrated further in Chapter 5, where a solution based on both traditions will be suggested. It is argued in this book that the legal borrowing Watson suggests is even more desirable on the Internet, with its blurred boundaries and jurisdiction issues.

(b) *Property Rights vs Obligations*

When discussing the concept of property, one should inevitably refer to obligations, especially the law of contracts, as its correlative concept. This is particularly significant for this book, as most of the currently recognised rights of users in their digital assets are contractual (as demonstrated in the following chapters).

Based on Roman law concepts, most authors in common and civil law systems would use the terms '*in rem*' and '*in personam*' when referring to property and obligations. In common law, the term 'obligations' is rare although

[107] California Civil Code, s 657.

[108] See generally DA Thomas, 'Anglo-American land law: Diverging developments from a shared history – part III: British and American real property law and practice – a contemporary comparison' (1999–2000) 34 *Real Property, Probate and Trust Journal* 443.

[109] Penner, *Idea of Property* (n 58) 107.

it has recently come into frequent use by courts and scholars. Instead, common law jurisprudence refers separately to the notions of contracts, torts and unjust enrichment. There has been, as some argue, a reception of obligations as a category in English law where more judges and academics speak of them when addressing one of these three categories.[110]

Civilian lawyers would commonly use the terms 'real' and 'personal rights', a usage that should not be confused with that of real and personal property in common law (both real and personal property belong to *in rem* property rights in common law, the first about land and the second about everything else). Property rights, as rights *in rem*, are rights against the whole world, a potentially infinite number of persons, while contracts, rights *in personam*, according to the doctrine of privity of contract in common law, and statutory rules and theory in civil law, bind only the parties to the contract, not third parties.[111] Thus, rights *in rem* are often referred to as absolute rights, whereas rights *in personam* are relative; their effect pertains only to the contract parties (with some exceptions).[112]

In an attempt to differentiate rights *in rem* from rights *in personam*, Reid suggests three unique features of real rights: real rights concern things; they can be enforced against the whole world; and the obligation correlative to a real right is negative (to refrain from doing something).[113] American authors Merrill and Smith identify 'four differentiating features of in rem rights' that could be subsumed under the three elements identified by Reid.[114] In civilian systems, the border between property and obligations is relatively straightforward. This clarity can be attributed to the *numerus clausus* principle, which states that all real rights are enumerated and defined in codes or statutes, and parties cannot invent new rights or modify existing ones (with the limitations discussed in previous sections).

110 See GH Samuel and J Rinkes, *Law of Obligations and Legal Remedies* (2nd edn, Cavendish 2001) 252, 254, 262–9.

111 Bridge (n 43) 26; Samuel and Rinkes (n 110) 364–7; *Barker* v *Stickney* [1919] 1 KB 121, 132; *McGruther* v *Pitcher* [1904] 2 Ch 306; *Taddy* v *Sterious* [1904] 1 Ch 354.

112 For a civilian perspective, see Ebke and Finkin (n 46) 228, 229. For mixed and common law systems, see P Sutherland and D Johnston, 'Contracts for the benefit of third parties' in R Zimmermann, D Visser and K Reid (eds), *Mixed Systems in Comparative Perspective* (Oxford University Press 2004) 208–39.

113 Reid (n 44) 227.

114 '(1) in rem rights apply to a large and indefinite class of dutyholders; (2) in rem rights attach to persons only insofar as they own particular "things" and not otherwise; (3) all persons hold in rem duties to a large and indefinite class of holders of such rights; and (4) in rem duties are always duties of abstention rather than performance.' See Merrill and Smith (n 64) 773–852, 789.

Thus, rights appearing in statutes in civilian systems as real rights (ownership, usufruct, securities and servitudes) are property rights, while others are obligations.[115] In civil law countries, obligations have a residuary nature, consisting of what is left after deducting real rights. In Reid's opinion, there are also categories of rights that are hard to classify, bearing in mind, on the one hand, their affinity with both real and personal rights (lease), and, on the other, their affinity with neither (trusts or IP). He suggests that while it is possible to attempt classification using the categories of real and personal rights for a trust, classification is impossible for IP and thus is mainly abandoned by authors.[116]

From the economic perspective, discussing the issue of costs concerning property rights and obligations, Merrill and Smith argue that 'information costs are key to understanding the features of a system of property rights'.[117] The advantage of property rights is that they enable low-cost identification and definition of resources, in the case where there is a large number of potential claimants to resources; thus, these *in rem* rights are governed by 'bright-line rules that allow large and indefinite numbers of people to identify owned resources at low cost'.[118] Obligations, on the other hand, are regulated by more flexible rules 'that minimise the costs of tailoring rights and obligations to each particular situation'.[119]

Crucially, property differs from contracts in that it is always transmissible to heirs on the owner's death. All property, personal and real, corporeal and incorporeal, to name but a few kinds, forms inheritance, the estate of a person, and transmits by the rules of succession to the deceased's heirs. In the UK, for instance, 'a person's estate is the aggregate of all the property to which he is beneficially entitled'.[120] In the US, 'probate assets are those assets of the decedent, includible in the gross estate under IRC § 2033, that were held in his or her name at the time of death'.[121]

[115] Reid (n 44) 228.

[116] Ibid. 229.

[117] Merrill and Smith (n 64) 833.

[118] Ibid. 793.

[119] Ibid. 798.

[120] Wills Act 1837, c 26, s 3 (this Act does not extend its effect to Scotland); Inheritance Tax Act 1984, c 51, s 5(1), applicable to England, Scotland, Wales and Northern Ireland. similarly Succession (Scotland) Act 1964, c 41, s 32 defines estate as property belonging to the deceased at the time of death.

[121] J Darrow and G Ferrera, 'Who owns a decedent's e-mails: Inheritable probate assets or property of the network?' (2006) 10 *New York University Journal of Legislation and Public Policy* 281. See also Sherrin et al., quoted in L McKinnon, 'Planning for the succession of digital assets' (2011) 27(4) *Computer Law and Security Review* 362, 362–7.

Conversely, obligations in principle do not persist on demise. In common law jurisdictions, purely personal obligations 'die with a person'.[122] This position, however, has been revised, and most of the personal rights of action arising from torts survive on death, according to the Law Reform (Miscellaneous Provisions) Act 1934. The only one that does not persist is defamation. As for contractual rights, personal contracts (e.g. employment contracts, contracts between an artist and a person commissioning them) will be discharged on death unless there is an opposite provision in the contract.[123] A contract that is not personal in nature is not discharged upon death, no matter whether it was broken or not; according to the reform mentioned above, it will survive for the benefit of the estate.[124] A personal representative stands in the position of the deceased without being a party to the contract.[125] In French law, with the notion of *patrimoine*,[126] comprising a person's rights and liabilities, all rights and liabilities pass on to the heir(s), who stand in the position of the deceased.[127] Like English common law, in French law, strictly personal contracts (either by the parties' agreement[128] or the nature of the contract[129]) end on death.[130] The same is true in Germany.[131]

Despite the differences presented, it has been noticed that there is a tendency to weaken the centrality of property rights to the advantage of contracts, torts or trusts in England. This tendency goes as far as to call for awarding

[122] Principle '*Actio personalis moritur cum persona*' in *Beker* v *Bolton* (1808) 1 Camp 439; 170 ER 1033, but the Law Reform (Miscellaneous Provisions) Act 1934, c 41 (as amended), revised the rule mandating that all personal rights will survive against and for the benefit of the estate, with the only exception of defamation and claim for bereavement. For the comparison between the US and German perspectives, see for example H Rosler, 'Dignitarian posthumous personality rights – an analysis of US and German constitutional and tort law' (2008) 26 *Berkeley Journal of International Law* 153.

[123] See *Farrow* v *Wilson* (1869) LR 4 CP 744, 746.

[124] See Law Reform (Miscellaneous Provisions) Act 1934, s 1(1); *Sugden* v *Sugden* [1957] 1 All ER 300.

[125] *Beswick* v *Beswick* (1966) Ch 538. For commentary about the contracts and succession, see AR Mellows, *The Law of Succession* (4th edn, Butterworths 1983) 295–6.

[126] B Nicholas, *The French Law of Contract* (2nd edn, Clarendon Press; Oxford University Press 1992) 29, 30.

[127] For more, see ML Levillard, 'France' in DJ Hayton (ed.), *European Succession Laws* (2nd edn, Jordans 2002) 219.

[128] Code civil, Article 1122.

[129] Ibid. Articles 1795, 2003.

[130] For more, see B Nicholas (n 126) 172.

[131] K Kuhne et al., 'Germany' in B Nicholas (n 126) 244, 257.

equal protection to personal rights and property rights.[132] A prominent example of this is the statement of Lord Nicholls in *Attorney-General* v *Blake*:

> Property rights are superior to contractual rights in that, unlike contractual rights, property rights may survive against an indefinite class of persons. However, it is not easy to see why, as between the parties to a contract, a violation of a party's contractual rights should attract a lesser degree of remedy than a violation of his property rights . . . it is not clear why it should be any more permissible to expropriate personal rights than it is permissible to expropriate property rights.[133]

In response to this tendency, some authors suggest an even more radical solution, proposing a unified civil remedy for property, contracts and trust, invoking the approximation of the main categories of private law.[134] To support this, they point to an increasing willingness of courts to use 'the full armoury of remedies' in English common law.[135] For instance, in the recent case of *Manchester Airport plc* v *Dutton*, the proprietary remedy was granted to the non-owner. The company hired by the owner to conduct clearing works on the land requested repossession (ejectment) from the demonstrators who occupied the land. The demonstrators claimed that the company was not entitled to this remedy since it did not have a title of possession. However, a majority of the Court of Appeal held that the company had a contractual right and was entitled to this remedy. The situation would look very different in the civil law systems, where a more precise division between *in rem* and *in personam* rights and remedies exists, and thus only the owner could claim an *in rem* remedy.[136] Some argue that, because English law has never actually developed proprietary remedies, that is, restitution and vindication, and uses torts to protect property (trespass, nuisance and conversion), it does not have such a strict division between real and personal rights, property and obligations.[137] Recognising the unclear picture regarding remedies applied, Samuel argues that perhaps the notion of obligations cannot be imported

[132] See D Pearce, 'Property and contract: where are we?' in Hudson, *New Perspectives on Property Law* (n 89) 109.

[133] [2001] 1 AC 268, 283.

[134] See Pearce (n 132) 109.

[135] Ibid. 116. Another example is *Manchester Airport plc* v *Dutton* [2000] QB 133, where the court allowed a person to use a proprietary remedy to repossess land belonging to another only on the basis of a contractual relationship.

[136] For a commentary, see G Samuel, *Understanding Contractual and Tortious Obligations* (Law Matters 2005) 110, 111.

[137] Ibid. 6.

into English law, which has different reasoning in respect to the law of things than Roman or Continental law.[138]

Others, conversely, argue that the two legal systems in Europe could be brought closer. Van Erp, for example, proposes a more flexible *numerus clausus*, '*quasi-numerus clausus*', where parties have more freedom to shape property rights and are given the freedom to create new property rights under certain strict conditions. In his opinion, these rights could be effective against certain interested third parties, but not the whole world. This result, according to him, would make property law a 'borderline law, a legal area in which traditional property law is further developed through contract and tort law'. Even more radically, van Erp asserts that the trend towards relaxation and flexibility of property rights 'is a *conditio sine qua non* for the development of property law in an era characterised by regional and global economic integration, with its resulting osmosis between national, European and global property law'.[139] This trend would also help settle the legal nature of the new types of assets, such as digital assets.

2.3 Theoretical Justifications for Property

A theory of property could be conceived in many ways. It could be defined as an attempt at a normative justification for allocating property rights at all or in a particular way (detecting which human interests are relevant to a particular way of allocation); it could provide reasons for allocating resources in a certain way; or it could specify the content of property rights at various levels of generality.[140] Similarly, Becker identifies three levels of property justifications: *general* – whether there should be property rights at all; *specific* – why there should be a specific sort of property right; and *particular* – why a particular person ought to have a particular property right in a particular thing.[141] The discussion in this book will mainly relate to the specific level of justifications. In other words, it will mainly attempt to use normative theories to ascertain whether property in digital assets can be asserted in particular cases, that is, emails, social network profiles, and so on.

The justification for property as a basis for normative and social action can be traced back to the works of most of the great philosophers and social

[138] Ibid.

[139] Van Erp (n 33) 21, 22.

[140] See GS Alexander and EM Peñalver, *An Introduction to Property Theory* (Cambridge University Press 2012) 6.

[141] LC Becker, *Property Rights: Philosophic Foundations* (Routledge and Kegan Paul 1977) 23.

thinkers, from the great Greek authors (Plato and Aristotle),[142] to Roman doctrine and law,[143] to natural law scholars, utilitarians, liberals and socialists, to name but a few.

It is important to note at the outset that, although these theories will not be elaborated further here, key Greek property concepts were used as a basis for later discussion about property and many thinkers used them as a starting point for their theories. Thus, the Greeks developed the idea of natural law, which evolved during the Roman period[144] and advanced throughout the Middle Ages, the Enlightenment and modern theories.[145] The natural rights theory considered individual rights derived from either the laws of God, nature or reason. It was incorporated into the American Declaration of Independence of 1776, whose second sentence reads, 'We hold these truths to be self-evident, that all men are created equal, that they are endowed by their Creator with certain unalienable Rights, that among these are Life, Liberty and the pursuit of Happiness'; and into the French Declaration of the Rights of Man and of Citizens of 1789, Article 2, which reads, 'The aim of all political association is the preservation of the natural and imprescriptible rights of man. These rights are liberty, property, security, and resistance to oppression.'

It is not my intention to discuss these theories in depth. The aim is to indicate the most relevant theories that could serve as a basis for later discussion about possible justifications for perceiving digital assets like property.[146] These theories could all be brought under the umbrella of three main groups, widely accepted and used, both in theory and practice. These theories for justifying private property are utilitarianism, the labour theory, and the

[142] For instance, Aristotle's definition of property provides that something 'is "our own" if it is in our power to dispose of it or keep it'. For more, see A Mossoff, 'What is property? Putting the pieces back together' (2003) 45 *Arizona Law Review* 371, 391. The difference between Plato and Aristotle was that the former was a communist when it came to property while the latter defended private property. See for example R Schlatter, *Private Property: The History of an Idea* (Allen & Unwin 1951) 9–21.

[143] Roman law scholar Barry Nicholas notes that there is no Roman definition of ownership, but there are Romanistic ones, usually emphasising enjoyment, and adapting usufruct by adding the right of abuse – *ius utendi fruendi abutendi*. In Mossoff (n 142) 391–2.

[144] Defined in Cicero's Republic or Institutes of Justinian. For more, see Schlatter (n 142) 21–33.

[145] For more, see A Ryan, *Property* (Open University Press 1987) 61–70.

[146] For a sound overview on some of these theories, concentrating mainly on the natural law ones, see S Buckle, *Natural Law and the Theory of Property: Grotius to Hume* (Clarendon Press 1991). For a discussion on Grotius', Pufendorf's and Locke's theories in relation to the bundle of rights and exclusive rights theory in common law scholarship, see Mossoff (n 142).

personhood theory (with the theory of human flourishing as, arguably, its subset).[147]

(a) Utilitarian Theories

The background assumptions of the utilitarian theory are that natural resources are scarce, people are demanding and of limited altruism, and labour is disagreeable and unpleasant. Therefore, there is a necessity to devise ways to make nature yield as much as it can, to be used in a way beneficial to the community. According to utilitarian theory, this aim cannot be achieved without property rules, since some will try to take the fruits of other people's efforts if they are not prevented. However, in the view of some authors, this argument does not readily distinguish between the need for property and the need for private property, since it is not certain whether, for example, capital would be best served in the hands of families or individuals.[148]

The principal exponent of the utilitarian justification of property, Jeremy Bentham, continued on the path traced earlier by Hume, who introduced the principle of utility, arguing that due to the selfish nature of people, and limited natural resources, it is helpful to respect the right of others in order to sustain our own and promote our happiness.[149]

In 1789, Bentham coined the term 'utilitarianism' and introduced the notion of a 'felicific calculus'.[150] This is the main principle of utilitarianism, looking for 'the greatest good for the greatest number'[151] and concentrating on the welfare approach to utility. This theory is, along with the labour theory, frequently used as justification for tangible and intangible property in the common law systems, especially in the US (by courts, academia and even the Constitution; see the discussion below).[152]

The underlying assumption is that people will create socially desirable objects only if granted appropriate incentives, some exclusive right, that is, property rights, so that 'free riders' do not enjoy the fruits of someone else's labour. Further, the theory assesses the goodness or badness of consequences regarding their tendency to maximise utility or welfare, where welfare maximises total net pleasure.

[147] Becker, *Property Rights* (n 141) 99–101; Harris (n 3) 168.

[148] See JS Mill and J Bentham, *Utilitarianism and Other Essays*, ed. A Ryan (Penguin 1987) 56.

[149] See Schlatter (n 142) 239–42.

[150] J Bentham, *An Introduction to the Principles of Morals and Legislation*, ed. JH Burns and HLA Hart (Athlone Press 1970) 12–13.

[151] Ibid.

[152] See also commentary in Alexander and Peñalver (n 140) 11.

For Bentham, the nature of utility is an individual, hedonistic pleasure. The problem that would arise in trying to maximise perverse pleasures, according to this theory, was solved by Mill, who classified them into higher and lower pleasures, giving more weight to higher pleasures when assessing decisions according to the felicific calculus. Hence his famous statement that 'It is better to be a human dissatisfied than a pig satisfied.'[153] If the decision concerns more than one person, the solution, according to Bentham, is to aggregate utility, to add up total net pleasure enjoyed by all the individuals in the group. This principle has been widely criticised on the grounds that it lacks sensitivity to unequal distribution,[154] therefore his principle would be satisfied if there is a total pleasure that only a tiny elite enjoys.

When applied to the justification of property, this theory argues that people need to individually acquire, possess, use and consume some things to achieve a reasonable degree of happiness. Security in possession and use of things is impossible unless enforced and unless modes of acquisition are controlled. The need for such control and enforcement amounts to the administration of a property rights system because of insecurity in possession and use and uncontrolled acquisition of the goods, which render individual achievement of a reasonable degree of happiness impossible. Therefore, a system of property rights is necessary.[155]

Based on the assumptions of the utilitarian theory, mainly in the US, the economic theory of property rights was developed. Many of these theorists refer to themselves as *wellfarists*, too. In response to the Benthamite individualist conception of pleasures, contemporary theorists adopted a weaker concept of goodness, the satisfaction of preferences, rather than pleasures in general. The idea is to filter for worthy and reasonable preferences, so that, in contrast to Bentham's conception, by concentrating on individual preferences, whatever they might be, later theorists tried to mitigate the absoluteness of pleasure, bringing it down to mere preferences, and only those worthy and reasonable, usually measured within a group rather than at the individual level. However, most of these theorists focus on the satisfaction of likely consequences rather than the actual consequence of the decision being evaluated.

In modern theory, the closest to Bentham's principle of aggregated utility is the Kaldor–Hicks criterion of efficiency.[156] According to this criterion, a social decision is superior to alternatives if the people who benefit from

[153] JS Mill, 'Utilitarianism' in Mill and Bentham (n 148) 260.
[154] See Alexander and Peñalver (n 140) 14.
[155] Becker, *Property Rights* (n 141) 57–8.
[156] K Nicholas, 'Welfare propositions in economics and interpersonal comparisons of utility' (1939) *Economic Journal* 49, 549–52.

the choice gain enough that they could, hypothetically, fully compensate those individuals who lose out from it such that the losers consider themselves no worse off than they were before. The Pareto principle states that a social choice is good if it makes at least one person better off without decreasing utility for anyone else.[157]

The biggest problem with assessing these principles is the gathering of necessary data. These methods vary from assessing the amount people are willing to pay to satisfy their preferences to conducting surveys and other empirical research. Thus, Alexander rightly argues that the value of any utilitarian prescription will only be as good as the empirical information on which it is based.[158]

Further, based on Benthamite assumptions, modern economic theories of property focus on explaining property in terms of economic factors, such as the efficiency achieved on the market, and are not normative like utilitarianism but rather explanatory.[159] In the best-known version of these theories, the inefficiency of common property is attributed to the tragedy of the commons. The 'tragedy of the commons' is a well-known and widely built upon concept in the US, created by Garrett Hardin.[160]

A tragedy of the commons is a situation appearing when too many owners have a privilege to use a resource, and no one has a right to exclude another. This leads to overuse and depletion of the resource. The theory is based on four assumptions: a community made up of rational actors who aim to maximise their individual material gain; a resource is rivalrous, that is, one who uses a resource progressively diminishes or degrades the remaining supply of the resource; users can keep all the benefits while they all bear the costs; and use of a resource is unregulated and open to all.[161]

On the other hand, as a critique, a theory of the 'tragedy of the anticommons' appeared, introduced by Michael Heller.[162] It is defined as a situation where 'multiple owners are each endowed with the right to exclude others from a scarce resource, and no one has an effective privilege of use. When too many owners hold rights of exclusion, the resource is prone to underuse – a tragedy of the anticommons.'[163] The example he uses is empty storefronts in transitional Moscow instead of metal kiosks appearing widely

157 Alexander and Peñalver (n 140) 14.

158 Ibid. 15. See also Becker, *Property Rights* (n 141) 68.

159 For more, see Mill and Bentham (n 148) 103–15.

160 G Hardin, 'The tragedy of the commons' (1968) 162 *Science* 1243, 1243–8.

161 Alexander and Peñalver (n 140) 28.

162 MA Heller, 'The tragedy of the anticommons: Property in the transition from Marx to markets reviewed' (1998) 111(3) *Harvard Law Review* 621, 621–88.

163 Ibid. 624.

in the same areas. He argues that the underuse in this example is caused by an inappropriate initial endowment of property rights, where multiple owners were assigned rights to exclude others, and no one had a right to control the resource individually. Thus, he suggests that bundles of rights should be allocated to individuals rather than allocating individual rights, to enable more efficient control of a resource. Another example is IP rights, where competing and restrictive patent rights in biomedical and pharmaceutical research, for instance, could disable the introduction of useful and cheaper products to the market.[164]

A similar theory to that of the tragedy of the commons was put forward by Demsetz, based on Blackstone's theory. It describes the invention of property as a response to scarcity. He illustrates his theory through the case of Native American hunters in the Hudson Bay area during the early colonial period when the Europeans' demand for furs created immense pressure to capture furred animals. Consequently, the Native Americans began to overhunt the common grounds, each hunter imposing 'external' costs on the others since all needed to deploy more hunting effort to catch the rare animals. Therefore, according to Demsetz, these indigenous hunters realised they could prevent overhunting by turning their common hunting grounds into private property. Once they had done so, he recounts, the individual owners appropriated wildlife resources on their respective territories, and the private hunting grounds became productive again. In Demsetz's more technical economic terms, property rights enabled people to 'internalise externalities'.[165]

The utilitarian justification is, understandably, and bearing in mind the dominant legal and political culture, most accepted in the US and countries that embrace liberal capitalist values. Thus, even the US Constitution in Article I, section 8, clause 8 says that the purpose of protecting IP rights is 'to promote the Progress of Science and useful Arts',[166] which is a utilitarian concept. Moreover, the US courts often use this justification in deciding IP-related cases.[167] This theory will be employed in the following chapters, where the utility of recognising digital assets as property will be assessed.

[164] MA Heller and R Eisenberg, 'Can patents deter innovation? The anticommons in biomedical research' (1998) 280 *Science* 698, 698–701.

[165] H Demsetz, 'Toward a theory of property rights' (1967) 57 *American Economic Review* 347, 347–9.

[166] This clause is known as the Patent and Copyright Clause. For more, see I Donner, 'The copyright clause of the U.S. Constitution: Why did the framers include it with unanimous approval?' (1992) 36(3) *American Journal of Legal History* 361, 361–78.

[167] See for example *Mazer* v *Stein*, 347 US 201, 219 (1954); *New York Times Co* v *Tasini*, 533 US 483, 495 (2001); *Precision Instrument Mfg Co* v *Auto Maint Mach Co*, 324 US 806, 816 (1945).

(b) Labour Theories

Labour theory was introduced and developed by John Locke. Locke has had the most significant influence on property theories in English-speaking countries, and his theory is often associated with libertarians.[168] His theory is mainly elaborated in chapter five of the *Second Treatise of Government*. In the introduction to the 1980 edition of the *Second Treatise*, Macpherson observes that nobody has made a more persuasive case for unlimited property rights than Locke, who defended the limited constitutional liberal state, and asserts that 'no one has come even near his skill in moving from a limited and equal to an unlimited and unequal property right by invoking rationality and consent' and thus providing a justification for a liberal capitalist state conception of property.[169]

Locke's central argument is that 'whatsoever (man) removes out of the state that nature hath provided and left it in, he hath mixed his labour with, and joined to it something that is his own, and thereby makes it his property'.[170] Before asserting this, Locke starts by elaborating his intention to show how men could have property in something that 'God gave mankind in common' and all that without any explicit consent from others, the commoners.[171] Further, he claims that to use a natural resource (in his example fruit or venison) for 'the best advantage of life, and convenience', it is necessary to appropriate it 'that another can no longer have any right to it'.[172] The justification for appropriation lies in Locke's claim that everyone has property in his or her own person, consequently in their labour, 'the work of his hands'. Therefore, whatever one removes from the commons and mixes their labour with ceases to be held in common and becomes their property.[173] This argument is not, however, without limitations.

Locke's famous principle of waste limitation is the requirement that the labourer is limited to 'as much as anyone can make use of to any advantage of life before it spoils'.[174] Becker defines it as the 'why not?' argument, meaning that a labourer has property rights if he produces something by his labour, and it is not against moral requirements for the labourer, and finally, other

[168] Alexander and Peñalver (n 140) 35.

[169] CB Macpherson, 'Editor's introduction' in J Locke, *Second Treatise of Government: Essay Concerning the True Original Extent and End of Civil Government*, ed. with an intro. CB Macpherson (Hackett 1980) xxi.

[170] Locke (n 169) § 27, 19.

[171] Ibid. § 25, 18.

[172] Ibid. § 26, 19.

[173] Ibid. § 27.

[174] Ibid. § 56.

members of society do not incur loss from being excluded from enjoying the fruit of labour.[175]

The final limitation is Locke's 'enough and as good' proviso, meaning that there should be enough and as good left in common for others after appropriation. Note, however, that Locke revises these limitations when writing of the introduction of money as property when all three limitations were removed – spoilage, 'enough and as good' and mixing labour – justifying unlimited private property.[176] Money does not spoil, so the first limitation is removed.[177] The second limitation is abandoned with the development of commerce and the consent to use money. Locke explains it by referring to the value of appropriated and cultivated land, which is at least ten times more than that of unappropriated and uncultivated land, and thus, even if there is not enough land left for others, there is *produce* for everyone.[178] The advent of commerce then induced each man to appropriate more and exchange the surplus for money, 'beyond the use of his family'.[179]

Penner criticises Locke's theory because it does not make a real difference between contracts and property based on consent. Moreover, according to him, the theory is flawed since it presupposes one's right to control or the ability to act freely, which is not always the case (the problem of slavery or ownership of goods created by employees).[180]

Nozick offered one of the most famous critiques of Locke's theory. It is interestingly summarised in this widely cited quote:

> Why isn't mixing what I own with what I don't own a way of losing what I own rather than a way of gaining what I don't? If I own a can of tomato juice and spill it in the sea so that its molecules (made radioactive, so I can check this) mingle evenly throughout the sea, do I thereby come to own the sea, or have I foolishly dissipated my tomato juice?[181]

Becker, for instance, shares this view,[182] whereas Alexander responds to this objection using the example of a stream, soup and tomato juice. Contrary to Nozick's example of the sea, in Alexander's illustration there is only a little water taken from the stream, so tomato juice adds much more value to the

[175] Becker, 'Moral basis of property rights' (n 18) 193.
[176] Macpherson, 'Editor's introduction' (n 169) xvii.
[177] Locke (n 169) § 37.
[178] Ibid. § 37; commentary in Macpherson, 'Editor's introduction' (n 169) xvii.
[179] Locke (n 169) § 48.
[180] Penner, *Idea of Property* (n 58) 187–8.
[181] R Nozick, *Anarchy, State and Utopia* (Basil Blackwell 1974) 175.
[182] Becker, *Property Rights* (n 141) 34.

water in making a soup. A further objection Alexander makes is collective labour, which is usually how things are produced.[183]

Another problem with Locke's theory is its application when the common is already appropriated. Throughout history, it has been used as a justification for various kinds of property objects, but many authors disregarded the fact that the theory applies only to the justification for things appropriated from the commons.[184] Locke's primary goal was to justify the appropriation of Native American land. He made it quite clear that he spoke of nature's state and not of his contemporary society.[185] This can be seen in his example of the commons in England, where the common is created by 'the law of the land' and to be used by all countrymen, who already have their property and participate in commerce. Hence, no one can appropriate this land without consent as it is 'in the beginning and first peopling of the great common of the world'.[186] This objection is particularly relevant to the discussion on digital assets, as it is challenging to identify the relevant commons there.

As hinted above, Locke's work has been used by a variety of scholars in efforts to justify diverse kinds of property relations, institutions and objects. The arguments supported by this theory have been used by opposing theories and practices. Thus, the nineteenth-century reading of Locke supported egalitarian and redistributive efforts and policies, whereas, conversely, the twentieth-century readings paint a picture of Locke as a defender of capitalist accumulation and rights of property.[187]

Locke's theory has been used as a starting point and an essential reference in discussions on IP and information as property (see 'Property in emails' in Chapter 6). This book will use it as one of the theories that might justify property in certain digital assets.

[183] Alexander and Peñalver (n 140) 48.
[184] Ibid. 37.
[185] Locke (n 169) § 51. See also Schlatter (n 142) 156.
[186] Locke (n 169) § 35, 22.
[187] See CB Macpherson, *The Political Theory of Possessive Individualism: Hobbes to Locke* (Wynford edn, new edn, Oxford University Press 2011); Alexander and Peñalver (n 140) 53; and Nozick and Epstein as the most influential contemporary American libertarian thinkers: Nozick (n 181) and R Epstein, 'One step beyond Nozick's minimal state: The role of forced exchanges in political theory' (2005) 22 *Social Philosophy and Policy* 286. See J Tully, *A Discourse on Property: John Locke and His Adversaries* (Cambridge University Press 1980) 172. Becker, *Property Rights* (n 141) 43. Becker asserts that Locke's theory provides more justification for socialist than capitalist societies.

(c) Personality Theory

Personality (personhood) theories justifying property originated from Hegel's conception of property as an extension of personality.[188] It is 'the relation of personality to the external sphere of things, understood in terms of the free will'.[189] Also, 'A person must translate his freedom into an external sphere in order to exist as an idea.'[190] Further, free will in every stage of development is embodied in something externalised, and since things have no will, there is an absolute right of appropriation. Therefore, a person with a will has a right to appropriate and determine the use of a thing that is considered as not having a will. This relates to the first appropriation. The following person who wants to appropriate it is confronted by the will of another embodied in possession of a thing.[191] Hegel, however, did not specify what types of property should exist, which is a lack in his theory.[192]

Modern personhood theories mainly focus on personality and human rights, invoking autonomy, liberty, identity and privacy as values that could not be effectively protected without property rights; in other words, these values are intrinsically connected to property interests. Thus, as Munzer notes, personality theorists advocate private property rights that should be recognised to advance a broad range of interests and promote human flourishing. He summarises these interests as peace of mind, privacy, self-reliance, self-realisation (as a social being and as an individual), security and leisure, responsibility, identity, citizenship and benevolence.[193]

In the cluster of modern personhood theories, one of the most significant and influential is Radin's personhood theory.[194] Radin classifies property as fungible and personal, arguing that property is an essential vehicle for the development of personality and, therefore, that the property which is incredibly close to a person's self-definition (e.g. his home, a wedding ring) deserves special legal protections and precedence over other property rights.[195] Critics,

[188] GWF Hegel, *The Philosophy of Right*, trans. TM Knox (Oxford University Press 1967). For a sound elaboration and critique, see Penner, *Idea of Property* (n 58) 169–86.

[189] See Penner, *Idea of Property* (n 58) 173.

[190] Hegel (n 188) para 41.

[191] Penner, *Idea of Property* (n 58) 174. For more, see Alexander and Peñalver (n 140) 59–61.

[192] Alexander and Peñalver (n 140) 65.

[193] SR Munzer (ed.), *New Essays in the Legal and Political Theory of Property* (Cambridge University Press 2001) 189–90; here he refers to personhood theorists, Waldron, Fried, Rose, Radin, Green etc.

[194] MJ Radin, 'Property and personhood' (1982) 34 *Stanford Law Review* 957; Waldron (n 12).

[195] Radin (n 194).

however, suggest that the shortcoming of her theory is that Radin only referred to the autonomous self, individual development, and had nothing to say about the relational, interpersonal aspect of property and self-development.[196]

This theory is also an essential underpinning of the discussions on whether information and digital assets can be considered property. In addition, it is closely linked to theories of autonomy and privacy, explored in Chapter 3, and it will be referred to further there.

2.4 Concluding Remarks

In conclusion, recognising an object or phenomenon as property brings some general benefits to the rights holder. These advantages include the *in rem* effect against the whole world and not only between parties to a contract; remedies applicable to property; and, importantly, the possibility to transmit it on death (with the reservations discussed above).[197] Regarding the last element, if an environment is extensively regulated by contracts (e.g. terms of service of Internet developers and service providers), which are strictly personal or explicitly forbid transmission on death, according to the rules mentioned above, they cannot be transmitted on death. Therefore, if their social and economic value is such that transmission on death is desirable, the property regime would be more suitable. This is, nevertheless, a provisional conclusion, dependent on the findings in the following chapters, where the nature and value of individual digital assets are discussed. Each chapter will either confirm or reject the proposition that digital assets can be considered property and therefore generally transmitted on death like any other form of property.

We could provisionally conclude that new forms of property could fit more easily into some of the English categories (choses in action), founded on the bundle of rights theory of property. However, notwithstanding the rigid 1885 (in *Colonial Bank* v *Whinney*) categorisation of personal property in English law, many authors would argue that, unlike in civil law, common law property is capable of expansion and inclusion of new categories.[198] Lord Wilberforce supports this in the *National Provincial Bank Ltd* v *Ainsworth* statement, cited in the previous section. Also, as Ball rightly notes, lack of a principle of unity of property in English law, lack of limitative definitions of

196 See Alexander and Peñalver (n 140) 69.

197 See for example Honoré (n 5); Becker, 'Moral basis of property rights' (n 18); *OBG Ltd* v *Allan* [2007] UKHL 21; [2008] 1 AC 1, 309.

198 WG Friedmann, *Law in a Changing Society* (2nd edn, Penguin 1972) 94; K Moon, 'The nature of computer programs: tangible? Goods? Personal property? Intellectual property?' (2009) *European Intellectual Property Review* 396, 407.

property, and the bundle of rights conception of property make English law liberal and prone to fragmentation and the manipulation of property rights by lawyers.[199]

Nevertheless, nowadays, theory no longer reflects reality as the courts have refused to create new forms of property in the last century.[200] In addition to the English example of confidential information, discussed in more detail later in Chapter 6, there is electricity. Even legal recognition of full property rights for choses in action, recognised as property in English law (see the discussion earlier in this section), has been denied because this property is not tangible. Thus, in *OBG Ltd* v *Allan*,[201] the House of Lords, by a 3:2 majority, denied applying the tort of conversion to anything other than chattels. However, this is not the case in the US, where the courts in some states have abandoned this traditional view, and some information (e.g. fresh news, trade secrets) is considered property. This development will be discussed further in Chapter 6.

Theories of property presented in this chapter will be examined systematically in each case study chapter to analyse whether doctrinal law supports the property status of digital assets and whether the theory, policy and ethics suggest that property should be recognised in such assets.

199 Ball (n 59) 4.

200 '[E]lectricity . . . is not capable of ownership' in *Low* v *Blease* [1975] Crim LR 513. See commentary in Moon (n 198) 406–7.

201 [2007] UKHL 21.

3

Theoretical Underpinnings: Autonomy, Testamentary Freedom and Post-Mortem Privacy

This chapter examines the primary underpinning value of the book, namely autonomy, and its relationship with the concept of post-mortem privacy. This analysis will be relevant to the case studies of emails and social networks due to the prevalence of personal data and privacy issues in these digital assets. The analysis can also apply to any other highly personal digital asset, any aspect of digital legacy and remains that intrinsically relates to what we consider our 'self', who we are, or, as Floridi puts it, our 'informational body'.[1] The issue of post-mortem privacy is less relevant to games and virtual worlds since players usually take up imaginary identities and do not share their personal data and the real-life identities therein. It is also less relevant to highly monetary assets, such as virtual currencies.

In my earlier work, I have set up foundations for the theory and law of post-mortem and, later, postmortal privacy.[2] The discussion in this chapter will consolidate these foundations and deepen the analysis of all the relevant concepts, including autonomy, privacy and data protection.

[1] L Floridi, 'Distributed morality in an information society' (2013) 19(3) *Science and Engineering Ethics* 727; L Floridi, *The Ethics of Information* (Oxford University Press 2013); L Floridi, *The Fourth Revolution: How the Infosphere Is Reshaping Human Reality* (Oxford University Press 2014).

[2] L Edwards and E Harbinja, 'Protecting post-mortem privacy: Reconsidering the privacy interests of the deceased in a digital world (2013) 32(1) *Cardozo Arts & Entertainment Law Journal* 101; E Harbinja, 'Does the EU data protection regime protect post-mortem privacy and what could be the potential alternatives?' (2013) 10:1 *SCRIPTed* 19; E Harbinja, 'Post-mortem privacy 2.0: Theory, law and technology' (2017) 31 *International Review of Law, Computers & Technology* 26; E Harbinja, 'The "new(ish)" property, informational bodies, and postmortality' in M Savin-Baden and V Mason-Robbie (eds), *Digital Afterlife: Death Matters in a Digital Age* (Taylor & Francis 2020) 89–106.

As discussed in Chapter 1, various stakeholders are concerned with the issues and the analysis in this book (users, families, service providers, friends, society). When considering choices amongst their interests, both doctrinal law and theoretical justifications for recognising the property status of digital assets do not always give a clear answer. I thus take a normative stance and promote the user's interests over their family or intermediaries in this instance. The reason is that autonomy is asserted as the key concept driving the development of the law in this area, as seen in the discovery of post-mortem privacy. Simultaneously, the technology market has a clear drive to provide such autonomy via Google Inactive Account Manager or Facebook Legacy Contact. Furthermore, the US Uniform Law Commission work in the area and some data protection statutes in Europe illustrate a significant policy drive towards greater recognition of post-mortem privacy.

I contend that if one of the digital assets analysed in the subsequent chapters can be considered property, then the answer is clear, and they do transmit on death. Conversely, if this conclusion cannot be established, then the user's interests and autonomy might not be met. In such circumstances, reform of the law might be required. Ideally, this reform will advance post-mortem control and steps to foster user choice and autonomy. Consequently, each of the assets will be analysed against the background set out in the previous chapter and here, and if an asset does not meet doctrinal and normative aspects of property, then I will aim to identify whether post-mortem privacy could be used as a tool to enable protection, user choice and control over these assets.

The book bases its findings and reform proposals on the proposition that user autonomy and privacy online should be recognised and strengthened. In particular, the suggested code–law–market solutions and the concept of post-mortem privacy have their firm grounding in autonomy.

Post-mortem privacy (PMP) builds on the conception of privacy as an aspect of one's autonomy. The proposition is that autonomy should, in principle, transcend death and allow individuals to control their privacy/identity/personal data post-mortem. PMP is a more recent phenomenon in legal scholarship, and, therefore, we will discuss it from a doctrinal point of view as well, as opposed to the primarily theoretical analysis in the earlier chapter. This approach will enable a holistic conceptualisation of PMP, encompassing its theoretical underpinnings (i.e. autonomy) and doctrinal arguments (i.e. the protection of personal data, testamentary freedom) for its legal recognition.[3] This is the starting point of the theory. It will later be developed

[3] Harbinja, 'Post-mortem privacy 2.0' (n 2).

using additional philosophical, sociological and legal arguments to evolve into what I have earlier called 'postmortal privacy'. This phenomenon helps explain some of the more recent technological developments, including the creation and sharing of deepfakes and chatbots of the deceased.[4]

PMP, rights of privacy for the dead, is not a recognised term of art or category in succession law or privacy literature. Edwards and Harbinja conceptualise it as 'the right of a person to preserve and control what becomes of his or her reputation, dignity, integrity, secrets or memory after death'.[5] PMP is a recognised phenomenon in psychology, counselling, anthropology, and other humanities and social sciences. However, as noted by Edwards and Harbinja, the notion has received little if any attention from legal scholarship.[6] Edwards, Harbinja and McCallig[7] argue that it is an appropriate topic of public and scholarly legal concern, 'particularly due to the growth in creation, sharing and acquisition of *digital assets* which often have a peculiarly personal and intimate character, and also happen to be voluminous, shareable, hard to destroy and difficult to categorise under current legal norms of property rights'.[8]

To set the foundations for the analysis, we will first briefly look at the most significant theories of autonomy. These theories will be subsequently discussed in relation to the conceptions of privacy, with the primary aim of restating the link between the two concepts and then relating it to the notion of post-mortem privacy. It is argued here and throughout the book that autonomy should be further extended on death, *inter alia*, in the form of post-mortem privacy. The analogy drawn to support this argument is that of testamentary freedom. This concept implies extending a person's autonomy on death by disposing of their property through a will.[9]

3.1 A Brief Conceptualisation of Autonomy

Autonomy, like property, is difficult to define, and it takes various meanings and conceptions based on different philosophical, ethical, legal and other

[4] E Harbinja, L Edwards and M McVey, 'Chatbots that resurrect the dead: Legal experts weigh in on "disturbing" technology' *The Conversation* (1 March 2021) <https://www.theconversation.com/chatbots-that-resurrect-the-dead-legal-experts-weigh-in-on-disturbing-technology-155436> last accessed 1 August 2021.

[5] Edwards and Harbinja, 'Protecting post-mortem privacy' (n 2) 103.

[6] Ibid.

[7] D McCallig, 'Private but eventually public: Why copyright in unpublished works matters in the digital age' (2013) 10:1 *SCRIPTed* 39, 43–4.

[8] Edwards and Harbinja, 'Protecting post-mortem privacy' (n 2) 103–4 (original emphasis).

[9] Harbinja, 'Post-mortem privacy 2.0' (n 2).

theories.[10] The theories of autonomy draw both from deist and secular ethical stances, will and interest theories of rights, natural law and its opposing views, explaining autonomy in relation to liberty, dignity, self-realisation, social contract, public interest and moral.[11] We will look at the conceptions of autonomy briefly and to the extent that this discussion can subsequently be utilised in the privacy and post-mortem privacy analysis later in the chapter.

The etymology of autonomy is based on the Greek words *autos* (self) and *nomos* (rule or law).[12] A definition similar to the linguistic meaning of the term has been offered by Raz, who maintains that 'The ideal of autonomy is that of the autonomous life . . . to be maker or author of [one's] own life',[13] or Rao, who argues that autonomy 'evokes images of self-rule, self-determination, and self-sovereignty'.[14]

Most classical thinkers explore this concept, relating it to freedom, ethics, personhood, dignity and other values. This book focuses on personal autonomy and not on 'moral autonomy', as used in Kant's work and Kantian scholarship. However, it is still necessary to refer to Kant's theory first, as his discussion of autonomy is one of the most comprehensive and influential of all times.[15]

Kantian autonomy is closely linked to ethics and represents the revolutionary thinking of Western morality in the eighteenth century. His theory is still highly influential and provides a focal point for contemporary scholarly discussions on ethics.[16] Kant's morality is based on self-governance and autonomy. According to Kant, human beings are rational, autonomous and self-governing, and they themselves legislate moral law.[17] This action by their will is a precondition for their obedience of the moral law.[18] For Kant, 'Whatever will is to be good if it is taken universally and reciprocally must not cancel

[10] See for example RH Fallon Jr., 'Two senses of autonomy' (1994) 46 *Stanford Law Review* 875, 876; R Rao, 'Property, privacy, and the human body' (2000) 80 *Boston University Law Review* 359, 360.

[11] For a useful commentary on the development of autonomy, see JB Schneewind, *The Invention of Autonomy: A History of Modern Moral Philosophy* (Cambridge University Press 1998).

[12] G Dworkin, *The Theory and Practice of Autonomy* (Cambridge University Press 1988) 12.

[13] J Raz, *The Morality of Freedom* (Clarendon Press 1986) 372.

[14] Rao (n 10) 360.

[15] See Schneewind (n 11) 550–5.

[16] Ibid. 3–11.

[17] I Kant, *Observations on the Feeling of the Beautiful and the Sublime*, trans. JT Goldthwait (2nd edn, University of California Press 2003) 31.10, 25.14.

[18] Ibid.

itself.'[19] Kant also discussed the relationship between the individual and the general public will, arguing that an action is morally just if it arises from the general will.[20] Furthermore, when explaining the relationships between these two wills, he refers to inner perfection that stems from 'the subordination of the totality of powers and sensibilities under the free will'.[21] He concludes with a sentence that sums up the relationship: 'This will contains both the merely private and the general will or man observes himself immediately in consensus with the general will.'[22]

In his later work, Kant refines his theory and introduces two principles: *Rechtspflichten* – governing duties of law, and *Tugendpflichten* – governing duties of virtue or morality. The first principle mandates that human beings act externally only to allow 'the freedom of the will of each to coexist together with the freedom of everyone in accordance with a universal law'.[23] The second principle means that we are to 'act according to a maxim of *ends* which it can be a universal law for everyone to have' and these ends are our perfection and happiness of others. This principle is also known as Kant's categorical imperative.[24] Finally, Kant believes that acts to which someone has a right may be obtained by compulsion, whereas the adoption of ends and virtue must result from free choice.[25]

The work of thinkers that was explored in the discussions on the theories of property will also be looked at from the perspective of their conceptions of autonomy. Like Kant, John Locke engages in contemplating morals and free will. According to him, the will is the power of deciding on an action, and our will engages only when we think there is good or bad at stake.[26] Willing to him is 'preferring an Action to its absence'.[27] Bentham also talks about will and autonomy in the context of his utilitarian writing on the greatest happiness principle, explored in the previous chapter in the context of property. According to Bentham, we must overcome a divergence between duty and interest by our actions. This means that we will pursue morally sound goals if legislation clarifies that it is in our own interest.[28]

19 Ibid. 67.5, 53.1.
20 Ibid. 154.4, 116.1.
21 Ibid. 145.16, 116.19.
22 Ibid.
23 I Kant, *The Metaphysics of Morals*, trans. M Gregor (Cambridge 1991) 6.230, 56.
24 Ibid. 6.395, 198 (original emphasis).
25 Ibid. 6.381, 186.
26 J Locke, *An Essay Concerning Human Understanding*, ed. P Nidditch (Oxford 1979) II.XXI. 31–8, 250–6.
27 Ibid. II.XXI. 21, 244.
28 J Bentham, *A Fragment on Government*, ed. W Harrison (Oxford 1948) X.5–7, 10; VII.1.

As noted in Chapter 2, some theories of property refer to autonomy and free will in their attempt to justify the concept of property. Hegel, for instance, understands property as an extension of personality and one's free will.[29] For him, property is 'the relation of personality to the external sphere of things, understood in terms of the free will'.[30] Also, 'A person must translate his freedom into an external sphere in order to exist as an idea.'[31] Further, free will in every stage of development is embodied in something externalised, and since things have no will, there is an absolute right of appropriation. Therefore, a person with a will has a right to appropriate and determine the use of a thing that is considered as not having a will.[32] Similarly, Radin classifies property as fungible and personal, arguing that property is an essential vehicle for personality development.[33] Radin bases these arguments on the notion of the autonomous self and individual development, that is, autonomy.[34]

Contemporary legal scholars use the notion of autonomy based on the classical concept of liberty.[35] Therefore, autonomy can be based on John Stuart Mill's theory as expressed, for instance, in his classical work *On Liberty*, where Mill argues:

> the only freedom which deserves the name is that of pursuing our own good in our own way . . . Each is the proper guardian of his own health, whether bodily or mental and spiritual. Mankind are greater gainers by suffering each other to live as seems good to themselves than by compelling each to live as seems good to the rest.[36]

Raz and Rawls follow this line of argument and emphasise the individual as the author of his own life, including a degree of control and leading to happiness and good life.[37] For Raz, an autonomous person is one who 'is a (part)

[29] GWF Hegel, *The Philosophy of Right*, trans. TM Knox (Oxford University Press 1967), or for a sound elaboration and critique, see J Penner, *The Idea of Property in Law* (Oxford University Press 1997) 169–86.

[30] See Penner (n 29) 173.

[31] Hegel (n 29) para 41.

[32] Penner (n 29) 174. For more, see GS Alexander and EM Peñalver, *An Introduction to Property Theory* (Cambridge University Press 2012) 59–61.

[33] MJ Radin, 'Property and personhood' (1982) 34 *Stanford Law Review* 957.

[34] See Alexander and Peñalver (n 32) 69.

[35] JP Safranek and S Safranek, 'Can the right to autonomy be resuscitated after Glucksberg?' (1998) 69 *University of Colorado Law Review* 737, 738. See also P Bernal, *Internet Privacy Rights: Rights to Protect Autonomy* (Cambridge University Press 2014) 30.

[36] JS Mill, *On Liberty*, ed. G Himmelfarb (Penguin 1984) 72.

[37] Raz (n 13) 369; J Rawls and SR Freeman, *Collected Papers* (Harvard University Press 1999) 365.

author of his own life'[38] and autonomy is a 'constituent element of the good life'.[39]

Therefore, many classical and contemporary Western philosophers and social theorists consider autonomy one of the central values and the basis of their ethical and social theories. This book builds on the literature and further explores the relationship between autonomy and privacy to justify its normative stance and solutions proposed in the concluding chapter. The conceptions of autonomy used to underpin the arguments of this book are those of personal autonomy as explained in the works of Hegel, Mill, Bentham, Raz, Rawls, Rao et al. The reason for this is that the individual, the user, is the main focal point of this book, and their interests are to be advanced in the first place, notwithstanding the potentially conflicting public interest to which we return in the final chapter.

3.2 Autonomy and Privacy

Many authors consider autonomy and privacy inseparable and use autonomy as a building block of the conceptions and definitions of privacy. Ortiz, for instance, argues that privacy defines 'the scope and limits of individual autonomy'[40] and links privacy to property. Property includes autonomy as dominion over things and the physical sphere, whereas privacy represents dominion over oneself.[41] Henkin has offered a similar view,[42] which is closely related to Radin's theory of property and personhood, discussed in Chapter 2 and mentioned above. A rich scholarship on privacy, autonomy, dignity and personhood makes similar links and interrelations.[43] Recent UK privacy scholarship follows a similar line of argument as well. Bernal, for instance, maintains that 'privacy is a crucial protector of autonomy',[44] basing his approach on Raz's and Rawls's conceptions of autonomy.[45]

[38] Raz (n 13) 369.

[39] Ibid. 408.

[40] DR Ortiz, 'Privacy, autonomy, and consent' (1988) 12 *Harvard Journal of Law and Public Policy* 21, 92.

[41] Ibid.

[42] L Henkin, 'Privacy and autonomy' (1974) 74 *Columbia Law Review* 1410, 1425.

[43] AJ Rappaport, 'Beyond personhood and autonomy: Moral theory and the premises of privacy' (2001) *Utah Law Review* 441, 443; J Feinberg, 'Autonomy, sovereignty, and privacy: Moral ideals in the Constitution?' (1983) 58 *Notre Dame Law Review* 445, 483; RM Smith, 'The constitution and autonomy' (1982) 60 *Texas Law Review* 175; Henkin (n 42). 1425; GR Nichol, 'Children of distant fathers: Sketching an ethos of constitutional liberty' (1985) *Wisconsin Law Review* 1305, 1309.

[44] Bernal (n 35) 9.

[45] Ibid.

Some of the most prominent US privacy theorists, such as Nissenbaum[46] and Solove,[47] also discuss the relationship between privacy and autonomy, setting the discussion in the digital environment. For Nissenbaum, privacy is an aspect of autonomy over one's person and privacy that frees us from the 'stultifying effects of scrutiny and approbation (or disapprobation)', contributing to an environment that supports the 'development and exercise of autonomy and freedom in thought and action'.[48] Nissenbaum further asserts that privacy is essential for making effective choices and following them through, which is an essential aspect of autonomy understood as explained in the above section.[49] Eventually, therefore, privacy is about control, as much as autonomy and property are.[50] Similarly, Rosen adopts an even more radical 'privacy as negative liberty' stance.[51]

Cohen, on the other hand, offers a critique of this liberal conception of the autonomous self, noting the post-modernist critique or social constructivism and calling for a more nuanced theoretical account of privacy 'in a world where social shaping is everywhere, and liberty is always a matter of degree'.[52] Cohen criticises these approaches fiercely in some of her more recent works, too.[53] Schwartz belongs to the group of scholars who see privacy in a positive liberty manner, arguing that there should be constraints on day-to-day autonomy and privacy so that one's capabilities can be developed and one can make better long-term choices.[54] This is known as the 'constitutive privacy' school of thought, which recognises autonomy as the core of privacy and requires external enablement and protection because of the societal influences on the core of the autonomous self.[55] In addition, scholars put collective and communitarian interests, welfare and security before individual autonomy and

[46] HF Nissenbaum, *Privacy in Context: Technology, Policy, and the Integrity of Social Life* (Stanford Law Books 2010) 2.

[47] DJ Solove, '"I've got nothing to hide" and other misunderstandings of privacy' (2007) *San Diego Law Review* 744, 745–72.

[48] Nissenbaum (n 46) 83.

[49] Ibid. 82–3.

[50] See also Bernal (n 35) 35.

[51] J Rosen, *The Unwanted Gaze: The Destruction of Privacy in America* (Vintage 2001) 166.

[52] JE Cohen, *Configuring the Networked Self: Law, Code, and the Play of Everyday Practice* (Yale University Press 2012) 7.

[53] JE Cohen, *Between Truth and Power: The Legal Constructions of Informational Capitalism* (Oxford University Press 2019).

[54] PM Schwartz, 'Privacy and democracy in cyberspace' (1999) 52 *Vanderbilt Law Review* 1609, 1660–2.

[55] AL Allen, 'Coercing privacy' (1999) 40 *William & Mary Law Review* 723; LE Cohen, 'Examined lives' (2000) 52 *Stanford Law Review* 1373; Schwartz (n 54).

privacy.[56] Regan, Rao, and Bennett and Raab argue that privacy promotes equality, while Solove maintains that privacy serves multiple individual and collective purposes bound up with everyday experience.[57]

Based on these conceptions of privacy as an extension of autonomy, Bernal has proposed the concept of Internet privacy rights, restating their grounding in autonomy:

> To protect our autonomy, to have influence over what happens to us online, over what we see online, over what decisions are made about us and for us, we need to have protection over our data online. That means protection over how data is gathered about us, how that data is used, who can hold that data and so forth.[58]

To achieve this, *inter alia*, Bernal supports the concept of the right to delete, as opposed to the right to be forgotten online. For Bernal,

> The essence of the right to delete personal data is a simple one: that the default position should be that people are able to have their personal data deleted. Specifically, rather than making the person who wishes their data to be deleted justify that deletion, those wishing to continue to hold that data should need to justify that holding.[59]

Bernal also introduces exceptions to reconcile the right to delete with free speech, security, and other individual and public interests.[60] His conception of Internet privacy rights essentially relates to informational privacy, which is one of the most significant aspects of digital privacy. Solutions put forward in the concluding chapter of this book build on Bernal's suggestions and extend the right to delete post-mortem, notwithstanding the post-mortem privacy interests discussed further in the following section.

[56] For the communitarian argument, see A Etzioni, *The Limits of Privacy* (Basic Books 2000). For the argument from a security perspective, see RA Posner, 'Privacy, surveillance, and law' (2008) 75 *University of Chicago Law Review* 245.

[57] See CJ Bennett and CD Raab, *The Governance of Privacy: Policy Instruments in Global Perspective* (MIT Press 2006); RC Post, 'The social foundations of privacy: Community and self in the common law tort' (1989) 77 *California Law Review* 957; P Regan, *Legislating Privacy: Technology, Social Values, and Public Policy* (University of North Carolina Press 1995); DJ Solove, *Understanding Privacy* (Harvard University Press 2008).

[58] Bernal (n 35) 15.

[59] Ibid. 18.

[60] Ibid. 19.

3.2 Post-Mortem Privacy

(a) Early Theory: Testamentary Freedom and PMP

The conception of post-mortem privacy was established in my earlier research. It means that autonomy should, in principle, transcend death, allowing individuals to control their privacy/identity/personal data post-mortem, analogous to their post-mortem control of property through the concept of testamentary freedom.[61]

Legal families do not share an understanding of the meaning and limits of testamentary freedom. In comparative academic discussions on succession laws, it is common knowledge that freedom of testation as a concept is much more limited in the civilian systems than in common law countries.

The practically unlimited freedom of testation is considered inviolable in common law,[62] stemming from liberal, *laissez-faire* economic and social thought revolving around liberty and autonomy, which were explored in the section above.[63] Examples of thinkers who explicitly support freedom of testation include Bentham, Mill and Locke.[64] Blackstone, for instance, maintains that wills are 'necessary for the peace of society' and testamentary freedom is a 'principle of liberty'.[65] It has been said that testamentary freedom 'crystallised eighteenth-century liberal thinking in relation to property' and was seen as 'a means of self-fulfilment'.[66] Case law has developed similar stances.

[61] Harbinja, 'Post-mortem privacy 2.0' (n 2).

[62] RF Atherton and P Vines, *Australian Succession Law: Commentary and Materials* (Butterworths 1996) 34.

[63] See for example F du Toit, 'The limits imposed upon freedom of testation by the boni mores: lessons from common law and civil law (continental) legal systems' (2000) *Stellenbosch Law Review* 358, 360; MJ de Waal, 'A comparative overview' in KGC Reid, MJ de Waal and R Zimmermann (eds), *Exploring the Law of Succession: Studies National, Historical and Comparative* (Edinburgh University Press 2007) 1–27, 14.

[64] John Locke regarded the power of bequest as part of paternal authority. See J Locke, *Two Treatises of Government*, ed. T Cook (Hafner 1947) 'Second treatise' 156. Mill maintained that 'each person should have power to dispose by will of his or her whole property'. See JS Mill, *Principles of Political Economy* (8th edn, Longmans, Green, Reader and Dyer 1878) 281. In his 'Principles of the Civil Code', Bentham asserted, 'The power of making a will . . . may . . . be considered as an instrument of authority, confided to individuals, for the encouragement of virtue and the repression of vice in the bosom of families.' See J Bentham, 'Principles of the civil code' in *The Works of Jeremy Bentham*, ed. J Bowring (William Tait 1843) Vol 1, 337.

[65] W Blackstone, *Commentaries on the Laws of England (1765–1769)* (18th edn, S. Sweet etc. 1829) Book II 489, 437–8.

[66] R Atherton, 'Expectation without right: Testamentary freedom and the position of women in nineteenth century New South Wales' (1988) 11 *University of New South Wales Law Journal* 133, 134.

For instance, Cockburn CJ observed in the 1870 case of *Banks* v *Goodfellow*, 'The law of every civilised people concedes to the owner of property the right of determining by his last will, either in whole or in part, to whom the effects, which he leaves behind him shall pass.'[67]

In civilian countries, this principle is considerably limited by the notion of forced heirship, giving certain family members indefeasible claims to a part of the testator's estate. Justifications for limiting the principle of testamentary freedom originate from ethical, philosophical and natural law thoughts, arguing for 'solidarity between generations'.[68]

Looking at freedom of testation from another perspective, more individual and personal, some authors argue that freedom of testation is an aspect of the testator's personality rights. As such, it cannot be detached from an individual, delegated or transferred from another person.[69] Similarly, others characterise freedom of testation as the manifestation of autonomy, having a considerable effect on the emancipation of the individual.[70] Therefore, if we share these views and see freedom of testation as another personality right, it could seem somewhat odd that countries that provide more protection for personality rights, in general, restrict freedom of testation more (e.g. Germany). Conversely, countries that arguably, provide less protection for personality rights (e.g. UK and US states) value and protect freedom of testation more.[71] This conclusion could only bring us back to the economic and market rationale in explaining the 'unlimited freedom of testation' in common law countries, giving a little space for personality arguments. Along the same lines, civilian countries limit freedom of testation for similar reasons, economic and social, putting personality rights arguments to one side.

We have briefly defined freedom of testation to relate this general concept to post-mortem autonomy and PMP. This section, however, did investigate details about the laws surrounding freedom of testation, as the conceptual comparisons were the focus of the section. The argument proposed in this book is that freedom of testation should translate to the online environment, where digital assets mainly comprise informational and personal data content. These assets are a counterpart of offline assets and wealth. Therefore,

67 42 (1870) 5 LR QB 549, 563, quoted in ibid.

68 De Waal (n 63) 15.

69 See JC Sonnekus, 'Freedom of testation and the aging testator' in Reid, de Waal and Zimmermann (n 63) 78–99, 79.

70 De Waal (n 63) 16; LM Friedman, 'The law of the living, the law of the dead: Property, succession and society' (1966) *Wisconsin Law Review* 340, 355.

71 See analysis and comparison in Edwards and Harbinja, 'Protecting post-mortem privacy' (n 2).

an individual should be able to exercise their autonomy online and decide what happens to their assets on death. As Bentham puts it in his 'auto-icon' description, 'Every man is his best biographer.'[72] I agree with this proposition and develop it further in relation to digital assets.

One of the most prominent objections to extending privacy post-mortem (where it has not already been extended, as found by Edwards and Harbinja[73]) is that the legal life terminates on death and legal personality ceases to exist.[74] However, as found by Naffine, legal personality is relative and varies from branch of law to branch of law and from legal family to legal family. There is no clear-cut answer as to when legal personality dies.[75] Legal personality in some cases, such as testamentary freedom, does extend beyond death, even impliedly by allowing a deceased person to control their wealth by the wishes they expressed pre-mortem. Similarly, Simes observes that 'though death eliminates a man from the legal congeries of rights and duties, this does not mean that his control, as a fact, over the devolution of his property has ceased. A legal person he may not be, but the law still permits his dead hand to control.'[76] Tur is even more critical of the definition of legal personality and its ending on death, arguing that

> We do not even have . . . any clear idea of when a legal person comes into being or when he ceases to exist . . . Nor should we regard physical death as marking the termination of legal life, if for no other reason than the existence of a legal will, through which the physically dead person seeks to control the disposition of his property.[77]

[72] N Naffine, 'When does the legal person die? Jeremy Bentham and the "auto-icon"' (2000) *Australian Journal of Legal Philosophy* 25.

[73] Edwards and Harbinja, 'Protecting post-mortem privacy' (n 2).

[74] Naffine (n 72) states that 'English law proceeds upon the basis that the deceased as a legal person does not survive his physical death.' Paton's *Jurisprudence* is cited as authority for the proposition that 'most modem legal systems lay down the rule that, in cases where legal personality is granted to human beings, personality begins at birth and ends with death'. See O Wood and GL Certoma, *Hutley, Woodman and Wood Succession: Commentary and Materials* (4th edn, Law Book Co 1990) 309. But also 'In the Anglo-American system of law, the dead have neither rights nor duties . . . We may appoint a guardian ad litem to protect the expectant interests of the unborn. There is no guardian ad litem for the deceased because he has no interest.' See L Simes, *Public Policy and the Dead Hand* (University of Michigan Law School 1955) 1.

[75] Naffine (n 72); also see R Tur, 'The "person" in law' in A Peacocke and G Gillett (eds), *Persons and Personality: A Contemporary Inquiry* (Basil Blackwell 1987) 122.

[76] Simes (n 74) 1.

[77] Tur (n 75) 123.

This argument can further be related to Hegel's and Radin's personhood theories of property. Thus, if property is an extension of an individual's personhood and a necessary precondition for its development, then this personhood transcends death in the same way that property does, through a will. Moral rights provide further support for this argument. As a personal aspect of copyright, moral rights extend on the death of a creator, perpetually (e.g. France), as long as the economic rights last, or for a lesser period with an option of waiving these rights (e.g. the UK and the US).[78] This evidence again supports the proposition that aspects of personality, such as dignity, integrity and autonomy, survive death, sometimes even for an unlimited period, as in France. Therefore, legal personality does extend beyond death, and so should privacy.[79] Other examples where aspects of personality, autonomy or memory survive death include burials, organ donation and medical confidentiality.[80] I and other influential authors have considered these examples, so we will not explore them in detail in this book.

(b) Other Influential PMP Scholarship

PMP scholarship has grown significantly in the last decade. Proponents of the legal recognition of this concept have attempted to address some of the most significant objections to PMP, namely the lack of subject and the problematic nature of harm.

Some of the most potent arguments against recognising PMP refer to the lack of actual harm to the individual, that is, the deceased cannot be harmed or hurt.[81] The analysis above rejects this argument and draws an analogy with the option to bequeath one's property. Following a similar line of argument, the deceased should not be interested in deciding what happens to their property on death as they will not be present to be harmed by the allocation. The interests advanced here are not only family and society interests in the distribution of wealth as freedom of testation is upheld to a lesser or greater degree in most systems, even where not congruent with the interests or desires of

[78] For more details, see Edwards and Harbinja, 'Protecting post-mortem privacy' (n 2) 129.

[79] Harbinja, 'Post-mortem privacy 2.0' (n 2).

[80] See T Davey, *Until Death Do Us Part: Post-Mortem Privacy Rights for the Ante-Mortem Person* (PhD thesis, University of East Anglia 2020); E Harbinja, 'Posthumous medical data donation: The case for a legal framework' in J Krutzinna and L Floridi (eds), *The Ethics of Medical Data Donation*, Philosophical Studies Series, vol 137 (Springer 2019) 97–113; E Harbinja and H Pearce, 'Your data will never die, but you will: A comparative analysis of US and UK post-mortem data donation frameworks' (2020) *Computer Law and Security Review* 36.

[81] See for example Beverley-Smith's contention that 'reputation and injured dignity are generally of no concern to a deceased person'. See H Beverley-Smith, *The Commercial Appropriation of Personality* (Cambridge University Press 2002) 124.

heirs or society. I have submitted that users do have interests in what happens after their death and that in the digital realm, this interest is more significant than in the traditional world due to the prominence and volume of personal data disclosed online and the importance of digital assets in creating one's online identity.[82] Therefore, I have argued that similar notions to testamentary freedom in relation to real-world property should be developed in online environments for digital assets.[83]

PMP harm has been the subject of a helpful analysis put forward by Davey.[84] Davey looks at the long-standing principle law and the theory that the dead cannot be harmed due to lack of knowledge and subjectivity. For Davey, 'no harm actually has to occur to the "dead", and lack of knowledge is not an issue, as the harm is to the living whilst alive because of the knowledge that in death her privacy can be invaded'.[85] Additionally, Davey argues that the protection of post-mortem privacy follows death culture, intuition and the notion of effecting assurances.[86] Davey then goes on to develop her conception of post-mortem privacy.

In summary, Davey proposed the extension of the protection of privacy afforded by Article 8 of the European Convention on Human Rights and introduced the definition of PMP as 'the right of the person to respect for her private and family life post-mortem'.[87] Davey contends that this extension of Article 8 could be achieved by using the ECtHR teleological approach to interpretation in the digital age and readiness to extend the scope of Article 8 to a degree in certain other situations.[88] She also argues that this extension should include 'relational post-mortem privacy'. She builds this aspect of PMP on the harm principle related to the living relatives and refers to some of the recent ECtHR and UK jurisprudence,[89] 'to include private matters about the deceased which affects the privacy interests of the relatives themselves'.[90]

I accept the suggestion to extend the scope of Article 8 of the ECHR put forward by Davey. It is a valuable contribution to the development of

[82] Harbinja, 'Post-mortem privacy 2.0' (n 2).

[83] Ibid.

[84] Davey (n 80).

[85] Ibid. 180.

[86] Ibid. 225.

[87] Ibid. 226; European Convention for the Protection of Human Rights and Fundamental Freedoms 1950.

[88] Ibid. 226. See *Putistin* v *Ukraine* [2013] ECHR 1154.

[89] *Dzhugashvili* v *Russia* [2014] ECHR 1448; *Éditions Plon* v *France* [2004] ECHR 200; *Lewis* v *Secretary of State for Health* [2008] EWHC 2196; *Putistin* v *Ukraine* ECHR 1154; Davey (n 80) 184.

[90] Davey (n 80) 222.

post-mortem privacy scholarship and law. In particular, I accept arguments of 'the death culture, intuition and the notion of effecting assurances'[91] as valid underpinnings of the post-mortem privacy that I have also recognised in my earlier work. I also believe that there is a strong argument for the protection of relational post-mortem privacy. However, the limitation of Davey's theory is the subject of the PMP being the ante-mortem person and the deceased's surviving relatives. While these are relevant, they do not go far enough. In developing the notion of postmortal privacy, I will demonstrate that the deceased themselves can and should be the subject of protections, that is, their 'immortal' persona and their informational body. Regarding surviving relatives, the subjects of relational PMP have not been defined further in Davey's work. It is not clear who these relatives are, whether they are heirs, next of kin or friends.

Buitelaar has put forward another influential theory.[92] He aimed to develop a theory that would justify 'protection for the various forms of post-mortem presence that are likely to subsist in the future'.[93] Buitelaar thus endows a person with a 'digital double' and states that this post-mortem digital persona should be afforded 'an appropriate locus in the legal framework that governs the survival or extinction of the rights and duties of subjects'.[94] In his theory, this digital double is effectively the bearer of the 'continuation of the privacy rights of the ante-mortem owner'.[95] The argument develops in that due to the 'overwhelming persistence of digital persona on the internet without there being a living counterpart', the post-mortem digital persona should be ascribed the 'appropriate locus'.[96]

Buitelaar accepts that such a conception of the subject and PMP is beyond the present law. However, he argues that in the future, 'fundamental human rights need not be limited to the rights of the living human beings'.[97] Davey accepts these arguments as helpful and forward-looking but adds that 'unless the nature of "fundamental human rights" changes, they are grounded in foundational values of which dignity and autonomy are uppermost'.[98] I also find Buitelaar's arguments convincing, adding a layer of postmortality later in this chapter.

[91] Ibid. 222, 145–80.

[92] JC Buitelaar, 'Post-mortem privacy and informational self-determination' (2017) 19(2) *Ethics and Information Technology* 129.

[93] Ibid. 131.

[94] Ibid. 135.

[95] Ibid. 139.

[96] Ibid. 135.

[97] Ibid. 131.

[98] Davey (n 80) 124.

More recent research in the area investigates empirical aspects of post-mortem privacy. I myself am part of an ongoing research project looking at, among other things, perceptions, attitudes and practices of PMP amongst individuals, lawyers, companies and regulators/policymakers.[99]

Morse and Birnhack's empirical inquiry represents an exemplary quantitative insight, focusing on Israeli Internet users' approaches and behaviours in managing digital remains.[100] At the time of writing, it is the only investigation of this kind to explore post-mortem privacy issues directly, focusing on the persistence of the privacy paradox after death, that is, the gap between 'people's stated interest in their online privacy and their actual behaviour'.[101] The authors surveyed a population sample to better understand perceptions, preferences, and actions to protect users' digital remains and PMP. Findings suggest the existence of a posthumous privacy paradox, where users either wish to deny all access to their digital remains but, in practice, enable partial or full informal access; or they wish to allow only part of this content, but instead enable full access.

The research reveals that the posthumous privacy paradox is a complex phenomenon. Significantly, findings demonstrate the presence of an inverted posthumous privacy paradox. In this case, there is a mismatch between the preferences and behaviour of users who might wish to share their personal data on death with loved ones. However, these wishes are likely to be overridden by 'current policies of online platforms, absence of legal framework and [the user's] own uninformed inaction'.[102] Morse and Birnhack point to several other exciting features of the management of digital remains. For example, even for users aware of data processing systems, there may be a 'lack of technological know-how, as to how to manage one's personal data that would become digital remains'.[103] Where online tools exist to manage digital remains (as shown later in this book), the authors suggest that users'

[99] Leverhulme Trust project, 'Modern technologies, privacy law and the dead', 2020–3.

[100] T Morse and M Birnhack, 'The posthumous privacy paradox: Privacy preferences and behavior regarding digital remains' (2020) *New Media and Society* 1.

[101] The term 'privacy paradox' was first defined in PA Norberg and DR Horne, 'The privacy paradox: Personal information disclosure intentions versus behaviors' 41(1) (2007) *Journal of Consumer Affairs* 100. However, the gap between people's stated interest in their online privacy and their actual behaviour was first identified in S Spiekermann, J Grossklags and B Berendt, 'E-privacy in 2nd generation e-commerce: Privacy preferences versus actual behavior' in *Proceedings of the 3rd ACM Conference on Electronic Commerce*, Tampa Bay, Florida, 14–17 October 2001 <https://www.dl.acm.org/doi/10.1145/501158.501163> last accessed 1 August 2021.

[102] Morse and Birnhack (n 100) 18–19.

[103] Ibid. 6.

reluctance to activate these may also be due to an unwillingness to contemplate their own death. The reluctance to contemplate death is a phenomenon that keeps emerging in investigations of PMP and death studies generally. It has probably been one of the guiding principles of tech companies in deciding not to 'advertise death' and their services for the disposition of digital legacy. It is, however, still an anecdotal argument. Further, Morse and Birnhack argue that users need to be empowered to make decisions about their digital remains, and as such 'a top-down, one-size-fits-all law will frustrate the wishes of large segments of the user population'.[104] This is an essential finding for any future legal framework, and we will reconsider it in the final chapter.

The empirical findings of this study could also provide a comprehensive methodological template for other empirical studies on post-mortem privacy online and then a useful comparator when such a study is completed. It offers potential pathways for other future research, where the focus of study might include users' perceptions of the corporate collection and processing of personal data post-mortem rather than social interaction between people. Given the intricacies and subjective experiences at play with decision-making approaches on digital remains, it is clear that there is also an urgent need for complementary qualitative research to capture the deeper understandings of digital remains management preferences and the social, cultural and legal norms that might influence approaches. Morse and Birnhack suggest utilising Terror Management Theory (TMT) from social psychology to investigate decision-making in the face of death.[105] We will certainly incorporate some of these considerations in the UK inquiry, which I have mentioned above.

(c) Laws to Date

Research demonstrates that the US and UK laws, in principle, do not protect PMP.[106] Protection has been awarded by different legal institutions to some aspects of the phenomenon, such as privacy laws, breach of confidence, IP, personality, publicity, defamation, succession, executry and trusts, and data protection. However, this protection is more prominent and encompassing in civil law countries, aiming to protect values such as autonomy, dignity and reputation, especially of the creators.[107] In the English and the US common

[104] Ibid. 19.

[105] See for example J Greenberg and J Arndt, 'Terror management theory' in PAM Van Lange, AW Kruglanski and ET Higgins (eds), *Handbook of Theories of Social Psychology: Volume One* (SAGE 2011).

[106] Harbinja, 'Post-mortem privacy 2.0' (n 2); Edwards and Harbinja, 'Protecting post-mortem privacy' (n 2); Davey (n 80).

[107] Edwards and Harbinja, 'Protecting post-mortem privacy' (n 2) 121.

law systems, the principle has traditionally been *actio personalis moritur cum persona*, meaning personal causes of action die with the person (e.g. defamation claims, breach of confidence claims, wrongful dismissal claims).[108] This principle has been revised by legislation mainly in many contexts for reasons of social policy.[109]

PMP is not protected in English law.[110] Although in principle, the same could be said for the US,[111] some traces of PMP protection may be found in individual states' laws. According to the Restatement (Second) of Torts, there can be no cause of action for invasion of privacy of a decedent, except 'appropriation of one's name or likeness'.[112] Some states protect so-called publicity rights (rights that usually protect celebrities, but sometimes all individuals' rights to name, image, likeness) post-mortem, up to the limit of seventy years after death.[113]

On the other hand, interestingly, US states have been the most active jurisdictions in the past two decades in legislating issues of the transmission of digital assets on death. The initial phase of the digital assets legislation started in 2005, with more than twenty US states having attempted to regulate the area of transmission of digital assets on death over the past ten years. These laws seem to have been inspired by the publicity around the Ellsworth case and similar controversies.[114] We will explore this case in detail

108 *Baker* v *Bolton* (1808) 170 Eng Rep 1033 (KB).

109 The principle has been revised in the United Kingdom and now pertains only to causes of action for defamation and certain claims for bereavement. See generally Law Reform (Miscellaneous Provisions) Act 1934, c 41; Race Relations Act 1976, c 74; Sex Discrimination Act 1975, c 65; Disability Discrimination Act 1995, c 50; Administration of Justice Act 1982, c 53.

110 Edwards and Harbinja, 'Protecting post-mortem privacy' (n 2).

111 In the Restatement (Second) of Torts (1977), the American Legal Institute takes a stance similar to English law that a person's privacy interest ends upon death. See also *Fasching* v *Kallinger* 510 A.2d 694, 701 (NJ Super Ct App Div 1986); *Miller* v *Nat'l Broad Co*, 232 Cal Rptr 668, 680 (Ct App 1986); *Hendrickson* v *Cal Newspapers, Inc*, 121 Cal Rptr 429, 431 (Ct App 1975).

112 See Restatement (Second) of Torts (1977) § 652I.

113 For a survey of which states provide for the protection by common and statute law, see Edwards and Harbinja, 'Protecting post-mortem privacy' (n 2) 124. Also, for an interesting proposal of creating publicity rights in Scots law, which would extend beyond death but only if registered pre-mortem for the benefit of the beneficiaries according to the deceased's will, see G Black, *A Right of Publicity in Scots Law* (PhD thesis, University of Edinburgh 2009) 226–38; G Black, *Publicity Rights and Image: Exploitation and Legal Control* (Hart 2011) 160–70.

114 See A Kulesza, 'What happens to your Facebook account when you die?', *Blog* (3 February 2012) <http://www.blogs.lawyers.com/2012/02/what-happens-to-facebook-account-when-you-die/> last accessed 1 August 2021; Associated Press release, *justinellsworth.net*

in Chapter 6 related to the disposition of emails. Legislative responses that followed the case were partial and piecemeal rather than comprehensive and evidence-based solutions.[115]

The answer to this scattered legislation and possible conflicts of law has been an attempt at harmonisation within the US. In July 2012, the US Uniform Law Commission formed the Committee on Fiduciary Access to Digital Assets. The goal of the Committee was to draft an act and/or amendments to Uniform Law Commission Acts (the Uniform Probate Code 1969, the Uniform Trust Code 2000, the Uniform Guardianship and Protective Proceedings Act 2017 and the Uniform Power of Attorney Act 2006) that would authorise fiduciaries to manage and distribute, copy or delete, and access digital assets. Starting from 2012, for Committee meetings, the Uniform Fiduciary Access to Digital Assets Act 2014 (UFADAA) had been drafted and published online on multiple occasions.[116] The process included fierce lobbying efforts by the big tech companies (e.g. Google and Facebook), connected through a think tank called NetChoices. The companies even moved on to lobby for a completely different act, which would replace the UFADAA, resulting in the Privacy Expectation Afterlife and Choices Act 2015 (PEAC). The Uniform Law Commission then decided to revise the UFADAA, and incorporate some of the industry concerns and pro-privacy stances, adopting the Revised UFADAA (RUFADAA) in 2015.[117]

Although this initiative was an attempt to improve and develop the existing statutes aiming to consider the full range of digital assets, there were many open issues that the Committee needed to address when drafting the RUFADAA. For instance, in the Prefatory Note for the Drafting Committee in the February 2013 Draft, the drafters identify the most critical issues to be clarified, including the definition of digital property (s 2) and the type and nature of control that can be exercised by a fiduciary (s 4). It seems that some of the most controversial issues were being disputed within the Committee, such as clarifying possible conflicts between contract and executry law and between heirs, family and friends.[118]

(21 April 2005) <https://www.justinellsworth.net/email/ap-apr05.htm> last accessed 1 August 2021.

[115] See AB Lopez, 'Posthumous privacy, decedent intent, and post-mortem access to digital assets' (2016) 24(1) *George Mason Law Review* 183.

[116] Ibid.

[117] Ibid.

[118] E Harbinja, *Legal Aspects of Transmission of Digital Assets on Death* (PhD thesis, University of Strathclyde 2017).

The RUFADAA includes significant powers for fiduciaries regarding digital assets and estate administration. These powers are limited by a user's will and intent expressed in their choice to use online tools to dispose of their digital assets (e.g. Google Inactive Account Manager). The user's choice overrides any provisions of their will. If the user does not give direction using an in-service solution but makes provisions for the disposition of digital assets, the RUFADAA gives legal effect to the user's directions. If the user fails to give any direction, the provider's terms of service (ToS) will apply. The Act also gives the service provider a choice of methods for disclosing digital assets to an authorised fiduciary, under their ToS (i.e. full access, partial access, or a copy in a record). Finally, the Act gives personal representatives default access to the 'catalogue' of electronic communications and other digital assets not protected by federal privacy law (i.e. the content of communication which is protected and can only be disclosed if the user has consented to the disclosure or if a court orders disclosure).

Additionally, the RUFADAA, s 9 aims to resolve the potential violations of criminal and privacy legislation. It also tackles jurisdiction, mandating that the choice of law provisions in ToS do not apply to fiduciaries. Apart from that, the new draft abandoned the digital property notion altogether and left only the digital assets, comprising both the content and the log information (information about electronic communication, the date and time a message has been sent, the recipient's email address).

So far, a vast majority of states have introduced and enacted the RUFADAA.[119] Most of these states already had their own digital assets statutes; however, this legislation was not harmonised before the RUFADAA. The Act thus contributed to harmonising divergent laws – at least in the states that enacted it. Notably, California, where the most prominent service providers are based and whose laws apply to the ToS, has not introduced the legislation. It is to be hoped that the Act will achieve wider adoption and application in the individual states or even initiate similar efforts in other countries. An acceptable legal solution for the transmission of personal digital assets will ideally follow the rationale behind the RUFADAA. It should aim to recognise technology to dispose of digital assets as a more efficient and immediate solution online. The solution would also consider technological

[119] US Uniform Law Commission, 'Fiduciary Access to Digital Assets Act, Revised (2015): 2018 Introductions & Enactments' <http://www.uniformlaws.org/Act.aspx?title=Fiduciary%20Access%20to%20Digital%20Assets%20Act,%20Revised%20(2015)> last accessed 1 August 2021.

limitations, users' autonomy, and the changing landscape of relationships online.[120]

The Uniform Law Conference of Canada followed this approach and enacted a similar act: the Canadian Uniform Access to Digital Assets by Fiduciaries Act 2016 (UADAFA).[121] This Act provides a more robust right of access for fiduciaries than the RUFADAA. There is default access to the digital assets of the account holder. In UADAFA, the instrument appointing the fiduciary determines a fiduciary's right of access rather than the service provider's. The Canadian Act has a 'last-in-time' priority system, whereby the most recent instruction takes priority over an earlier instrument.

Interestingly, however, a user who already has a will, but nominates a family member or a friend to access their social media account after their death, restricts their executor's rights under the will. This is similar to the US RUFADAA, whereby the deceased's will takes priority in any case, and the difference is in the mechanism. The RUFADAA is more restrictive than the UADAFA in honouring ToS without a user's instruction. Service providers are obliged only to disclose the catalogue of digital assets and not the content. This solution is more suitable for the online environment, particularly where assets are intrinsically tied to one's identity (communications, social networks, multiple accounts with one provider such as Google; these create a unique profile and identity of a user).

In the Digital Republics Act 2016, France has adopted a solution quite similar to the RUFADAA.[122] Article 63(2) of the Act states that anyone can set general or specific directives for preserving, deleting and disclosing their personal data after death.[123] These directives would be registered with a certified third party (for general ones) or with the service provider who holds the data (e.g. Facebook and its policy described above). Even though the implementing decree that would operationalise this law has not been adopted yet, it is quite a surprising development that brings the US and French approaches

[120] E Kasket, 'Access to the digital self in life and death: Privacy in the context of posthumously persistent Facebook profiles' (2013) 10:1 *SCRIPTed* 7, 10; E Kasket, *All the Ghosts in the Machine* (Robinson 2019); N Pennington, 'You don't de-friend the dead: An analysis of grief communication by college students through Facebook profiles' (2013) 37 *Death Studies* 617.

[121] Uniform Law Conference of Canada, Uniform Access to Digital Assets by Fiduciaries Act (2016) <https://www.ulcc-chlc.ca/ULCC/media/EN-Uniform-Acts/Uniform-Access-to-Digital-Assets-by-Fiduciaries-Act-(2016).pdf> last accessed 1 August 2021.

[122] Loi n° 2016-1321 du 7 octobre 2016 pour une République numérique.

[123] For more, see L Castex, E Harbinja and J Rossi, 'Défendre les vivants ou les morts? Controverses sous-jacentes au droit des données post-mortem à travers une perspective comparée franco-américaine' (2018) 4(210) *Réseaux* 117.

to post-mortem privacy closer. This is even odder if we consider the conventional and extremely divergent approaches of these jurisdictions to protecting the personal data of living individuals.[124]

We will not see similar developments in the UK, unfortunately. The Law Commission has recently initiated the reform of the law of wills in England and Wales. Their consultation brief asserts that digital assets 'fall outside the sort of property that is typically dealt with by a will'[125] and that digital assets are primarily a matter of contract law and could be addressed in separate law reform. This suggestion fails to future-proof the law of wills as these assets become more common and valuable. In the future, we will see conflicts between wills and the disposition of digital assets online, and this reform is a chance for UK law to show foresight in anticipating these issues and follow good examples in other countries, as explained above. Edwards and I have argued that the Commission should consider digital assets in the ongoing reform to forestall rather than create unclarity and confusion. We will see quite soon whether the Commission will take our suggestion on board and take this opportunity to bring about some clarity in the law.

Regarding other countries that partly protect PMP, Malgieri's research usefully categorises these regimes into three theoretical scenarios: 1) the 'data freedom' or 'commodification' scenario; 2) the quasi-propertisation model (IP-like); and 3) the full or weak PMP model.[126] In the 'data freedom' scenario, the data controller can process the deceased's personal data as they wish on death of the data subject.[127] English law, explained above, is an example that Malgieri uses to illustrate this scenario. For the second scenario, quasi-property or IP-like, Malgieri uses the example of the former Estonian data protection law, where limited rights of the heirs exist for thirty years post-mortem of the data subject.[128] He argues that data is treated and inherited in this scenario as '(digital) goods or as Intellectual Property rights on intangibles'.[129] This is limited with moral rights protected in the European IP regime, so full propertisation is impossible. In his last scenario, the post-mortem

[124] Ibid.

[125] Law Commission, 'Making a will' (Consultation paper 231, 2017) <https://www.s3-eu-west-2.amazonaws.com/lawcom-prod-storage-11jsxou24uy7q/uploads/2017/07/Making-a-will-consultation.pdf> last accessed 1 August 2021.

[126] G Malgieri, 'R.I.P: Rest in privacy or rest in (quasi-)property? Personal data protection of deceased data subjects between theoretical scenarios and national solutions' in R Leenes, R van Brakel, S Gutwirth and P de Hert (eds), *Data Protection and Privacy: The Internet of Bodies* (Hart 2018) 143.

[127] Ibid. 145.

[128] Ibid. 154.

[129] Ibid. 155.

privacy one, PMP is protected more or less stringently. Like many other scholars I mentioned above, Malgieri notes the problem of the interested subject that can be harmed, that is, the problem of the 'interest', 'harm' and the 'narrator'.[130]

For an intermediate scenario with a weaker PMP, he exemplifies the Italian Data Protection Code (which has implemented Directive 95/46/EC). Article 9(3) of the Code states that the data subject's rights 'where related to the personal data concerning a deceased, *may be exercised by any entity that is interested* therein or else acts to protect a data subject or for *family-related reasons* deserving protection'.[131] He further defines this model as a 'Kantian' model, where legitimate subjects can act on behalf of the deceased, similar to burial cases in common law systems.[132] This way, he argues, the problem of the subject has been solved to an extent. The example includes 'weak' protections of PMP because the deceased themselves cannot express their directives to process their personal data on death.[133] Regarding this scenario, he concludes by saying that this model does not help in the case of conflict between different interested parties, such as family members or heirs.

For the strong PMP protections, Malgieri quotes the French law Loi pour une République numérique. In his view, this is the most advanced statute in the area, which has resolved the 'problem of the subject' (i.e. the problem of the interest, the harm and the narrator) through advance directives whereby the data subject can preventively express their decisions on the post-mortem processing of their personal data and designate a person that can actively exercise data protection rights, respecting their directives on behalf of the deceased.[134] The law also includes the distinction between personal data and 'digital goods', whereby the heirs can 'receive communication of *digital goods* or data amounting to family memories, transmissible to the heirs', unless there is a directive of the deceased that states otherwise.[135] Further, heirs can have access to digital goods just if there were no directives of the deceased, meaning that 'personality interests always prevail under the French Law'.[136] Finally, copyright law still applies, and the heirs can exercise economic and moral rights for works authored by the deceased person, but the deceased can also designate different persons for exercising these rights

[130] Ibid. 147.
[131] Ibid. 156 (emphasis added by Malgieri).
[132] Ibid.
[133] Ibid.
[134] Ibid. 148.
[135] Ibid. 159 (original emphasis).
[136] Ibid.

in a will.[137] I have analysed the French law earlier in my work with Castex and Rossi, where we discuss the French pro-PMP regime and its similarities with the US RUFADAA (analogised above) in the effects the laws produce on the protection of PMP.[138] We conclude that the PMP regime of these two countries is much more approximate than their juxtaposed regimes of the protection of privacy more generally.

A similar example to the French one is the Catalan law (Ley 10/2017) that introduces *voluntats digitals* (digital wills), comparable to the *directives* in the French law. These can be a part of a will or registered in an electronic register. If a person has not written a will or included a stipulation in the electronic register, then ToS or contractual clauses apply between the service provider and the data subject (user).[139] If the *voluntats digitals* does not explicitly mention the right of the executor to access personal data after the deceased's death, the executor (or the heir) needs a court order to access such data. Unlike French law, Malgieri finds that traditional wills and digital wills are never in conflict here, that is, digital wills can be part of a person's will.[140]

Malgieri has looked at several examples of post-mortem privacy legal regimes that were available at the time of his writing. His categorisation is helpful, albeit incomplete. If we were to build on Malgieri's categorisation, we would need to add a purely patrimonial or succession regime that applies to digital assets, including personal data that constitutes a digital account such as a social media account. An example of this regime is in Germany. In a critical case in Germany, Facebook refused to grant access to a deceased girl's Facebook account to her parents, arguing its duties of confidence were solely owed to her. The Court of Appeal in Berlin supported Facebook's stance, but the Federal Court of Justice overturned this decision, relying on the German Civil Code (BGB) and its principle of universal succession (i.e. that heirs step into the deceased's shoes for all their rights and obligations). The Court rejected Facebook's argument that this was a contract of a personal nature and, therefore, rights did not transmit to heirs.[141] Edwards and Harbinja find it intriguing, as in common law jurisdictions it has been assumed, without binding precedent, 'that contracts with social media platforms would be of

[137] Ibid.

[138] Castex et al. (n 123).

[139] Malgieri (n 126) 160.

[140] Ibid.

[141] Kammergericht, Urteil vom 31. Mai 2017, Aktenzeichen 21 U 9/16 <https://www.berlin.de/gerichte/presse/pressemitteilungen-der-ordentlichen-gerichtsbarkeit/2017/pressemitteilung.596076.php> last accessed 30 January 2022; appealed BGH, 12 July 2018, Docket No III ZR 183/17.

such a highly personal nature (the doctrine of *delectus personae* in English law) and therefore rights and duties would both come to an end with the death of the subscriber'.[142] This argument was rejected in the German Facebook case.

Furthermore, Malgieri categorises laws that belong to various areas (data protection, succession and wills, regulation of technologies and IP) under the same umbrella categories. These categories are hardly comparable in such a manner, as they usually overlap and complement each other, even in the same jurisdiction. They also conflict with one another in a given jurisdiction, meaning the categorisation is incomplete unless we have examined a more comprehensive range of laws. For example, certain countries can exclude PMP protection in one area of law and envisage it simultaneously in a different area, albeit impliedly. A clear example of this is the US, analysed further below, where RUFADAA offers implicit protection of PMP, yet privacy and data protection do not extend on death. The situation in the US is further complicated by the fact that each state has different laws on succession, publicity, property and confidential information. It is therefore challenging to consider PMP as a singular phenomenon since it has not been defined in general legal principles or theory. The piecemeal laws are all there is now, so Malgieri's categorisation contributes to further thinking about PMP.

Post-Mortem Data Protection

In addition to the laws investigated above, where implicit explicit recognitions of PMP exist, it is helpful to examine data protection and PMP protection in the EU. This area has changed quite significantly since the introduction of the General Data Protection Regulation (GDPR), despite the GDPR's failure to harmonise it.

Do data protection rights survive one's death? We have investigated the human rights aspect of post-mortem privacy above. We will not turn to investigate data protection law in so far as it applies to the deceased and confers on them or other parties certain rights. Erdos has surveyed the protection of the deceased's personal data in three generations of data protection law in the EU. The first generation data protection law, in the early 1990s, referred to concepts such as 'individual', 'natural person' or 'a person in physical terms', 'rendering it somewhat ambiguous whether the deceased were meant to be directly referred to or not'.[143]

[142] L Edwards and E Harbinja, '"Be right back": What rights do we have over post-mortem avatars of ourselves?' in L Edwards, B Schafer and E Harbinja (eds), *Future Law: Emerging Technology, Regulation and Ethics* (Edinburgh University Press 2020) 273.

[143] D Erdos, 'Dead ringers? Legal persons and the deceased in European data protection law' (2021) 40 *Computer Law & Security Review* 13.

The GDPR's predecessor, the Data Protection Directive (DPD), applied only to living individuals, protecting the personal data of 'natural persons'.[144] However, the Directive left discretion in implementation to EU member states to extend this minimum protection, which was guaranteed.[145] Some EU states used this possibility, and their data protection laws offer some kind of post-mortem data protection, limited in its scope and post-mortem duration.[146] McCallig found that twelve states protect the deceased's personal data (Bulgaria, Czech Republic, Denmark, Estonia, France, Italy, Latvia, Lithuania, Portugal, Slovakia, Slovenia and Spain); four states expressly exclude the deceased (Cyprus, Ireland, Sweden and the United Kingdom); ten states refer to personal data of a natural person (Czech Republic, Denmark, France, Italy (both natural and legal person), Latvia, Lithuania, Portugal, Slovakia, Slovenia and Spain) and one state provides a temporal limit for protection of the deceased's personal data (Estonia, thirty years on consent).[147] The rationale behind not protecting the deceased's personal data is the lack of the ability to consent to data processing.[148] Conversely, Erdos finds that nine EEA states include *sui generis* provisions for the deceased's data in national law, with similar levels of protection as found by McCallig.[149] In this generation of data protection law, Ireland, the UK, Sweden and Cyprus establish that online, the living individuals are within data protection laws.[150]

The GDPR did not clarify this patchy protection of the deceased's data in the EU. It does not explicitly provide for post-mortem data protection;

[144] Article 2 a) of Directive 95/46/EC of the European Parliament and of the Council of 24 October 1995 on the protection of individuals with regard to the processing of personal data and on the free movement of such data OJ L 281, 23/11/1995 P. 0031–0050 (the Data Protection Directive).

[145] Case C-101/01, *Criminal Proceedings Against Lindqvist* [2003] ECR I-12971, I-13027 (European Court of Justice decision deferring to the national court's resolution of the issue).

[146] Edwards and Harbinja, 'Protecting post-mortem privacy' (n 2) 131, 132.

[147] D McCallig, 'Data protection and the deceased in the EU' (Presentation at the Computer Privacy and Data Protection 2014 Panel: Exploring post-mortem privacy in a digital world, 21–23 January 2014) (on file with the author).

[148] 'Dead persons cannot give consent to use or changes in their personal data or contribute to any balancing of interests which may be required. Rights as data subjects should in general extend only to living individuals, but should be exercisable for a limited period after the death of the data subject by personal representatives.' House of Lords Select Committee on the European Communities, *Report on the Protection of Personal Data* (HMSO 1993).

[149] Erdos (n 143) 14.

[150] Ibid.

instead, it delegates regulatory decisions on this issue to the member states.[151] Many EU member states have legislated for post-mortem data protection in different forms, while few member states explicitly exclude this protection (e.g. Ireland and Sweden). Erdos has conducted a comprehensive study of data protection laws whose provisions extend on the death of the data subject.[152] He finds that twelve EEA countries have provided protection for the deceased's data in their new data protection acts. This protection varies significantly and includes the following broad types of protection: the extension of the validity of the deceased's consent for a limited time (Estonia); the requirement for a legal basis of processing, including consent by heirs or the extension of or other people with a sufficient legal interest (Slovakia, Slovenia – provided that the deceased has not prohibited this in writing); the extension of all or some data subject rights (France, Italy, Portugal, Spain, Hungary, Bulgaria, Switzerland); and the extension of the application of the data protection law as a whole (Iceland, Denmark). The categorisation is mine, and it is slightly different from the one Erdos has provided.[153] The UK has retained its previous approach to the deceased's data. The UK Data Protection Act 2018 in s 1 defines personal data as 'data which relate to a living individual', denying any post-mortem rights and following the approach taken in the Data Protection Act 1998. The rationale behind not protecting the deceased's personal data in the UK has historically been the lack of the deceased's ability to consent to data processing.[154] This is not a solid reason, however, since many other counties have found mechanisms to address this issue. As seen above, consent can be expressed pre-mortem, recorded in a will or technology, or given by an heir, personal representative or another party. We will return to this in the final chapter.

3.3 Future Law and Theory: Informational Body, Digital Immortality and Postmortal Privacy

In more recent research, I have begun to develop the notion of PMP further, looking at the notions of informational bodies (a philosophical concept), immortality and postmortal society (sociological concepts), to support the

[151] Recital 27 of Regulation (EU) 2016/679 of the European Parliament and of the Council of 27 April 2016 on the protection of natural persons with regard to the processing of personal data and on the free movement of such data, and repealing Directive 95/46/EC (General Data Protection Regulation) OJ L 119, 04.05.2016; cor OJ L 127, 23.5.2018.

[152] Erdos (n 143).

[153] Ibid. 11.

[154] UK House of Lords Select Committee on the European Communities (n 148).

concept of 'postmortal privacy'.[155] Postmortal privacy is qualitatively different from post-mortem privacy. As seen above, the latter in legal scholarship has relied on the legal conceptions of personality, data protection and privacy, with normative considerations of privacy, autonomy and testamentary freedom. The postmortal privacy framework goes beyond post-mortem privacy and includes protecting the informational body and aspects of digital immortality.

The aim is to consider theories and concepts beyond just digital assets, theories of property, IP and privacy, and to offer a comprehensive framework and more nuanced normative support for future policy and law.[156] The framework, thus, does not apply to the case studies in this book specifically, but it offers grounding for considering digital remains holistically. This theory goes beyond data protection and privacy, as conceived in some of the theories and laws set out in this chapter. It not only includes and protects information and personal data but aims to encompass the entirety of the deceased's identity and 'self', as curated, stored and left behind in the digital realm. Therefore, to be able to understand this complex concept of digital remains and legacy, I have borrowed from the influential philosophical and sociological scholarship.

In the new conception, post-mortem privacy is conceptually building upon Floridi's notion of the 'informational body'.[157] According to Floridi, human beings exist through information related to their identity. Thus Floridian ethics maintain that a person has a 'right to control one's personal identity . . . an informational structure, constituted by everything that defines this identity'[158] (memories, search history, etc.). Individuals are, essentially, constituted and exist through their own information and thus 'their personal data are their informational bodies' so data should be seen as being 'ours' as in 'our body' as opposed to 'our car'.[159] This informational body exists for the living and the dead and is applied regardless of a person's awareness of having their privacy compromised.[160]

155 Harbinja, 'The "new(ish)" property' (n 2).
156 Ibid.
157 Floridi, 'Distributed morality' (n 1); Floridi, *Ethics of Information* (n 1); Floridi, *Fourth Revolution* (n 1).
158 C Öhman and L Floridi, 'The political economy of death in the age of information: A critical approach to the digital afterlife industry' (2017) 27 *Minds and Machines* 639, 650.
159 Ibid.
160 Ibid. 651.

Therefore, infringement of informational privacy is an act of aggression to the specific person and humanity and, more generally, 'human dignity'.[161] For Floridi, maintaining one's dignity is key to remaining the master of one's existence in the world.[162] Öhman and Floridi argue that 'the dead's informational body continues to have the right to be treated with respect and dignity worthy of human existence even after the end of their physical existence'.[163] Here, there is also an analogy with the 'protection that the law traditionally offers to the physical body and its integrity post-mortem, as well as the fact that the organic body is not considered property in most legal systems'.[164] If we treat the human body with respect after death, by analogy we should provide the same treatment for the informational body, underpinned by dignity and autonomy. Postmortal privacy protects the integrity and dignity of the informational body.

Moreover, the physical body decays naturally, and the informational body arguably does not as it persists for as long as technology permits it. Parts of this postmortal informational body are dispersed in the digital realm and are more or less easily accessible by many individuals and companies. Here, therefore, we find aspects of immortality, as conceptualised in the sociological and philosophical literature, which we will explore briefly.

Related to preserving one's informational body and identity, Dow examined archival immortality, which includes preserving artefacts related to the self, saved and achieved in totality (letters, emails and digital data).[165] More generally, Jacobsen's conception of 'digitalised immortality' or 'electronic immortality' means that the memory of the deceased can be kept alive through memorial pages; players can restart their lives in games and virtual reality. More remarkably, we could store and transfer neural energy from the deceased, hoping to keep them artificially alive after their physical death.[166] Similarly, Kastenbaum introduces the concept of assisted immortality, posing a philosophical question of whether technologically assisted immortality would be a meaningful form of survival and whether individuals would be willing to use it, if available.[167]

161 L Floridi, 'On human dignity as a foundation for the right to privacy' (2016) 29 *Philosophy and Technology* 307.

162 Ibid. 310.

163 Öhman and Floridi (n 158) 651.

164 Harbinja, 'The "new(ish)" property' (n 2) 94.

165 EH Dow, *Electronic Records in the Manuscript Repository* (Scarecrow Press 2009).

166 MH Jacobsen (ed.), *Postmortal Society: Towards a Sociology of Immortality* (Routledge 2017).

167 R Kastenbaum, *On Our Way: The Final Passage through Life and Death (Life Passages)* (University of California Press 2004).

Notably, Brown sets out his four pathways to immortality, namely survival of the body, survival of the mind, survival of the genes, and survival of the memes (understood as memories or cultural genes stored and passed on internally and externally through technology).[168] Survival of the memes is enabled by the technological and cultural transmission of memories. For Brown, whether this would count as survival depends on the concept of the self. This concept evolves with time and space, and it could mean different things to different individuals. It depends on whether they identify with their genes, memes, bodies, mind, consciousness, or all of these. Survival of the memes, our memories, or our identity understood by Brown as 'what we feel counts as ours' and whether we can identify with our memes in other people does not have to depend on whether 'in reality' we survive by these memes.[169] All these considerations Jacobsen usefully labels 'immortality by proxy', an umbrella term that encompasses all the different ways of survival, including technology.[170] For this book, digital immortality is immortality reached in the digital realm due to a symbolic proxy or technology.[171]

In summary, postmortal privacy aims to protect the informational body expressed, stored, mediated and curated through technology (Figure 3.1). This body, consisting of information, memes and data, exists in the digital afterlife or the New Elysium,[172] thus attaining aspects of immortality understood as immortality by proxy. This new concept further solidifies the need to consider very personal identity and dignity interests when drafting policies and laws in this area. It is argued that the concept deserves attention because it offers a comprehensive and future-facing prospect for digital remains. It is based on multidisciplinary arguments and thus provides a solid normative underpinning for law-makers. Finally, it goes beyond a single digital asset and looks at the totality of the digital remains of an individual. The theory will not be used in considering case studies in this book. Instead, it is a novel theoretical perspective underpinning some of the solutions in the final chapter of the book.

Moreover, the theory is applicable to some more recent phenomena of chatbots, deepfakes and other forms of reviving the deceased using their data. MyHeritage is a more recent example of a service offering the creation of deepfakes of the deceased.[173] If recognised in law, postmortal privacy would

[168] B Brown, 'Individualised immortality in liquid-modern times – teasing out the topic of symbolic immortality in the sociology of Zygmunt Bauman' in Jacobsen (n 166) 40.

[169] Ibid.

[170] Jacobsen (n 166).

[171] Harbinja, 'The "new(ish)" property' (n 2).

[172] Kasket, *All the Ghosts in the Machine* (n 120).

[173] MyHeritage <https://www.myheritage.com/deep-nostalgia> last accessed 1 August 2021.

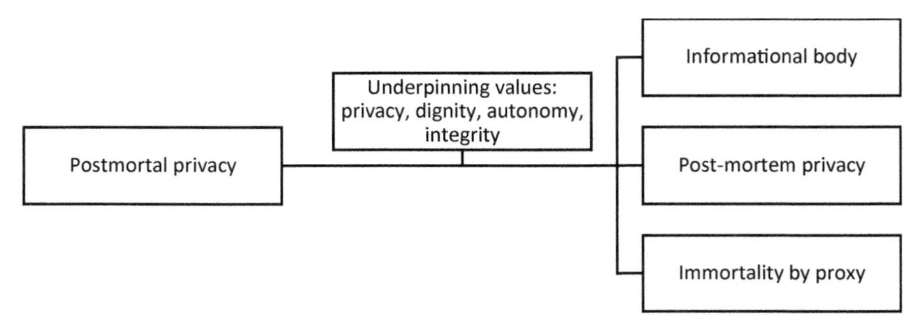

Figure 3.1 Postmortal Privacy[174]

help protect the deceased's remains against unauthorised use of their data and the creation of chatbots and deepfakes. We will consider the exact mechanisms for this in the final chapter.

3.4 Concluding Remarks

The discussion above reviewed the role of autonomy as a value and then discussed how it supports privacy. I follow the pro-autonomy stance of Nissenbaum, Bernal et al. as justification for the hard choices herein favouring users' rights, rather than those of platforms or families.

Clearly, the law typically recognises a person's autonomy and, as a connected phenomenon, that person's right and ability to dispose of their wealth and property. This, however, has arguably not been translated to the online world. As will be shown in greater detail in the case study chapters, neither a user's rights of ownership over digital assets nor their rights to allocate these assets after death are routinely recognised. It can be argued that in the online world, digital assets are more closely related to privacy interests than in the online world and thus are much more closely related to the personal and autonomy interests of the user. It is therefore argued here that separate from the general consideration of property status and thus transmissibility, testamentary freedom should in principle extend to digital assets created in the online world.

I argue throughout the book for recognition of at least some degree of PMP and the right of an individual to dispose of or control their personal data post-mortem. Of course, like all user interests, PMP rights will need to be balanced with other considerations, including the same privacy interests of others and the social and personal interests in free speech and security, and so on. It is not the ambition of this book to analyse the potential exceptions

[174] Harbinja, 'The "new(ish)" property' (n 2) 97.

in more detail. The aim is to discuss if the transmission of personal digital assets on death is justified on doctrinal or theoretical grounds. In discussing this challenging and grey question, this book will take the view that autonomy interests play a vital part and that a framework for recognising PMP, which will assist in the transmission of digital assets on death, is essential. However, the position set out in this chapter is principled, and the practical solution will be discussed more in the last chapter. The counterbalancing of such autonomy and property interests by countervailing interests is a further issue that will be dealt with in my future work.

Admittedly, however, some digital assets might not be so intertwined with the user's privacy, for example a poem written on Facebook or a short story in an email. This would be primarily an IP issue, and the relevant case study chapter suggests appropriate solutions to tackle their transmission.

Finally, I have put forward a novel concept of postmortal privacy, relevant for the totality of one's digital remains, one's postmortal self, existing in and through technology. The concept is less relevant for individual case studies. Instead, it offers a grounding for considering digital remains more comprehensively, especially in the context of digital resurrection, ghostbots, post-mortem deepfakes and other technology that offers ways of reviving the deceased. I will consider this in more detail in my future work.[175]

[175] Harbinja et al. (n 4).

4

Social Networks

4.1 Conceptualisation and a Brief History of Social Networks

Social network sites (SNSs) can be defined as:

> web-based services that allow individuals to (1) construct a public or semi-public profile within a bounded system, (2) articulate a list of other users with whom they share a connection, and (3) view and traverse their list of connections and those made by others within the system.[1]

boyd and Ellison use the term 'social network sites' as opposed to the term 'social networking sites' that is often considered its synonym. They argue that these terms are different in that 'networking' emphasises relationship initiation, often between strangers, which is not the primary purpose of social network sites, 'nor is it what differentiates them from other forms of computer-mediated communication (CMC)'.[2] Instead, social networks are primarily used to maintain and continue existing offline relationships between their users.[3] This varies across SNSs and is more accurate for Facebook than for Instagram, where users follow and interact with a more significant number of 'strangers' who choose to leave their profiles open.

Grimmelmann, in his comprehensive early study on Facebook, accepts this definition and adds the feature of 'explicitness', noting that social networks are 'the *explicit representation* of connections among users'.[4] These

[1] d boyd and NB Ellison 'Social network sites: Definition, history, and scholarship' (2007) 13(1) *Journal of Computer-Mediated Communication* 210, 1.

[2] Ibid. 2.

[3] JTL Grimmelmann, 'Saving Facebook' (2009) 94 *Iowa Law Review* 1137, 1154; d boyd, 'Why youth (heart) social network sites: The role of networked publics in teenage social life' in D Buckingham (ed.), *Youth, Identity, and Digital Media* (MIT Press 2009) 119–29, 126 <http://www.mitpressjournals.org/doi/pdf/10.1162/dmal.9780262524834.119> last accessed 1 August 2021.

[4] Grimmelmann (n 3) 1143 (original emphasis).

connections and interactions, according to Grimmelmann, have three most important aspects: identity (they enable users to create and build their identities, so they are 'as much performative as informative'[5]), relationship and community.[6] Regarding the relationship aspect, research finds social networks have significant social impact, including their use to maintain social ties, revive 'dormant' relationships and avoid social isolation.[7] Social networks carry many negative connotations and consequences, such as addiction, bullying, harassment and trolling. A great range of credible research has emerged over the years to evidence these phenomena. However, this aspect of SNSs is outside the scope of this book.

Another critical aspect of SNSs is that they facilitate the posting and sharing of user-generated content (UGC), discussed in Chapter 1. The individual terms in the UGC phrase take the following meanings: user – a computer or Internet user and amateurs; generated – created by these users, including a degree of creativity, something not merely uploaded or copied; content – digital content, the content available online.[8] White, for example, when defining UGC, notes that 'Blogs, wikis, social-networking sites and video-sharing sites (for example, YouTube) are among the most popular UGC technologies.'[9] From a technological point of view, Shirky calls the code behind social networks 'social software', that is, 'software that supports group communications'.[10]

Notwithstanding the standard features, social networks are very different in terms of their purpose and the content posted, shared or created therein. Some are primarily used for social interactions with friends, families and others, facilitating the exchange of various kinds of content, such as text,

[5] Ibid. 1153.

[6] Ibid.

[7] See Pew Research Center, 'Social networking fact sheet' <http://www.pewinternet.org/fact-sheets/social-networking-fact-sheet/> last accessed 1 August 2021. The emancipatory aspect of social networks has been a subject of fierce critique as well. See for example J Hasanović and E Adilović, 'The double life of virtual: Emancipation as immobilization in an isolated age' in ŞŞ Erçetin, ŞN Açıkalın and E Vajzović (eds), *Chaos, Complexity and Leadership* (Springer Proceedings in Complexity 2020).

[8] S Hetcher, 'User-generated content and the future of copyright: Part two – agreements between users and mega-sites' (2008) 24 *Santa Clara Computer & High Technology Law Journal* 829, 870–3.

[9] E White, 'The Berne Convention's flexible fixation requirement: A problematic provision for user-generated content' (2012–13) 13 *Chicago Journal of International Law* 685, 691.

[10] C Shirky, 'Social software and the politics of groups' *Networks, Economy, & Culture Mailing List* (9 March 2009) <http://www.shirky.com/writings/group_politics.html> last accessed 1 August 2021. Other kinds of social software include blogs, wikis and media-sharing sites, like Flickr and YouTube.

photos, personal data, videos, games, and so on (Facebook, Twitter). Others focus on the exchange of photos and videos (YouTube, Instagram, Flickr, TikTok), some focus on professional interactions (LinkedIn), and some are music-oriented (Spotify, LastFM, MySpace). All this content can have a very diverse legal nature, which depends, *inter alia*, on the different relationships and options available within the intermediaries that facilitate these social interactions.

Essentially, SNSs are online platforms that enable and facilitate communication, sharing and other types of interaction between their users. Communications and sharing are the key features looked at in this book through the lenses of different legal concepts (IP, data protection, property, contracts). These interactions trigger the analysis of whether traditional legal concepts apply to SNSs.

The popularity of social networks in the Western world nowadays is tremendous.[11] The UK Office for National Statistics finds that in 2020, 70 per cent of all adults participated in social networking, which makes it the fifth most popular online activity after sending emails, finding information, Internet banking and using instant messaging services.[12] Similarly, in the US, Pew Research Center finds that 72 per cent of online adults in the US use social networks.[13] This chapter focuses on the most widely used and representative social networks in the Western world, Facebook and Twitter. These SNSs have the most extensive user base, and their social and cultural importance for users is invaluable. Alongside Instagram and TikTok, they are still the primary platforms used to share UGC worldwide.[14]

Facebook is an open social network, and anyone with an email address and claiming to be aged thirteen or older can join.[15] Facebook offers different

[11] This is not to say that the popularity is not similar in the other parts of the world. See for example *Statista*, 'Social media in Asia Pacific – statistics & facts' (8 June 2021) <https://www.statista.com/topics/6606/social-media-in-asia-pacific/#:~:text=The%20favored%20social%20media%20app,prominent%20mark%20on%20the%20industry> last accessed 1 August 2021.

[12] See Office for National Statistics, 'Internet access – households and individuals 2020' (7 August 2021) <https://www.ons.gov.uk/peoplepopulationandcommunity/householdcharacteristics/homeinternetandsocialmediausage/datasets/internetaccesshouseholdsandindividualsreferencetables> last accessed 1 August 2021, 6.

[13] See Pew Research Center, 'Social media fact sheet' (7 April 2021) <https://www.pewresearch.org/internet/fact-sheet/social-media/> last accessed 1 August 2021.

[14] Statista, 'Most popular social networks worldwide as of April 2021, ranked by number of active users' <https://www.statista.com/statistics/272014/global-social-networks-ranked-by-number-of-users/> last accessed 1 August 2021.

[15] C Abram, 'Welcome to Facebook, everyone' *Facebook Blog* (26 September 2006) <http://blog.facebook.com/blog.php?blog_id=company&m=9&y=2006> last accessed 1 August

tools for users to search and add potential friends.[16] A user's profile page has a 'timeline' where other users can post messages (so-called status updates), photos, videos and other content (provided that the privacy settings set by the user allow this). The timeline includes a cover photo, profile picture, timeline stream and different information a user decides to share (personal information, interests, hobbies and various other applications such as games or events). A private chat and messaging system, 'Messenger', acts as a standalone application, now integrated in Instagram. Another important feature is 'Photos', a photo-sharing functionality with a tagging system: users click on a face in a photo (posted by them or someone else) and enter the person's name. If that person is a Facebook user, the photo will be linked to their timeline or photostream (if allowed by privacy settings). These activities generate a stream of event notifications, and since September 2006, that stream is visible to users. A user's homepage displays a 'Feed' (formerly 'News Feed'), a list of the most recent notifications from their friends. Facebook's 'Platform' feature enables developers to create 'Applications' that plug into the Facebook site. The Platform includes an interface for providers to issue instructions to Facebook and gathers information from it,[17] along with a custom mark-up language that enables notifications and an interface shown to users with the Facebook look and feel.[18] Facebook has constantly been growing and innovating, introducing additional features for groups, adverts, shopping and games.

Twitter, conversely, has been conceived as a 'conversational microblog', where users post messages that appear in the streams of all the people who are subscribed to them (who 'follow' these users). Users who subscribe to and receive one's messages are one's 'followers' or people who are following them. In turn, the people whom a user is following are called their friends. The maximum length of the message, or 'tweet', has grown from the initial 140 to 280 characters only, which puts Twitter in the microblogging category. In order to address someone on Twitter, users use the functionality of @reply, including a user's username, to indicate that the tweet is specifically intended for them (e.g. a tweet including @EdinaRl would be directed to my Twitter account

2021; Facebook, 'Terms of use' <http://www.facebook.com/terms.php> last accessed 1 August 2021.

[16] Facebook, 'Find people you know on Facebook' <https://www.facebook.com/help/146466588759199 (search for users)> last accessed 1 August 2021; F Ratiu, 'People you may know' *Facebook Blog* (2 May 2008) <http://blog.facebook.com/blog.php?post=15610312130> last accessed 1 August 2021.

[17] Facebook Wiki, '*API*, Facebook Developer Wiki' <http://fbdevwiki.com/wiki/Facebook_Developer_Wiki> last accessed 1 August 2021.

[18] Facebook Wiki, '*FBML*, Facebook Developer Wiki' <http://fbdevwiki.com/wiki/Category:FBML> last accessed 1 August 2021.

and shown on its main page). The tweet is still public, but now the addressee is known, and the flow of the conversation is clearer. Another important feature on Twitter is a hashtag, identified by the # sign. The hashtag is a descriptive keyword, and by using or searching for a hashtag, users can join or follow the conversation on particular topics (e.g. #digitalassets would contribute to the conversation on digital assets). Hashtags are, however, not Twitter's invention but that of a similar service called Jaiku.[19] The action of retweeting means using someone else's tweet and rebroadcasting it with attribution to that user so that the retweeter's own followers can see it. Finally, users can send private messages with the same character limit and attach photos and videos to their tweets.

Creating content – primarily images, videos, notes, status updates and tweets – is one of the essential functions of social networks. Therefore, this chapter will look at the content of social network (SN) accounts in terms of private messages, images, videos, status updates or tweets, personal data and information. The focus will not be on some other features, for instance Facebook groups, events or games. Games could arguably follow the line or arguments established in Chapter 5, especially as the use of virtual reality features in social networks increases. The focus will be on the private, individual content shared and created through an SN account, as the whole book looks at the relevant post-mortem issues from a user perspective. User accounts will be explored in relation to terms of service and how they restrict or enable access to the content. The focus is not in the interface and current application features of these SNSs because of the tremendous pace at which these features change, on the one hand, and the importance of the phenomenon rather than technicalities, on the other.

The analysis in this chapter will include copyright, property, contracts and privacy issues. Like games and VWs and emails in later chapters, SN accounts represent a complex set of legal relations, between users and the platform or intermediary, between users themselves, and even between users and third parties (advertisers, government, media).

In contrast with Chapter 5, where assets in games and VWs are looked at from a perspective of three layers, the case study of SNSs requires a perspective similar to the one in Chapter 6, discussing emails. There are two critical layers here. The first one is the developers' code, which entitles the SNS providers to own the underlying system and account created to be able to use the system. The second layer predominantly includes copyrightable material.

[19] V Barash and S Golder, 'Twitter: Conversation, entertainment and information, all in one network!' in D Hansen, B Shneiderman and M Smith, *Analyzing Social Media Networks with NodeXL: Insights from a Connected World* (Morgan Kaufmann 2010) 147.

All the six main issues around post-mortem transmission of other assets analysed in this book apply to social networks (i.e. legal definition; access; conflicts with criminal legislation; jurisdiction; conflicts between various interests; and conflicts between succession laws and digital solutions). These issues are, understandably, manifested differently. The chapter will consider these differences, applying the same conceptual approach and focusing on the issues of a legal nature, access to the content, and different conflicts arising in the transmission of SNS content.

4.2 Illustration Through Case Law

Unfortunately, there has not been comprehensive, relevant litigation and precedent in the UK or US that would answer some of the questions posed in these and similar cases, more specifically the legal nature of this content and whether it transmits on death. There has been a growing number of relevant court cases worldwide, but most of them have raised more questions than they have answered so far. We will explore some of these and illustrate critical issues by looking at the media reports and cases that have unfortunately not reached the courts.

In one of the first cases reported by the media, Karen Williams, the mother of Loren Williams, who was killed in a motorbike accident in 2005 at the age of twenty-two, requested access to her son's account.[20] Karen asked Facebook not to delete her son's account after she obtained his password through a friend of her son. Soon after she began logging in, the password was changed or deactivated by Facebook, and she could not access the account any more.[21] Karen started negotiating with Facebook through her lawyer, and they agreed that she would be able to access Loren's account for ten months. In 2007, Karen also obtained a court order from Multnomah County Circuit Court, Oregon, giving effect to the agreement.[22]

Another case that has only been known from its media coverage again illustrates some of the issues and the *ad hoc* response Facebook has to the issues surrounding accounts of deceased users. Facebook has launched a 'Look Back' feature that creates a video generated by popular moments on a

[20] L Gambino, 'In death, Facebook photos could fade away forever' *Associated Press* (1 March 2013) <http://news.yahoo.com/death-facebook-photos-could-fade-away-forever-085129756--finance.html> last accessed 1 August 2021.

[21] Huff Post Tech, 'Karen Williams' Facebook saga raises question of whether users' profiles are part of "digital estates"' *Huffington Post* (15 March 2012) <http://www.huffingtonpost.com/2012/03/15/karen-williams-face book_n_1349128.html> last accessed 1 August 2021.

[22] Ibid.

person's profile. John Berlin, the father of Jesse, who died in 2012 at the age of twenty-two, posted a YouTube clip asking Mark Zuckerberg, Facebook's founder, to create a Look Back video for his son. Berlin did not have access to his son's account and thus could not create one himself. After widespread media support for Berlin, Facebook agreed to create one on his behalf using content Jesse had posted publicly, again implying its policy of protecting users' privacy, even upon death. Facebook also noted that 'This experience reinforced to us that there's more Facebook can do to help people celebrate and commemorate the lives of people they have lost' and said that it will share more about this in the future.[23] Facebook has come up with some changes in this regard, and we will look at these later in the chapter. There have been, reportedly, other cases where deceased users' videos have been provided to their families upon request, and the request for a deceased's Look Back video has now been incorporated in Facebook's terms.[24]

The case of Sahar Daftary illustrates the issue of international jurisdiction in these cases.[25] Although it is not within the scope of this book to discuss the jurisdiction issue in depth, it is important to note here that Facebook refused to grant access to the account to Sahar's family without a court order, and the family initiated a request to subpoena the records in the Californian courts. The court found that the US Stored Communications Act[26] prevents a US service provider from disclosing stored communications in civil proceedings.[27] The court has extended the effect of the US statute to a foreign citizen, stating that there was no duty to provide stored communications for the foreign proceedings. The Court held, 'It would be odd, to put it mildly, to grant discovery related to foreign proceedings but not those taking place in the United States.'[28] The court also noted that Facebook could disclose the records to the family voluntarily, as this is in accordance with the Act. It has not been reported if Facebook has done so, but bearing in mind its terms of use, it is unlikely that it did. This case thus serves as an example where precedence has been given to the deceased's privacy over the claimed property right

[23] D Lee, 'Facebook reviews family memorials after dad's plea' *BBC* (6 February 2014) <http://www.bbc.co.uk/news/technology-26066688> last accessed 1 August 2021.

[24] K Wagner, 'Facebook will make "Look Back" videos for deceased users' *Mashable* (21 February 2014) <http://mashable.com/2014/02/21/facebook-look-back-video-deceased/> last accessed 1 August 2021.

[25] *In re Request for Order Requiring Facebook, Inc to Produce Documents and Things*, C 12-80171 LHK (PSG) (ND Cal 20 September 2012).

[26] 18 USC § 2701.

[27] See *In re Request for Order Requiring Facebook, Inc to Produce Documents and Things* (n 25), citing *Theofel* v *Farley-Jones*, 359 F.3d 1066, 1074 (9th Cir 2004) 2.

[28] Ibid.

of the family and heirs. This is contrary to the German case where a dead girl's parent fought Facebook over access to her account. As noted in the previous chapter, succession claims prevailed over the privacy defence that Facebook used.[29]

There has been exciting but scarce case law in the US regarding Twitter, addressing proprietary or privacy interests in tweets concerning criminal investigations and the Stored Communications Act.[30] In *New York* v *Harris*,[31] Twitter sought to quash the subpoena issued by the New York County District Attorney's Office in January 2012. The subpoena required Twitter to provide user information (email addresses etc.), and tweets tweeted from the account @destructuremal allegedly used by Malcolm Harris. Harris was charged with disorderly conduct after participating in the Occupy Wall Street march on the Brooklyn Bridge. After getting the District Attorney's order, Twitter informed Harris that his account had been subpoenaed and, subsequently, Harris filed a motion to quash the subpoena. Twitter decided that it would not comply with the subpoena until the court ruled on this motion. The court order upheld the subpoena in April 2012. The court held that the defendant had no proprietary interest in the user information on his Twitter account, and he lacked standing to quash the subpoena.[32] The court also stated that by agreeing to Twitter's terms of service agreement, the user 'was granting a license for Twitter to use, display and distribute the defendant's Tweets to anyone and for any purpose it may have'.[33]

Following this decision, Twitter moved to quash the April 2012 court order and had not complied with the order by then. At the same time, on 17 May 2012, Twitter revised its terms of service agreement to add 'You retain your rights to any Content you submit, post or display on or through the Services.' It could be argued that Twitter changed its agreement between the April and June 2012 court orders in response to the April order.[34] However, in the June 2012 order, the court granted the motion to quash in part and denied it in part. It ordered Twitter to disclose all non-content and content

29 Kammergericht, Urteil vom 31. Mai 2017, Aktenzeichen 21 U 9/16 <https://www.berlin.de/gerichte/presse/pressemitteilungen-der-ordentlichen-gerichtsbarkeit/2017/pressemitteilung.596076.php> last accessed 30 January 2022; appealed BGH, 12 July 2018, Docket No III ZR 183/17.

30 See analysis in J Lamm, 'Defending your ownership and privacy in Twitter (and other online accounts)' *Digital Passing Blog* (25 July 2012) <http://www.digitalpassing.com/2012/07/25/defending-ownership-privacy-twitter-online-accounts/> last accessed 1 August 2021.

31 *People v Harris*, 36 Misc 3d 613 (NY Crim Ct 2012).

32 Ibid.

33 Ibid.

34 Ibid.

information older than 180 days, but content information less than 180 days old may only be disclosed under a search warrant.[35] It is interesting to note that, similarly to Facebook in the Daftary case and Yahoo! in the Ellsworth case, Twitter decided to defend the user's privacy and refuse to disclose the information until it had exhausted the legal challenges. However, even if not a subject matter of this case, the court found neither proprietary interests nor reasonable expectations of privacy in tweets. The analysis in this chapter will follow a similar line of argument, with a difference in considering copyright as a tool.

These cases and real-world examples illustrate only a limited number of issues identified in the section above (property, jurisdiction, privacy). This chapter will refer back to these examples and look at other issues not articulated in these cases (copyright, technology).

4.3 Legal Nature of the Content of Social Network Accounts

The main concepts to consider relevant to the legal nature of SNS account content and following the approach adopted in the book are property, copyright, contracts and privacy. This chapter will consider two alternative paradigms for the nature of this content: 1) SNS content is protected by copyright as literary or artistic works; and 2 the content is property (which takes us to the debate about whether information can be property; see Chapter 6).

Prima facie, this content predominantly includes literary and artistic works created by their authors, SNS users. Therefore, copyright appears to be one of the most obvious answers when determining the legal nature of SNSs. The following section will thus discuss copyright in SNS content in relation to transmission on death. Subsequently, the analysis will include property issues in a type of SNS content not susceptible to copyright protection.

(a) Copyright in SNSs and Post-Mortem Transmission

Social networks contain vast amounts of potentially or actually copyrighted materials. These include, for instance, photos and videos uploaded on Facebook and Twitter; tweets; Facebook status updates; and notes on Facebook in the forms of short stories, comments and poems.

The question of copyright in the content posted on SNSs has been relatively straightforward for many academics.[36] In Mazzone's opinion, 'poems,

[35] *People* v *Harris*, 2012 NY Slip Op 22175 [36 Misc 3d 868].

[36] 'In the US Copyright protection subsists . . . in original works of authorship fixed in any tangible medium of expression, now known or later developed, from which they can be perceived, reproduced, or otherwise communicated, either directly or with the aid of a machine or device.' See US Copyright Code 17 USC § 102(a) (2006). Digital works are eligible for

essays, photographs, videos, commentary, and even status updates are all potentially eligible for copyright protection'.[37] He also rightly observes that 'users do not depend upon the social networking site to obtain intellectual property rights',[38] Similarly, Darrow and Ferrera and Tarney all assert even more firmly that videos and pictures on social networks are copyrightable and consequently transmissible on death.[39]

Nevertheless, one should not assume that all content will automatically qualify for copyright protection. This depends on the fulfilment of legal requirements. In most countries, these are publication, originality and fixation. One issue that could arise concerning copyright and social networks is whether the fixation in an electronic form on a remote computer or server would satisfy the requirement of fixation. The fixation requirement is discussed in more detail in Chapter 6 and my earlier work,[40] but it is clear that electronic fixation does meet the legal requirements of US and UK copyright law.[41] White rightly asserts that UGC, such as tweets, posts on Facebook and blogs, will often meet these requirements. She notes that this content can be perceived and reproduced from a medium, namely a computer or servers. She also argues that they also are available for more than transitory duration. Tweets, for instance, 'update constantly, [but] do not automatically delete, nor do they overwrite each other when a new Tweet is posted. Tweets that are not on the immediate screen are archived and retrievable.'[42] In addition, many websites store tweets, including the US Library of Congress.[43]

---

copyright protection. See ibid. § 101 ('A work is "fixed" in a tangible medium of expression when its embodiment in a copy or phonorecord, by or under the authority of the author, is sufficiently permanent or stable to permit it to be perceived, reproduced, or otherwise communicated for a period of more than transitory duration').

[37] J Mazzone, 'Facebook's afterlife' (2012) 90 *North Carolina Law Review* 1643, 1651, citing § 102(a) (setting out the classes of work eligible for copyright protection).

[38] US Copyright Code 17 USC § 201 (2006) ('Copyright in a work protected under this title vests initially in the author or authors of the work').

[39] See J Darrow and G Ferrera, 'Who owns a decedent's e-mails: Inheritable probate or property of the network?' (2006) 10 *New York University Journal of Legislation and Public Policy* 281, 282–3, 287–9; US Copyright Code 17 USC § 102(a); T Tarney, 'A call for legislation to permit the transfer of digital assets at death' (2012) 40 *Capital University Law Review* 773, 783.

[40] E Harbinja, 'Social media and death' in L Gillies and D Mangan (eds), *The Legal Challenges of Social Media* (Edward Elgar 2017).

[41] White (n 9) 697.

[42] Ibid.

[43] R Adams, 'All your Twitter belongs to the Library of Congress' *Guardian* (14 April 2010) <http://www.theguardian.com/world/richard-adams-blog/2010/apr/14/twitter-library-of-congress> last accessed 1 August 2021.

The same could be argued for Facebook postings and blogs; they are updated and moved from a Feed, but they are also easily retrievable from a user's timeline.[44]

The second copyright requirement is originality, and the same analysis from Chapter 6 and my earlier work applies.[45] If tweets, Facebook posts, updates, and so on contain single words or short phrases or titles, they would most likely not meet the originality requirement in US law. The situation is less evident in UK and EU law. However, most of the posts on Facebook and Twitter are longer than that and most probably satisfy this requirement, provided that a user has created them.

Regarding photographs, another familiar type of Facebook and Twitter content, a similar originality threshold is required. A photograph would be considered original in the US if it includes a small degree of composure and positioning.[46] Under UK copyright law, photographs are protected as artistic works under section 4 of the Copyright, Designs and Patents Act (CDPA) 1988. The UK requirement for originality has been similar to the US one (the labour and skill or 'sweat of the brow' test) but differs from the Court of Justice of the European Union's 'author's own intellectual creation' test, which requires a higher level of creativity.[47] Concerning photographs, in particular, it could be argued that the lower threshold of originality remains (including e.g. composition, positioning the object, choice of the angle of shot, lighting and focus, being at the right place at the right time).[48] Therefore, it could be argued that many (but not all) of the photos uploaded on Facebook and taken by a particular user could be protected by copyright. Conversely, much content would include the cases where users copy someone else's works, as in quotes (a widespread type of content on SNSs, where users express their moods and opinions quoting different authors), links to different content on other websites (news portals, blog posts, quotation pages, etc.), music (usually links to YouTube, Spotify, TikTok, etc.), articles (scholarly or news

[44] White (n 9) 698.

[45] Harbinja (n 40).

[46] The main cases are *Burrow-Giles Lithographic Co* v *Sarony*, 111 US 53, 59 (1884); *Mannion* v *Coors Brewing Co*, 377 F.Supp.2d 444, 455 (SDNY 2005), interpreting US Copyright Code 17 USC § 101.

[47] *Infopaq International A/S* v *Danske Dagblades Forening* (C-5/08) [2012] Bus LR 102 (16 July 2009) 33–7.

[48] See *Antiquesportfolio.com Plc* v *Rodney Fitch & Co Ltd* [2001] ECDR 5, 29–39; the unified test of *Infopaq* and *University of London Press* has been adopted by the Court in *Temple Island Collections Ltd* v *New English Teas Ltd* [2012] EWPCC 1, where the judge held, 'Ultimately however the composition of the image can be the product of the skill and labour (or intellectual creation) of a photographer and it seems to me that skill and labour/intellectual creation directed to that end can give rise to copyright.'

articles) and photos taken by others. This category of content (user-uploaded or user-copied content) is not in the scope of this chapter, as the focus is on the content created by users and not the external content copyrighted by someone else. Users would not have any rights in this content and could, potentially, be liable for infringing copyright belonging to someone else. For this reason, this content is not the relevant one in relation to transmission on death.

Some SN content could resemble joint work or works of joint authorship in copyright law.[49] Users create and post content; other users comment on it, share it further, tag it, and so on. It is argued here that this analogy is not appropriate as the concept of joint work requires a high degree of integrity so that the contributions of individual authors are 'inseparable or interdependent parts of a unitary whole'[50] or 'not distinct'.[51] The contributions are easily distinguishable and separable on a social network, as they are all tagged by an author's name and can be edited, deleted or deactivated at any time.[52]

The emphasis here is on the unpublished works of authorship and materials generated and posted on Facebook or Twitter only. This case is very different from emails as, on Twitter, most of the content is public and definitely published, and therefore protected as regular literary works, provided it meets the other requirements discussed above. In the case of Facebook, it is less clear, since publishing to a limited number of people is not making the content available to the public and so would not qualify in the cases where privacy settings are set to 'friends only' and only a limited number of users can access the content.[53]

If the content is deemed unpublished, the same findings as in emails and my earlier research apply (PMP used as an argument against the default publication of personal data).[54] These works would potentially transmit on death, according to CDPA 1988, s 93 but it is argued that the provision would need to be changed or technology solutions need to be recognised as an 'entitlement' for the purpose of CDPA 1988, s 93.[55]

49 See US Copyright Code 17 USC § 101; UK Copyright, Designs and Patents Act 1988, c 48, s 10.

50 US Copyright Code 17 USC § 101.

51 UK Copyright, Designs and Patents Act 1988, c 48, s 10.

52 Hetcher (n 8) 888.

53 See the US case *Getaped.com, Inc* v *Cangemi*, 188 F.Supp.2d 398, 62 USPQ.2d (BNA) 1030 (SDNY 2002), where publication on the website, available to all, constituted publication for the purpose of US Copyright Code 17 USC § 101. This interpretation would arguably comply with the UK Copyright, Designs and Patents Act 1988, c 48, s 175.

54 Harbinja (n 40).

55 Ibid.

However, if the works are considered published, they are protected by copyright, and the next of kin should be able to inherit and benefit from them for seventy years post-mortem of the author. Content published elsewhere and accessible to the personal representative, executor or next of kin is not problematic. The estate will benefit from this content, and the usual rules for the succession of copyright apply.

Furthermore, social network authors of literary or artistic works would be entitled to moral rights, in addition to the copyright as an economic right.[56] In the UK, unless waived, therefore, users would have moral rights for seventy or twenty years post-mortem, depending on the type of right. In principle, moral rights in the UK transmit on death, but there are further relevant issues in relation to Facebook in particular. Whereas Facebook, for instance, does not require the waiving of moral rights in its terms of service, the access of a user's heirs to this content is limited. Since we do focus on unpublished work in this chapter (as published works can be accessed elsewhere), the problem with passing them on is the one identified in the paragraph above, concerning copyright, that is, access and contracts.

In summary, the most significant issue when considering the copyright and transmission of SN content is access and relevant contractual terms. In this regard, Mazzone draws an analogy with letters and the division between physical and intellectual property, arguing that even if users have copyright in social network content, the physical property would belong to the operator of the social network and 'the heir would have no right to obtain a copy of the materials'.[57] Later in this chapter, we will address these issues in more detail.

(b) Property in SNS Content

Some commentators firmly believe that social network accounts and content are essentially the property of the user. For them, a social network account 'is, like any online account, intangible property'.[58] This argument simplifies the different features of SN content and relationships between users and SN sites, as discussed later in this chapter. It also favours the American approach to intangible property, explored in Chapter 6, and fails to account for IP as a distinct legal concept. In addition, to rebut this argument, we could resort to Benkler's description of peer production, applicable to UGC in social networks, defined as a mode of 'information production that is not based on exclusive proprietary claims, not aimed toward sales in a market for either motivation or information, and not organized around property and contract

[56] Ibid.
[57] Mazzone (n 37) 1644.
[58] Ibid. 1650.

claims to form firms or market exchanges'.[59] In Grimmelmann's view, 'that's a fair description of Facebook culture: users voluntarily sharing information with each other for diverse reasons, both personal and social', rejecting the IP protection of their posts or trading in their social capital and information.[60] However, he asserts that the information commons is not desirable in the case of private information, as Facebook, with its features of sharing, large user base, and so on, is 'a privacy nightmare'.[61] This chapter will note the information commons feature of Facebook and Twitter, take into account Grimmelmann's fears, and provide a different account of the legal nature of SN account content.

This chapter will use the analysis of property in information and personal data set out in Chapter 6. This analysis is chiefly relevant for that chapter, and therefore it is set out therein, but for the reader's benefit, we will summarise the main findings here. As in emails, in SN accounts, information would include non-copyrightable material such as short phrases, single words, jokes in status updates on Facebook or tweets that will not meet the requirements for copyright protection. Additionally, personal data represents a significant amount of SN content. In the case of Facebook, for instance, there is personal data in the 'About' section (name, place of birth, address, education, age, sex, relationship status, religious and political beliefs, pictures, etc.), but also in the user's albums, notes and status updates. A vast amount of this data belongs to the category of sensitive data (religious and political beliefs, sexual orientation, etc.).[62] On Twitter, personal data is less prominent, but users still share some of it (in their general profile data, names, location, interests, etc.).

Regarding information and personal data, findings from Chapter 6 are applicable here. The non-copyrightable content of SNS, that is, information and personal data, is not (doctrinal argument) and should not be (normative argument) considered property. Instead, other safeguards established for information and personal data should be utilised to protect this content (breach of confidence, trade secrets, data protection).[63] This, tentatively, means that the non-proprietary character of SNS content to a considerable extent precludes its post-mortem transmission. The argument against the default

[59] Y Benkler, 'Siren songs and Amish children: Autonomy, information, and law' (2001) 76 *New York University Law Review* 23.

[60] Grimmelmann (n 3) 1188.

[61] Ibid.

[62] Article 8 of Directive 95/46/EC of the European Parliament and of the Council of 24 October 1995 on the protection of individuals with regard to the processing of personal data and on the free movement of such data OJ L 281, 23/11/1995 P. 0031–0050 (the Data Protection Directive); Data Protection Act 1998, c 29, s 2.

[63] Harbinja (n 40).

transmission of SNS content on death is further supported by the issues in transmitting copyright and the phenomenon of post-mortem privacy (PMP). Consequently, considering the issues with property and copyright in SNS content, the more relevant concept concerning the legal nature of this SN content is PMP, discussed further in this chapter.

4.4 Allocation of Ownership in Social Network Sites

We have established so far that most SN content is copyright and therefore potentially transmissible. This section will analyse ownership, property and copyright allocation in users' SN account content as established by service provider contracts (Facebook and Twitter). After discussing whether this content is property or work protected by copyright, this section will answer the question of who gets the copyright, if applicable, according to the contracts users conclude before starting to use their SN accounts.

Facebook's terms of use and privacy policy are known as the 'Statement of Rights and Responsibilities' and the 'Data Use Policy'.[64] In addition, the labyrinth of terms governing users' behaviour on Facebook is also found in other specific terms, policy documents, guidelines and forms.[65] These terms are often revised, and proposed changes are posted to the Facebook Site Governance Page a minimum of seven days before the change is effective.[66] Apart from for German users (where German law applies), the 'laws of the State of California will govern' the contract in terms of jurisdiction.[67] However, all disputes arising from the contract will be resolved 'exclusively in a state or federal court located in the US District Court for the Northern District of California or a state court located in San Mateo County'.[68]

Facebook is clearly referring to the ownership of UGC when it states:

> You own the intellectual property rights (things such as copyright or trademarks) in any such content that you create and share on Facebook and the other Facebook Company Products you use. Nothing in these Terms takes away the rights you have to your own content.[69]

This term seems permissive compared with some other terms analysed in the following chapters, for emails in particular, as it recognises users' ownership

64 Facebook, 'Terms: Statement of rights and responsibilities' <https://www.facebook.com/legal/terms> last accessed 1 August 2021.
65 Ibid. s 5.
66 Ibid. s 14. Users must 'like' the page in order to receive a notification on their timeline.
67 Ibid. s 4.
68 Ibid. s 3.1.
69 Ibid.

and control of the content, but only for IP in the content created and shared by the user. However, looking at the extensive licence that users give Facebook for using their content, this control does not appear to be as strong as initially stated.[70] Furthermore, the somewhat incomprehensible term for an average user is related to the deletion of the content.[71] It follows from this provision that the user cannot be sure whether the content has actually been removed and what the 'reasonable amount of time' for which this content can persist really means. Also, the use Facebook makes of this particular content is unclear. Furthermore, while the user seemingly retains control and can remove the content at any time, this is not the case with the account. The account can be transferred only with Facebook's written permission, and only the user themself is entitled to access the account.[72]

Therefore, whereas Facebook notes that the user owns the content, Facebook owns the account, and we can identify the same legal implications as in email accounts. This diminishes users' control in what seems a relatively comprehensive way at first glance. However, it is also understandable, as the users use proprietary software to post and share their content. More control would arguably mean that users could download and transfer their content from one platform to another, which would be a property feature, as discussed earlier in this book. Also, the licence is imposed, and users cannot object to Facebook using their content. There are no negotiations in this regard, and users again lack control over their content.

Twitter also emphasises that users retain the right to 'any Content you submit, post or display on or through the Services. What's yours is yours – you own your Content.'[73] Twitter requires granting a broad licence to UGC, similar to that which Facebook requires.[74] Therefore, the analysis is similar to the above. The difference is privacy settings and how users share content on Twitter, which is public by default.[75] The underlying software is Twitter's ownership, and the user gets a non-assignable and non-exclusive licence to use it.[76] However, even if Twitter is ready to recognise property or copyright interests in tweets and content posted on its platform, the courts are less likely to make a similar decision. However, the matter is still very unclear, as the US cases on

[70] Ibid.

[71] Ibid.

[72] '[N]ot share your password, give access to your Facebook account to others or transfer your account to anyone else (without our permission).' See ibid.

[73] Twitter, 'Terms of service' <https://twitter.com/tos> last accessed 1 August 2021.

[74] Ibid.

[75] Ibid. 'This license authorizes us to make your Content available to the rest of the world and to let others do the same.'

[76] Ibid.

these issues primarily have pertained to subpoenas and employer–employee relationships. Even there, the courts have failed to provide clear guidance. There are no relevant UK cases at the time of writing.

(a) Intermediary Contracts and Transmission of SNS Content on Death

The essential issue relating to transmission on death is the non-transferable nature of SN accounts. Facebook's terms state that the agreement 'does not confer any third party beneficiary rights'.[77] Facebook accounts are non-transferable, including any 'Page' or 'application' users administer, without Facebook's written permission.[78] There is a clear prohibition of impersonation (using another user's account pretending you are that user), as password sharing is prohibited, and users are also banned from letting anyone else access their account.[79] Twitter also has a strict impersonation policy, a breach of which results in the permanent suspension of an account.[80] There are no clear Twitter rules on whether the account is transferable, but one can infer from the impersonation policy that this is not allowed. Having in mind property incidents identified in Chapter 2, where transferability is essential, it is clear that individuals cannot own accounts. However, the question of owning content is a separate one and will be looked at in more detail.

Facebook

Regarding deceased users, no provision expressly terminates the contract between Facebook and a deceased user. For a very long time, Facebook's terms, the 'Statement of Rights and Responsibilities' and 'Data Use Policy', contained only one provision relating to a deceased's account. This obscure provision was hidden in the 'some other things you need to know' section of the 'Data Use Policy'[81] and referred to the Facebook 'memorialization' process and the account closure under specific conditions.[82] The use of the term 'may' implied a vague promise by Facebook, without any criteria specified, to

[77] Facebook, 'Terms: Statement of rights and responsibilities' (n 64) s 5.6.

[78] Ibid. s 3.1.

[79] Ibid. s 3.1.

[80] Twitter, 'Impersonation policy' <https://help.twitter.com/en/rules-and-policies/twitter-impersonation-policy> last accessed 1 August 2021. For a more comprehensive survey of cloud service providers' terms regarding their deceased users, see JD Michels, D Kamarinou and C Millard, 'Beyond the clouds, part 2: What happens to the files you store in the clouds when you die?' Queen Mary School of Law Legal Studies Research Paper No 316/2019 (13 May 2019) <https://ssrn.com/abstract=3387398> last accessed 1 August 2021.

[81] Facebook, 'Data use policy, some other things to know' <https://m.facebook.com/policy/?page=other> last accessed 1 August 2021 (on file with the author).

[82] Ibid.

memorialise or close an account.[83] The insertion of this option in Facebook's terms resulted from a personal loss of a Facebook employee.[84] This once more confirmed the usual practice of dealing with digital assets on death: *ad hoc* solutions, provoked by media coverage (as in Look Back videos, for instance), personal losses of employees (memorialisation), political interests (US state laws) or court cases (Twitter and Harris case). Facebook's terms of service are now much clearer and clearly refer to memorialisation and Legacy Contact options explored later in the chapter.[85]

In addition to this provision within the actual agreement, all other details on Facebook's deceased policy are contained in various sections in Facebook's help centre and the options provided in several requests and contact forms. Bearing in mind their place and nature, Edwards and Harbinja question whether some of these forms and policies are 'merely statements of good practice' rather than binding contractual terms.[86] Therefore, it was suggested that the requests and help forms, not referred to in the general terms of service, are not a part of the contract between Facebook and its users, as they lacked some significant incorporation of terms requirements.[87] In this case, it would be incorporation by reference, and Facebook had not taken appropriate steps to bring these to users' attention. This has changed with the inclusion of the above term in the main terms, so the incorporation of terms is arguably present. Still, there is a problem with user awareness of the terms and the fact that help pages are not linked in the main terms of service.

Furthermore, like the general terms of service, these help centre pages and forms are often changed without notice to users, and it is difficult, if impossible, to keep track of the changes. McCallig argues that looking at Facebook's policies on deceased users, 'it seems clear that it is Facebook policy to memorialize the accounts of all deceased persons'.[88] However, technically,

[83] See D McCallig, 'Facebook after death: An evolving policy in a social network' (2014) 22(2) *International Journal of Law and Information Technology* 107, 114.

[84] HK Chan, 'Memories of friends departed endure on Facebook' *Facebook* (26 October 2009) <https://www.facebook.com/notes/facebook/memories-of-friends-departed-endure-on-facebook/163091042130> last accessed 1 August 2021.

[85] Facebook, 'Terms: Statement of rights and responsibilities' (n 64) s 5.5.

[86] L Edwards and E Harbinja, '"What happens to my Facebook profile when I die?": Legal issues around transmission of digital assets on death' in C Maciel and V C Pereira (eds), *Digital Legacy and Interaction: Post-Mortem Issues* (Springer 2013) 115–44.

[87] For example the requirement that these are brought to a user's attention before or at the time of the formation of contract, that is, when the user signs up to use Facebook. See *Olley* v *Marlborough Court Ltd* [1949] 1 KB 532; *Parker* v *South East Railway Company* (1877) 2 CPD 416.

[88] McCallig (n 83) 9.

Facebook does not know if someone has died unless it is notified.[89] It may have technical means to infer that from a user's inactivity, for instance, or their friends' posts in remembrance, but the approach of not taking steps unless 'formally' notified is better and provides more certainty.

Additionally, Facebook has no account inactivity policy, meaning that profiles might remain active for very long, if not permanently, and it will not delete inactive accounts. Therefore, the only way for the accounts to be memorialised or deactivated is after a user or non-user has reported the death to Facebook. Initially, the request could have been submitted by 'others' in addition to the user's family and friends. It was unclear who exactly could submit a request as 'other' – friends of friends, non-users, anyone else – so in June 2013, Facebook removed 'other' from the relationship with the deceased options on the memorialisation request form.[90] The current memorialisation policy again allows friends to submit the request, and arguably, others, too, but advises the person making the request to contact 'the person's family before requesting memorialisation'.[91]

The effects of memorialisation are that it prevents anyone from logging into the account, even those with valid login information and password.[92] While alive, the decedent's content remains visible to those with whom it was shared (privacy settings remain 'as is').[93] Only the Legacy Contact that the deceased has chosen can manage the account, and if the user has requested deletion before death, this option will not be available.[94] In allowing privacy settings to remain post-mortem, Facebook claims that it wishes to respect the deceased's privacy. Depending on the privacy settings, confirmed friends may still post to the decedent's timeline. Accounts (timelines) that are memorialised no longer appear in the 'people you may know' suggestions or other

[89] JC Martin, 'Have you ever wondered what happens to your Facebook account after you have passed away?' *Silicon Valley Estate Planning Journal* (27 February 2015) <http://johncmartinlaw.com/ever-wondered-happens-facebook-account-pass-away/> last accessed 1 August 2021.

[90] Facebook, 'Memorialization request' <https://www.facebook.com/help/contact/305593649477238> last accessed 1 August 2021; Harbinja (n 40).

[91] Facebook, 'Memorialization request' (n 90).

[92] For a history of memorialisation, see McCallig (n 83) 11–12.

[93] Initially, it was visible only to the user's friends, but this changed in February 2014. See L Fields, 'Facebook changes access to profiles of deceased' *ABC News* (22 February 2014) <http://abcnews.go.com/Technology/facebook-access-profiles-deceased/story?id=22632425> last accessed 1 August 2021; C Price and A DiSclafani, 'Remembering our loved ones' *Facebook Newsroom* (21 February 2014) <http://newsroom.fb.com/news/2014/02/remembering-our-loved-ones/> last accessed 1 August 2021.

[94] Facebook, 'Terms: Statement of rights and responsibilities' (n 64).

suggestions and notifications.[95] Facebook also removes 'sensitive information such as contact information and status updates' to protect the deceased person's privacy.[96] In addition, memorialisation also prevents the tagging of the deceased in future Facebook posts, photographs or any other content.[97] Unfriending (removing someone from one's friends list) a deceased person's memorialised account is 'permanent and there is no way for a renewed friend request to be approved'.[98] Seemingly, a friend cannot be added to a memorialised account or profile, which might be an issue for parents of deceased children who may not have added their parents as friends while alive.[99] As McCallig notes, however, it was not clear whether Facebook would consider or grant a 'special request' to be added as a friend if made, for example, by a bereaved parent (as it met the request of Mr Berlin and the access to his son's Look Back video).[100] It seems like the current provision has been updated to disallow any request but the removal of the deceased's account or memorialisation.[101]

Concerning deactivation and removal of a deceased's account, the procedure has been complex and vague for a long time, before its latest revisions in the last couple of years. Facebook provided this option,[102] but with very general statements and vague criteria, calling this a 'special request'. The option was available only to 'verified immediate family members' or an executor, and the relationship to the deceased needed to be verified. Again, Facebook only promised to 'process' these requests, without giving a firm promise of fulfilling special requests. This has recently been clarified, and the process is

95 Facebook, 'What happens when a deceased person's account is memorialized?' <https://www.facebook.com/help/103897939701143/> last accessed 1 August 2021.

96 M Kelly, 'Memories of friends departed endure on Facebook' *Facebook Blog* (26 October 2009) <https://www.facebook.com/blog/blog.php?post=163091042130> last accessed 1 August 2021.

97 S Buck, 'How 1 billion people are coping with death and Facebook' *Mashable* (13 February 2013) <http://mashable.com/2013/02/13/facebook-after-death/> last accessed 1 August 2021.

98 Death and Digital Legacy, 'Nebraska is latest state to address digital legacy' (20 February 2012) <http://www.deathanddigitallegacy.com/2012/02/20/nebraska-is-latest-state-to-address-digital-legacy/> last accessed 1 August 2021.

99 Facebook, 'Special request for deceased person's account' <https://www.facebook.com/help/contact/228813257197480> last accessed 1 August 2021.

100 Ibid.

101 Facebook, 'Special request for a medically incapacitated or deceased person's account' <https://www.facebook.com/help/contact/228813257197480> last accessed 1 August 2021.

102 Facebook, 'How do I ask a question about a deceased person's account on Facebook?' <https://www.facebook.com/help/265593773453448> last accessed 1 August 2021.

available to an immediate family member or executor of the account holder. Facebook requires the death certificate to process this request fast, or other documents if this is not possible (proof of authority: power of attorney, birth certificate, last will and testament, estate letter; proof that a person has passed away: obituary or memorial card).[103]

Researchers have argued that the procedure for removal of a deceased user's profile is incongruous with Facebook's purpose and features (primarily keeping in touch with one's friends). Kasket, for instance, questions the 'right' of parents (often not users' friends on Facebook) to request permanent removal when this digital bond with friends there and profiles are primarily co-constructed (through different interactions on Facebook, such as tagging, sharing or re-posting).[104] Although looking at a small sample size, Pennington finds that all her college-student research participants had never unfriended a deceased user, although the reasons for not doing so varied.[105] Research finds that most Facebook users did not have their parents or children on their friends list, but 93 per cent of them do have other relatives on their Facebook friends list.[106] Also, most users are connected to their offline friends, and only a small percentage has befriended individuals they have never met offline.[107] Deactivation, therefore, even more than memorialisation, poses a question of reconciling the interests of a deceased user's family and friends. Is it in a user's interest to allow family members who are not on their friends lists in these co-constructed profiles to request deletion of such a profile and loss of the valuable materials for other users without a user expressing their wish in this direction? We will return to this question again later in this chapter and Chapter 7.

Following the case of Karen Williams, Facebook does not permit a family member access to the account, as opposed to copies of the contents of the account, which is permitted in some instances. McCallig opines that this change is 'most likely linked to fears that doing so might breach the Stored Communication Act, a United States federal law which prohibits the

[103] Facebook, 'How do I request the removal of a deceased family member's Facebook account?' <https://www.facebook.com/help/1518259735093203/?helpref=related> last accessed 1 August 2021.

[104] E Kasket, 'Access to the digital self in life and death: Privacy in the context of posthumously persistent Facebook profiles' (2013) 10:1 *SCRIPTed* 7.

[105] N Pennington, 'You don't de-friend the dead: An analysis of grief communication by college students through Facebook profiles' (2013) 37 *Death Studies* 617, 625.

[106] M Duggan, 'Demographics of key social networking platforms' *Pew Internet* (9 January 2015) <http://www.pewinternet.org/2015/01/09/demographics-of-key-social-networking-platforms-2/> last accessed 1 August 2021.

[107] Ibid.

disclosure of electronic communications to third parties, except in limited circumstances'.[108] An example of how this works in practice can be found in the case involving Sahar Daftary. Notably, the judgment concluded with the obiter comment, 'Of course, nothing prevents Facebook from concluding on its own that Applicants have the standing to consent on Sahar's behalf and providing the requested materials voluntarily.'[109] Lamm is encouraged by this statement, stating, 'this sentence is ultimately beneficial because it strongly suggests (to me [James Lamm]) that this court would not oppose the executor of a deceased user's estate providing "lawful consent" under § 2702 of the Stored Communications Act'.[110] Lamm also reminds us of the location of the court, being in the Northern District of California, the chosen jurisdiction under Facebook's terms.[111] McCallig, on the other hand, warns that this obiter statement should be treated with caution, as first, 'it fails to acknowledge Facebook's fear of wrongly concluding that an administrator or executor has the power to consent in such circumstances'. Second, 'It also ignores the reality that even if such consent is lawful, Facebook is under no obligation to release those communications'[112] since the Act grants to the provider a discretionary power of whether to disclose the contents of the communications. In s 2702, regarding the effect of a user's consent to the disclosure of communications, the Act uses the phrase 'may divulge the contents of communication',[113] which does not mean that the provider is required to act and provide the communications. This interpretation was followed in the Daftary case, as well.[114] In addition, the contents of communication cannot be disclosed to anyone but the government, and therefore the only solution is a user's consent.[115] There is no similar case in the UK to interpret the similar provisions of Part 1, Chapter 1 of the Regulation of Investigatory Powers Act 2000.

Facebook's help page states that it may be possible for content from a deceased's account to be requested by an authorised representative of the

[108] Stored Communications Act 18 USC ss 2701–12.

[109] *In re Request for Order Requiring Facebook, Inc to Produce Documents and Things* (n 25) 2.

[110] J Lamm, 'Facebook blocks demand for contents of deceased user's account' *Digital Passing Blog* (11 October 2012) <http://www.digitalpassing.com/2012/10/11/facebook-blocks-demand-contentsdeceased-users-account/> last accessed 1 August 2021.

[111] Ibid.

[112] McCallig (n 83) 17.

[113] See 18 USC § 2702(b).

[114] *In re Request for Order Requiring Facebook, Inc to Produce Documents and Things* (n 25) and *United States* v *Rodgers*, 461 US 677, 706 (1983) ('The word "may," when used in a statute, usually implies some degree of discretion.').

[115] US Stored Communications Act § 2702(b).

deceased and with a court order in rare cases.[116] The help page then links to a request form, asking several questions and requiring the submission of proof of identity. It is worth noting that this is much more definite than the old version of the request, which permitted a request based on an obituary.[117] Further, even following this procedure and upon the provision of documents, Facebook does not guarantee the fulfilment of the request. This is a very similar situation to that of the deactivation and removal of an account.

Finally, Facebook seems to have followed Google's lead and Inactive Account Manager with its more recently announced option of Legacy Contact.[118] From 12 February 2015, Facebook allowed its US users to designate a friend or family member to be their Facebook estate executor and manage their account after they have died. This was then rolled out to the rest of its users worldwide. The Legacy Contact has a limited number of options: writing a post to display at the top of the memorialised timeline; responding to new friend requests; and updating the profile picture and cover photo of the deceased user.[119] In addition, a user 'may give their legacy contact permission to download an archive of the photos, posts and profile information they shared on Facebook'.[120] The Legacy Contact will not be able to log in to the account or see the deceased's private messages. All the other settings will remain the same as before memorialisation of the account. Finally, an option is that a user decides that their account is to be permanently deleted after their death.[121] The rationale behind this feature, according to Facebook, is to support both grieving individuals (it is not clear whether family, friends or all of them) and users who want to take more control over what happens to their account on death.[122]

This move from Facebook is, admittedly, a valuable development for its users. It does shift the balance of interests from family and next of kin to

116 Facebook, 'How do I request content from the account of a deceased person?' <https://www.facebook.com/help/123355624495297> last accessed 1 August 2021.

117 K Notopoulos, 'How almost anyone can take you off Facebook (and lock you out)' *BuzzFeed* (4 January 2014) <http://www.buzzfeed.com/katienotopoulos/how-to-murder-your-friends-on-facebook-in-2-easy-s#.xbLyLygo2> last accessed 1 August 2021; J Schofield, 'What happens to your Facebook account when you die?' *Guardian* (30 October 2014) <http://www.theguardian.com/technology/askjack/2014/oct/30/what-happens-to-your-facebook-account-when-you-or-a-loved-one-dies> last accessed 1 August 2021.

118 Facebook, 'Adding a legacy contact' *Facebook Newsroom* (12 February 2015) <http://newsroom.fb.com/news/2015/02/adding-a-legacy-contact/> last accessed 1 August 2021.

119 Ibid.

120 Ibid.

121 Ibid.

122 Ibid.

users. Users now have control over who their Legacy Contact is, and this can only be one of their Facebook friends. Legacy Contact does not take too much control over the deceased's account, as they cannot post on behalf of the user (apart from the one message in remembrance and changing the timeline and profile picture), and they need permission to download an archive of the deceased user's content. Initially, it was unclear whether this permission includes all the content or some categories. Recent changes have provided that the Legacy Contact can receive photos and videos the deceased uploaded, wall posts, profile and contact information, events and friends list. They will not receive messages, ads the person clicked, pokes, security and settings information, or photos they automatically synced but did not post. This is due to this content's private or sensitive nature, and I support this from a PMP stance. However, understandably, Facebook notes that it 'may provide access to this type of information in response to a valid will or other legal consent document expressing clear consent'.[123]

One of the issues is the obscure place of this option (as seen with other options about the deceased's account; see the discussion above). To designate a Facebook Legacy Contact, a user needs to go into 'Settings', choose 'Security', and then choose 'Legacy Contact' at the bottom of the page.[124] Moreover, under the existing policy, it is unclear whether this option will trump the options heirs and next of kin have (deactivation and memorialisation as set out above). I have argued that Facebook needs to make this clear in its terms of service.[125] This has been clarified to an extent, but still not reasonably as this information does not appear in the request form for removal. Also, there might be issues with conflicting interests of heirs or families with a friend designated as a Legacy Contact and having an option to download the archive of the deceased's content. For instance, if the heirs inherit copyright in the user's works, and the Legacy Contact has acquired this content with the user's permission, will this content be exempt from the provisions of the will or intestacy laws? With this option, Facebook notably shifts the balance and accounts more for the deceased's interests and decisions before death.

In the next round of revising its terms related to deceased users, in April 2019, Facebook introduced a 'Tributes' section. This came after a series of consultations with external stakeholders, including myself and other academics working in the area. The new provision aims to develop memorialisation further and provide the Legacy Contact with new powers. The Tributes side

[123] Facebook, 'What data can a legacy contact download from Facebook?' <https://www.facebook.com/help/408044339354739/?helpref=related> last accessed 1 August 2021.

[124] Ibid.

[125] Harbinja (n 40).

of the deceased's profile co-exists with their timeline, and the timeline is still visible as set by the deceased before their death, whereas the Tributes include posts created after death in the remembrance of the deceased. The Legacy Contact can alter the visibility of the Tributes and do the following: change who can post tributes; delete Tributes posts; change who can see posts in which the deceased is tagged; remove tags of the deceased that someone else has posted; and, if the deceased had turned on a timeline review, the Legacy Contact can turn it off for posts in the Tributes section.[126] Facebook also changed its policies to let parents who have lost underage children to request to become their Legacy Contact. This is most likely in response to the recent court and media cases, such as the Berlin court case or the case of Molly Russell's tragic death.[127] Finally, in this iteration of changes, Facebook has attempted to clarify the use of AI for the deceased's profiles that have not yet been memorialised. Facebook claims that it uses AI to 'keep it from showing up in places that might cause distress, like recommending that person be invited to events or sending a birthday reminder to their friends'.[128] Edwards and Harbinja have argued that the exact extent and specifics of the use of AI are still vague and it would be helpful if Facebook made this clearer in its terms of service and the help centre.[129]

These kinds of tools give users a chance to explicitly shape their own future by indicating perhaps what data they do or do not want preserved or deleted, or to whom that data should go. Many issues remain to be addressed with such technological solutions, including the issue of conflicts both with traditional wills and with standard terms of service.[130] Also, anecdotal evidence shows that both the Google (discussed in Chapter 6) and Facebook tools remain relatively obscure. Facebook and Google could both make the existing options more prominent and a part of their core terms of service

[126] Facebook, 'What are tributes on a memorialised Facebook profile?' <https://www.facebook.com/help/745202382483645> last accessed 1 August 2021.

[127] BBC News, 'Molly Russell: "Why can't I see my daughter's data?"' (6 February 2019) <https://www.bbc.com/news/av/technology-47143315/molly-russell-why-can-t-i-see-my-daughter-s-data> last accessed 1 August 2021.

[128] Facebook, 'Making it easier to honor a loved one on Facebook after they pass away' *Facebook Newsroom* (9 April 2019) <https://newsroom.fb.com/news/2019/04/updates-to-memorialization/> last accessed 1 August 2021.

[129] L Edwards and E Harbinja, '"Be right back": What rights do we have over post-mortem avatars of ourselves?' in L Edwards, B Schafer and E Harbinja (eds), *Future Law: Emerging Technology, Regulation and Ethics* (Edinburgh University Press 2020).

[130] This issue was a hot topic in the revision of the US model law UFADAA, which grants priority to service providers' terms of service and user choices over any other provisions, including a traditional will.

rather than part of their 'help' pages. Finally, the designated Legacy Contact might simply refuse to play their part or not be able to be located, which then defeats the initial good intention of the social network.[131]

Twitter
Similarly, Twitter's user agreement is spread over several pages, including 'Terms of Service',[132] 'Privacy Policy'[133] and 'Rules and Policies'.[134] These terms are not very visible, as they are linked to the user's profile help page. Also, Twitter's policy differs in that it includes a period of inactivity (six months) after which the account can be permanently removed.[135] Another difference is that Twitter has a single option policy concerning the deceased's account, set out in the 'General' section of the 'Rules and Policies'.[136] According to this section, essentially a help page rather than a firm contractual term, 'a person authorized to act on the behalf of the estate or with a verified immediate family member of the deceased' can request deactivation of the account.

In the earlier version of the form, interested parties were required to provide an extensive list of information and documents for their request to be considered. The documentation had to be sent by post to Twitter's address in San Francisco. Further communication could be conducted via email. This has been simplified recently, and in the first instance, much less information is required to request deactivation. After the online form has been submitted, Twitter promises to get in touch by email with further instructions and a request to provide information about the deceased, a copy of the requester's ID, and a copy of the deceased's death certificate. Twitter is explicit about access to the account, like Facebook, stating, 'We are unable to provide account access to anyone regardless of his or her relationship to the deceased.'[137]

Twitter terms thus offer fewer options than Facebook. Understandably, due to the features and nature of Twitter, it is unimaginable that similar options to Facebook's could be available. Followers on Twitter are not exactly

[131] Edwards and Harbinja, '"Be right back"' (n 129).
[132] Twitter, 'Terms of service' (n 73).
[133] Twitter, 'Privacy policy' <https://twitter.com/privacy> last accessed 1 August 2021.
[134] Twitter, 'Rules and policies' <https://help.twitter.com/en/rules-and-policies> last accessed 1 August 2021.
[135] Twitter, 'Inactive account policy' <https://help.twitter.com/en/rules-and-policies/inactive-twitter-accounts> last accessed 1 August 2021.
[136] Twitter, 'How to contact Twitter about a deceased family member's account' <https://help.twitter.com/en/rules-and-policies/contact-twitter-about-a-deceased-family-members-account#:~:text=In%20the%20event%20of%20the,of%20a%20deceased%20user's%20account> last accessed 1 August 2021.
[137] Ibid.

one's friends, and many are, in fact, complete strangers. The nature of the community on Twitter is very different, too (users sharing different interests and participating in discussions, not necessarily wanting to keep in touch and share personal information to the extent Facebook's users do). The option of getting the user's content, provided by Facebook in unclear circumstances, is not available on Twitter at all.

On the other hand, most tweets are public[138] and anyone can access them, therefore it is not necessary to gain access to a user's account. Only users themselves can download an offline archive of their tweets. Their family or friends could access the public tweets themselves, bearing in mind the period of inactivity after which the account will be inaccessible (currently six months). Issues similar to Facebook arise in the case of private tweets and protected accounts, and for these, some form of user choice is needed, as in Facebook.

Recently, Twitter attempted to make a move and remove the accounts of its inactive users, including the deceased, to 'free up' usernames and make the information on the network more up to date and credible.[139] This was met with a massive outcry amongst users and commentators, so Twitter decided to halt the plan and introduce a memorialisation policy instead.[140] At the time of writing, unfortunately, we have not heard any details as to what that policy may look like.

In conclusion, Twitter appears to have had a sensible approach to deceased users' accounts, given the nature and use of this network. The public nature of tweets is a mitigating factor compared with Facebook, as families can access tweets if they wish. In addition, they can request deactivation and, in exceptional circumstances, protection of the deceased's privacy. The factor that complicates possible communication between families of the deceased and Twitter is Twitter's requirement that the correspondence should be conducted by post.

[138] B Bosker and D Grandoni, '9 quirkiest facts about Twitter: Gaze into the soul of the Twittersphere' *Huffington Post* (10 November 2012) <http://www.huffingtonpost.com/2012/10/10/quirkiest-facts-twitter-users_n_1956260.html> last accessed 1 August 2021.

[139] C Welch, 'Twitter will remove inactive accounts and free up usernames in December' *The Verge* (26 November 2019) <https://www.theverge.com/2019/11/26/20984328/twitter-removing-inactive-accounts-usernames-available-date> last accessed 1 August 2021.

[140] C Welch, 'Twitter halts plan to remove inactive accounts until it can memorialize dead users' *The Verge* (27 November 2019) <https://www.theverge.com/2019/11/27/20986084/twitter-inactive-accounts-usernames-memorialize-deceased-users-not-removing> last accessed 1 August 2021.

4.5 Post-Mortem Privacy

As demonstrated in Chapter 3, a critical issue that arises when considering the transmission of SNS content (and email considered in Chapter 6) is post-mortem privacy, understood in terms of the liberal conception of autonomy and the conceptions of privacy as autonomy, informational body and immortality.

SN service providers refer to PMP repeatedly (without using the term itself), refusing to transfer a deceased person's account or allow for access, memorialisation or content, in court cases, the company's news items and conversations with the company.

It is important to note at the outset that Facebook must comply with the European Union (EU) data protection legislation. As its subsidiary Facebook Ireland Limited is the provider of services and data controller in the EU, the Irish data protection laws apply.[141] Moreover, in a German case, Facebook successfully claimed that Irish data protection law should apply to all its EU users as its headquarters are based in Ireland.[142] Recollecting the discussion in the previous chapter (where it was demonstrated that most EU member states recognise PMP to an extent in their data protection regimes, excluding Ireland; the UK and US do not protect it either),[143] this means that the legislation generally requires that only personal data of living individuals is to be protected by Facebook.[144] Despite this, in the process of memorialising an account, Facebook promises to remove 'sensitive information such as contact information and status updates' in order to protect the deceased's privacy.

Another instance where Facebook allegedly protects post-mortem privacy is requesting a Look Back video or provision of the deceased's account contents. In this case, Facebook can only provide a unique link to the deceased's confirmed friends who request the link without an option to share it.[145] Finally, its Legacy Contact option protects a user's choice and privacy by providing for an individual's control over their account. This is demonstrated in the prohibition of the Legacy Contact to log in to the deceased's account

[141] Data Protection Act, Number 7 of 2018.

[142] *Facebook Ireland Limited gegen ULD*, Az. 4 MB10/13, 8 B 60/12 (Beschwerdebegründung ULD) and *Facebook Inc gegen ULD*, Az. 4 MB 11/13, 8 B 61/12 (Beschwerdebegründung ULD).

[143] See also L Edwards and E Harbinja, 'Protecting post-mortem privacy: Reconsidering the privacy interests of the deceased in a digital world' (2013) 32(1) *Cardozo Arts & Entertainment Law Journal* 111.

[144] Data Protection Act, Number 7 of 2018.

[145] Facebook, 'Deactivating, deleting & memorializing accounts' <https://www.facebook.com/help/359046244166395/> last accessed 1 August 2021.

and in that this person cannot see the deceased's private messages.[146] It is further exemplified in the recent addition of Tributes, a separate page in remembrance of the deceased where posts can be shared, distinct from the timeline that remains 'as is'. All these features are helpful and supportive of PMP.

However, this *prima facie* post-mortem friendly policy is complicated because Facebook, in principle, does not allow a nuanced and granular choice, and there are limited options regarding the Legacy Contact feature. Further, memorialisation of an account is not something that a user can opt in or out of, but is the default if a user has not chosen Legacy Contact. The nexus of data protection regimes in the EU, and perhaps less in the US, is the user's informed decision and control over their data. This regime, in most cases, does not apply to the deceased, as their personal data and privacy are generally not protected. However, if SN providers wish to establish this protection contractually, as they claim in their provisions, they need to provide users with meaningful information and coherent options to control this while alive.

In the early days of Facebook, the issue of PMP was examined in a comprehensive review by the Office of the Canadian Privacy Commissioner in 2009.[147] Before the review, the Canadian Internet Policy and Public Interest Clinic (CIPPIC) complained about the accounts of deceased Facebook users. The Canadian Commissioner pointed out three specific issues: an opportunity to opt out of memorialisation of their profiles should be given to users; clear information should be contained in terms of service and privacy policy relating to the process of memorialisation; and a procedure should be provided for relatives of a deceased user to request the removal of a user's profile.[148] The Commissioner opined that most 'typical' Facebook users welcome memorialisation and the prospect of being posthumously remembered and honoured by their friends and that this is 'an important part of the Facebook experience'.[149] The Commissioner was satisfied that memorialisation meets users' reasonable expectations and that an opt-out mechanism was not required.[150] Initially, however, in her preliminary report, the Commissioner had recommended that Facebook 'provide, and notify users of, a means whereby they

[146] Facebook, 'Adding a legacy contact' (n 118).

[147] Office of the Canadian Privacy Commissioner, *Report of Findings into the Complaint Filed by the Canadian Internet Policy and Public Interest Clinic (CIPPIC) against Facebook Inc., under the Personal Information Protection and Electronic Documents Act* (16 July 2009) <https://www.priv.gc.ca/cf-dc/2009/2009_008_0716_e.asp> last accessed 1 August 2021.

[148] Ibid. 65.

[149] Ibid. 68.

[150] Ibid. 69.

may opt-out of Facebook's intended use of their personal information for the purpose of memorialising accounts'.[151] Facebook, however, rejected this recommendation.[152] The Commissioner was satisfied that due to the conclusion on users' reasonable expectations regarding the process of memorialisation, Facebook could rely on what she termed users' 'continuing implied consent to the practice'.[153] A similar conclusion would be (hypothetically in the lack of relevant case law and reports) drawn for the US, as privacy legislation there excludes protection of privacy of the deceased.[154] With the introduction of the Legacy Contact feature, the Commissioner's requirements have been implemented to an extent, and Facebook reconsidered its argument stated above.

In relation to deleting personal data from Facebook, it is again contradictory that, while expressly mentioning PMP at various points, Facebook currently offers this option to living users and to deceased users in the US. In addition, Facebook warns that deleting information may need to be balanced with the rights of other users who 'may wish to retain on their account information posted by others'.[155] Moreover, even in living users' requests for deletion, some of the content still remains on Facebook, such as posts in groups and private messages to their friends.[156] This balance can also be disturbed, for instance, when parents or next of kin request deletion of an account but friends would like to retain it and have it memorialised. Therefore, the argument seems to be contradictory and does not entirely promote PMP and users' autonomy.

The crux of the issue is how to balance the right of the 'owner' of information (the person who originally posted it) to control it with the rights of others who believe that this shared information is owned (jointly) by them. This is also where Facebook's terms, forms and help pages contradict each other. Thus, whereas information may be removed from a timeline by another, when Facebook defines a user's information, this includes items others have posted to the user's timeline.[157] This issue surfaced on the death of a

151 Ibid.
152 Ibid.
153 Ibid. 68.
154 Edwards and Harbinja, 'Protecting post-mortem privacy' (n 143).
155 E Mann, 'Comments from Facebook on the European Commission's proposal for a Regulation' *Github* (25 April 2012) <https://github.com/lobbyplag/lobbyplag-data/raw/master/raw/lobby-documents/Facebook.pdf> last accessed 1 August 2021, 5.
156 Facebook, 'Deactivating or deleting your account' <https://www.facebook.com/help/359046244166395/%20> last accessed 1 August 2021.
157 Facebook, 'What categories of my Facebook data are available to me?' <https://www.facebook.com/help/405183566203254/> last accessed 1 August 2021.

user and, according to Facebook's stance mentioned above, default memorialisation, without an opt-out option (except for the Legacy Contact), solves the problem of maintaining the information on the network.

Finally, concerning the third issue in the complaint to the Canadian Commissioner (a procedure for relatives to seek the removal of a deceased user's profile), Facebook confirmed that such a procedure was already in place. Facebook stated that it 'honor[s] requests from close family members to close the account completely' and that its 'policy leaves the choice of whether or not a profile is "memorialized" or retained indefinitely, to the next of kin'.[158] Consequently, while Facebook denied the user the option of deciding whether or not information should be deleted following death (except for the Legacy Contact), a family member or next of kin were considered suitable to make such a decision.[159] This policy has evolved since. Facebook notes that requests will not be processed if it cannot verify the requester's relationship to the deceased.[160] In terms of its effects, the removal request if granted 'will completely remove the timeline and all associated content'.[161] However, the process is discretionary, and it is unclear what criteria are used to decide whether removal is appropriate.[162] It is also unclear what happens to the competing requests for memorialisation and deletion when family members require different options or when a user wishes to have their content deleted in the Legacy Contact option.

Facebook, therefore, may have a genuine intention to protect PMP, but in reality, this is met with many issues and inconsistencies indicated above. The options provided in relation to the deceased's account seem to point to the opposite conclusion: Facebook protects the interests and wishes of the deceased user's *family* while providing only a limited option for a user to decide what happens to their account upon death. In addition to curtailing PMP, this power over a deceased user's profile is not under the general rule that no third-party rights are created or conferred. As demonstrated above, this option needs to be reconsidered carefully and developed in order for Facebook to create a coherent post-mortem policy. First and importantly, Facebook needs to decide whose interests should prevail, those of the deceased, their family and next of kin, or their Facebook friends. This decision is a basic presumption for implementing a coherent and sustainable policy. However,

[158] Office of the Canadian Privacy Commissioner (n 147) 66.

[159] Ibid.

[160] Facebook, 'How do I ask a question about a deceased person's account on Facebook?' (n 102).

[161] Ibid.

[162] Mazzone (n 37) 1661–2.

this primarily technological solution should be recognised in law, as is argued further in the following section.

Consequently, Facebook would be able to rightly assert that it fosters the user's autonomy and privacy coherently post-mortem. This coherent policy would then be implemented technologically through the Legacy Contact, for instance. By enabling users to control their profiles post-mortem and preventing others from circumventing the wishes of the deceased expressed technologically, Facebook would be respecting the autonomy that underpins Internet privacy rights (according to Bernal) and recognising the PMP rights of its users.

Twitter does not address personal data and privacy of deceased users in its privacy policy;[163] neither is the issue mentioned in its guidelines on contacting Twitter about a deceased user. Instead, the guidelines note, 'We are unable to provide account access to anyone regardless of his or her relationship to the deceased', invoking privacy of the deceased.[164] For Twitter, however, the issue is less prominent as the majority of content published there is public anyway, and users consent to this when accepting the terms of service.[165] Although public tweets are the default setting, users can make their tweets private and allow only approved followers to see them.[166] This is done by a small percentage of Twitter users,[167] as protecting tweets almost defeats the purpose of Twitter. Therefore, the PMP question would relate only to this small number of Twitter users, and the findings regarding Facebook would apply to these accounts, too.

PMP serves as an argument against the default transmission of SN account contents on death without the deceased's consent, that is, through intestacy laws or by requiring intermediaries to provide access to the deceased's emails.[168] This further justifies the court's decisions in the cases of Ellsworth

163 Twitter, 'Privacy policy' (n 133).

164 Twitter, 'Contacting Twitter about a deceased user or media concerning a deceased family member' <https://help.twitter.com/en/rules-and-policies/contact-twitter-about-a-deceased-family-members-account#:~:text=In%20the%20event%20of%20the,of%20a%20deceased%20user's%20account> last accessed 1 August 2021.

165 Twitter, 'Privacy policy', version 12 <https://twitter.com/en/privacy/previous/version_12> last accessed 1 August 2021.

166 Twitter, 'About public and protected Tweets' <https://help.twitter.com/en/safety-and-security/public-and-protected-tweets> last accessed 1 August 2021.

167 11.84 per cent of Twitter users had protected accounts on average. See Beevolve, 'An exhaustive study of Twitter users across the world' <http://www.beevolve.com/twitter-statistics/#c1. There is not more recent data, but anecdotal evidence suggests the figures have been steady.

168 Harbinja (n 40).

and Daftary (more impliedly, though) and the service providers' ToS, which implicitly recognise PMP. Recognition of PMP, and consequently autonomy, questions the default position of using transmission by way of the laws of succession for some kinds of digital assets (those containing a vast amount of personal data, such as emails and social networks). Rather than using the current offline defaults, it is argued here and in my earlier work[169] that more nuanced solutions for the transmission of SN account contents are needed. These solutions will be explored in the following sections and would aim to account for the privacy interest of the deceased and their autonomy. These interests are mostly not recognised, as the law favours the heirs, and the technology solution initially favoured the surviving families' interests. As information generally cannot be viewed as a property object (for more detail, see Chapter 6), and it represents a significant portion of the content online, laws that had a purpose of regulating the disposition of the traditional types of property (including copyright, but with some exceptions) should not apply by default. Autonomy and the privacy interests of the deceased based on autonomy should be considered much more when suggesting solutions for the transmission of digital assets in general.

4.6 Solutions for the Transmission of Social Network Content on Death

The final section will offer some tentative solutions concerning the transmission of SNS content on death. More general solutions will be offered in the final chapter.

Social network content has been a subject of the most extensive interest amongst scholars in the area of transmission of digital assets. The commentators attempt to address some of the issues analysed in this chapter, proposing legal, technological and market solutions.

McCallig underpins his proposal by a premise of 'the promotion of active testamentary choice', arguing that the default access rule should be overridden by the user's choice of 'a service opt-ins to a digital remains disposition scheme'.[170] He argues that the in-service feature recognising user choice or approved digital estate planning services should be utilised and recognised by statute, akin to the US example elaborated in the previous chapter (RUFADAA). He also proposes that users should be prompted to review their choices regularly and that this option should not be only a waiver added to terms of service. He submits that the options for users to opt in to other research and heritage schemes should be available for a limited time after

[169] Ibid.

[170] Ibid. 34.

death. He goes even further, introducing a granular approach where users would be able to choose the type of institution or research.[171] McCallig suggests that Facebook should implement policy changes on its network in order to benefit users, families and heirs, by granting them certainty but also by promoting preservation and heritage institution access.[172]

Along similar lines, Sherry proposes a checkbox solution, whereby the SN would prompt users to decide what happens to their SN assets on death. She, however, expresses concerns and pessimism about whether SN sites would implement these options voluntarily, calling for US state and federal statutory interventions.[173] In addition, she identifies some other options and further develops the existing ones, currently not included in terms of service or US legislation and legislative proposals, namely:

> (1) outright termination of a decedent's account by the social media service; (2) termination of the account by an executor; (3) allowing an executor to obtain the *contents* of an account; (4) allowing the executor *access for limited purposes*; (5) granting the executor uninhibited access to the account; and more.[174]

Beyer and Cahn[175] and Lamm et al. also argue that Congressional amendments to the Computer Fraud and Abuse Act and the Electronic Communications Privacy Act (in order to avoid criminal liability of service providers and fiduciaries) and uniform state law is the best holistic approach to solving all these issues.[176]

Mazzone proposes a solution in the form of 'a Facebook executor', a person that would be designated by a user and allowed by Facebook to take over the account or to decide what happens to the account after the user's death (e.g. close down the account or request closure from Facebook, curate materials, or leave all of the content).[177] In addition to these functions, the executor would be responsible for monitoring postings on the deceased's timeline and

[171] Ibid.

[172] Ibid.

[173] K Sherry, 'What happens to our Facebook accounts when we die?: Probate versus policy and the fate of social-media assets postmortem' (2013) 40(1) *Pepperdine Law Review* 185, 250 (original emphasis).

[174] Ibid. 235.

[175] GW Beyer and N Cahn, 'Digital planning: The future of elder law' (2013) 9 *NAELA Journal* 135, 137.

[176] JD Lamm et al., 'The digital death conundrum: how federal and state laws prevent fiduciaries from managing digital property' (2014) 68 *University of Miami Law Review* 385, 414–19; Electronic Communications Privacy Act, 18 USC §§ 2510 *et seq.*

[177] Mazzone (n 37) 1655.

maintain the account in general (this would probably mean memorialisation).[178] Mazzone, however, is sceptical as to Facebook's will to implement these changes on its own initiative. He maintains that Facebook is responsive to consumer pressure (of which we have offered many illustrations in this chapter). However, due to the lock-in effects (Facebook's popularity resulting in users' not wanting to move to a different service with more favourable terms) and users' aversion towards thinking and being reminded about their mortality, 'dissatisfaction with Facebook's current policy likely does not translate into a sufficient level of consumer pressure to force change'.[179] Mazzone, therefore, advocates a federal statute, which would impose these requirements and mandate some degree of control to users over their profiles post-mortem.[180] Mazzone warns, however, that protecting the interests of other users would depend on the user and their representative. Whereas some users will request memorialisation of a sort, those who would prefer deletion could be prevented by a statute from deleting all the content to enable protection of the competing interests of other users and their access to the content. One example that Mazzone uses to illustrate this suggestion is that the law could preserve access to content posted more than one year before the user's death so that only access to recent postings is limited.

Further, he proposes that the law could prohibit a representative from deleting or disabling access to content that has been shared with more than a specified number of other users. Finally, the law could limit the power of the representative to remove or prevent access to content that they consider harmful to the reputation of the deceased or that is sensitive.[181] While the proposal is a good step forward, it is difficult to see how a representative could implement these different options in practice. It seems rather impractical, bearing in mind the volume and nature of content shared on Facebook between millions of users.

In my earlier work, I have proposed law- and code-based solutions, arguing that a solution akin to Legacy Contact is acceptable, provided that greater consistency in terms of service has been achieved in the future. In addition, the solution must be supported by law reforms to address conflicts between traditional laws of succession and novel, code-based solutions.[182] I have repeatedly tried to access more concrete data about the uptake of Legacy Contact, but Facebook has not provided exact data at the time of writing. Anecdotally, the

[178] Ibid. 1579.
[179] Ibid. 1681.
[180] Ibid. 1685.
[181] Ibid. 1684.
[182] Harbinja (n 40).

uptake has been very low; probably not more than 10 per cent of users have considered the post-mortem options.

Facebook has, admittedly, implemented some of the scholarly suggestions set out above with the introduction of Legacy Contact and Tributes. The granularity of options has increased significantly in the past years, but inconsistencies are still to be resolved. Importantly, it seems like Facebook has been amongst the very few technology companies that have taken the issues surrounding their deceased users' account somewhat seriously. It has introduced changes based on input from stakeholders and scholars, and some of them mirror the ones explored in this book. We will return to solutions in the last chapter.

5

Games, Virtual Worlds and Virtual Realities

5.1 Conceptualisation and History of VWs and Games

(a) Definitions and a Brief Historical Account

The concept of virtual worlds (VWs) pre-dates the Internet. The history of VWs began with text-based, offline role-playing games, created based on different works of fiction, such as, for instance, JRR Tolkien's books and the idea of world-building.[1] The first text-based interactive computer game appeared in 1970, *Colossal Cave Adventure*, with real-time interactive computer games called multi-user dungeons (MUDs) appearing by the end of the 1970s.[2] These were the first VWs. *MUD1* was created by Richard Bartle and Roy Trubshaw in 1979, at Essex University, being the first online network computer game. However, the most famous game in this group (text-based VWs) was *LambdaMOO*, created by Pavel Curtis in 1990.[3]

The literature analysing social, economic, technological and legal aspects of virtual worlds starts from the late 1990s, concerning the text-based VWs,[4] and continues throughout the 2000s, discussing visually represented

[1] FG Lastowka and D Hunter, 'Virtual worlds: A primer' in JM Balkin and BS Noveck (eds), *The State of Play: Laws, Games, and Virtual Worlds* (NYU Press 2006) 13–28, 17–18; W Erlank, *Property in Virtual Worlds* (PhD thesis, Stellenbosch University 2012) 22–3 <http://ssrn.com/abstract=2216481> last accessed 1 August 2021.

[2] FG Lastowka and D Hunter, 'The laws of the virtual worlds' (2004) 92 *California Law Review* 1, 17.

[3] F Rex, 'LambdaMOO: An introduction' *LambdaMOO* <http://www.lambdamoo.info> last accessed 1 August 2021. For more details about the history and the development of computer games in general, see for example J Juul, 'A history of the computer game' *Blog* (2001) <http://www.jesperjuul.net/thesis/2-historyofthecomputergame.html> last accessed 1 August 2021; J Dibble, *My Tiny Life: Crime and Passion in a Virtual World* (Henry Holt 1998).

[4] See for example R Bartle, 'Hearts, clubs, diamonds, spades: Players who suit MUDs' (1996) 1(1) *The Journal of Virtual Environments* <http://mud.co.uk/richard/hcds.htm> last accessed 1 August 2021.

VWs and massively multiplayer online playing games (MMOPGs). The focus of the early literature was mainly on the technical, philosophical and governance issues of MUDs. More substantive legal discussion started at the beginning of the twenty-first century, with seminal works on the legal aspects of VWs, which tackle the following issues: economies and taxation;[5] governance of VWs;[6] property and IP;[7] contracts and consumer

[5] See for example E Castronova, 'On virtual economies' (2003) 3 *The International Journal of Computer Gaming Research* <http://www.gamestudies.org/0302/castronova/> last accessed 1 August 2021; E Castronova, 'Real products in imaginary worlds' (2005) 83(5) *Harvard Business Review* 20, 20–2; E Castronova, 'The right to play' (2004) 49 *New York Law School Law Review* 185; E Castronova, 'Virtual world economy: It's Namibia, basically' *Terranova* (3 August 2004) <http://www.terranova.blogs.com/terra_nova/2004/08/virtual_world_e.html> last accessed 1 August 2021; Lastowka and Hunter, 'Virtual worlds' (n 1) 9; MA Cherry, 'A taxonomy of virtual work' (2011) 45 *Georgia Law Review* 951.

[6] See for example Lastowka and Hunter, 'Virtual worlds' (n 1); V Mayer-Schoenberger and JR Crowley, 'Napster's second life? – The regulatory challenges of virtual worlds' (2006) 100 *Northwestern University Law Review* 1775; BJ Gilbert, 'Getting to conscionable: Negotiating virtual worlds' end user license agreements without getting externally regulated' (2009) 4 *Journal of International Commercial Law and Technology* 238; JM Balkin, 'Virtual liberty: Freedom to design and freedom to play in virtual worlds' (2004) 90(8) *Virginia Law Review* 2043.

[7] Lastowka and Hunter, 'Virtual worlds' (n 1); SH Abramovitch and DL Cummings, 'Virtual property, real law: The regulation of property in video games' (2007) 6(2) *Canadian Journal of Law and Technology* 73; J Fairfield, 'Virtual property' (2005) 85 *Boston University Law Review* 1047; E Castronova, 'Virtual worlds: A first-hand account of market and society on the cyberian frontier' (2001) 618 CESifo Working Papers Series; C Blazer, 'The five indicia of virtual property' (2006) 5 *Pierce Law Review* 137; R Vacca, 'Viewing virtual property ownership through the lens of innovation' (2008) 76 *Tennessee Law Review* 33; TJ Westbrook, 'Owned: Finding a place for virtual world property rights' (2006) *Michigan State Law Review* 779–812; Erlank (n 1); JM Moringiello, 'Towards a system of estates in virtual property' (2008) 1 *International Journal of Private Law* 3; *Kremen* v *Cohen*, 337 F.3d 1024 (9th Cir 2003); A Chein, 'A practical look at virtual property' (2006) 80 *St. John's Law Review* 1059; C Cifrino, 'Virtual property, virtual rights: Why contract law, not property law, must be the governing paradigm in the law of virtual worlds' (2014) 55 *Boston College Law Review* 235; MG Veloso III, 'Virtual property rights: A modified usufruct of intangibles' (2010) 4 *Philippine Law Journal* 82; J Slaughter, 'Virtual worlds: Between contract and property' (2008) 62 *Yale Student Scholarship Papers* <http://digitalcommons.law.yale.edu/student_papers/62> last accessed 1 August 2021; U Yoon, 'South Korea and indirect reliance on IP law: Real money trading in MMORPG items' (2008) 3(3) *Journal of Intellectual Property Law and Practice* 174; JW Nelson, 'Fiber optic foxes: Virtual objects and virtual worlds through the lens of Pierson v Post and the law of capture' (2009) 14 *Journal of Technology Law & Policy* 5; JW Nelson, 'The virtual property problem: What property rights in virtual resources might look like, how they might work, and why they are a bad idea' (2010) 41 *McGeorge Law Review* 281.

protection;[8] and virtual crime.[9]

There is a variety of academic literature discussing death and VWs from anthropological, sociological, psychological, educational and other perspectives,[10] but little, almost nothing, from a legal angle. Literature about VWs and games has been decreasing steadily in the last two decades. However, issues around their legal nature have remained.

Legal aspects of transmission of other digital assets on death (e.g. emails, social network accounts, online banking accounts, photos, domain names) have been explored to an extent following the growing importance of these assets in life and on the death of the users, only sporadically mentioning VW accounts as types of digital assets.[11] This literature has been explored in more detail in other chapters.

This chapter addresses the gap in the literature and sheds light on the post-mortem legal status of different in-game assets (e.g. avatars, weapons, houses, land). I have addressed this issue in my previous writings, and this

[8] A Jankowich, 'The complex web of corporate rule-making in virtual worlds' (2006) 8 *Tulane Journal of Technology and Intellectual Property* 1, 52–3; B Glushko, 'Tales of the (virtual) city: Governing property disputes in virtual worlds' (2007) 22 *Berkeley Technology Law Journal* 507; R Shikowitz, 'License to kill: MDY v Blizzard and the battle over copyright in World of Warcraft' (2009–10) 75 *Brooklyn Law Review* 1015; J Fairfield, 'Anti-social contracts: The contractual governance of virtual worlds' (2007) 53 *McGill Law Journal* 427; D Miller, 'Determining ownership in virtual worlds: Copyright and license agreements' (2003) 22 *Review of Litigation* 435; P Riley, 'Litigating Second Life land disputes: A consumer protection approach' (2009) 19(3) *Fordham Intellectual Property, Media and Entertainment Law Journal* 877; PJ Quinn, 'A click too far: The difficulty in using adhesive American law license agreements to govern global virtual worlds' (2010) 27 *Wisconsin International Law Journal* 757.

[9] See for example OS Kerr, 'Criminal law in virtual worlds' 2008 *University of Chicago Legal Forum* 415; Lastowka and Hunter, 'Virtual worlds' (n 1); AR Lodder, 'Dutch Supreme Court 2012: Virtual theft ruling a one-off or first in a series?' (2013) 6(3) *Journal of Virtual Worlds Research* 1; AV Arias, 'Life, liberty and the pursuit of swords and armor: Regulating the theft of virtual goods' (2008) 57 *Emory Law Journal* 1301.

[10] See for example R Ferguson, 'Death of an avatar: Implications of presence for learners and educators in virtual worlds' (2012) 4(2) *Journal of Gaming & Virtual Worlds* 137; M Jakobsson, 'Rest in peace, Bill the bot: Death and life in virtual worlds' in R Schroeder (ed.), The Social Life of Avatars (Springer 2002); JA Archinaco, 'Virtual worlds, real damages: The odd case of American Hero, the greatest horse that may have lived' (2007) 11(1) *Gaming Law Journal*; CJ Sofka, IN Cupit and KR Gilbert (eds), *Dying, Death, and Grief in an Online Universe: For Counselors and Educators* (Springer 2012); A Haverinen, *Memoria Virtualis – Death and Mourning Rituals in Online Environments* (PhD thesis, University of Turku 2014) <https://www.doria.fi/handle/10024/98454> last accessed 1 August 2021.

[11] The literature includes my own and other work cited throughout this book.

analysis will be primarily based on the arguments and analysis set out therein.[12] However, this analysis is more thorough, and the chapter addresses the topic at a greater length and depth than any of the earlier articles.

Following this book's principal and subordinate research questions, the chapter explores how the notion of property applies to VWs and games. It will attempt to determine if there is property in VWs and games, and if not, what would be an appropriate legal treatment of user rights and interests in virtual, in-game assets. The aim is to determine the possibility of transmission of virtual assets (VAs) or their value on the death of a player.

The term 'virtual assets' (VAs) is used here provisionally, trying to avoid any implications about the potential legal nature of these assets. Therefore, the analysis avoids the widely used term 'virtual property' (VP) at the moment. Later in this chapter, after exploring different legal concepts that could characterise these assets, the term might change and adapt to the findings. Until then, the term 'VAs' will be used to describe any item, object or asset found in VWs or games and used or created by players (e.g. avatars, weapons, land, houses, clothes, furniture, and anything else that could be found in different VWs). It is also vital to differentiate VAs from digital assets defined in the Introduction. VAs are only a subset of digital assets (DAs), defined as any asset of value online, capable of post-mortem transmission.

Therefore, the analysis will assess whether these assets could fit within the notions of property or some other relevant legal concepts (IP, servitudes, easements, the right of use), which would result in their being recognised as part of a user's estate. This first question aligns with the book's theoretical underpinning, that is, the discussion of whether a digital asset can and should be considered property and, consequently, transmit on death. The discussion and conceptual framework of PMP are not included in this chapter because currently, sharing and storing personal data is not a predominant feature of VWs, as it is in emails and social networks. Avatars or other items represent VWs and online game users, who usually do not publicly share their identities and personal data.

I do not share the views of most of the classical legal VWs literature, arguing for the recognition of 'virtual property' and referring to full ownership. Instead, this chapter proposes a compromise solution to reconcile different interests arising in VWs, primarily those of developers and players. Recognising a phenomenon of *constitutionalisation* of VWs and arguing for

[12] E Harbinja, 'Virtual worlds players – consumers or citizens?' (2014) 3(4) *Internet Policy Review* <http://policyreview.info/articles/analysis/virtual-worlds-players-consumers-or-citizens> last accessed 1 August 2021; E Harbinja, 'Virtual worlds – a legal post-mortem account' (2014) 11:3 *SCRIPTed* 273.

better recognition of players' in-game interests, the chapter identifies a solution entitled 'VWs usufruct', a personal right of a player against the VW provider in second layer assets. If VA exchanges are legal on recognised auction sites, the right will only be transmissible as a monetary claim. If no such auction sites exist or ToS do not permit them, then monetisation is impossible, and neither is the right to compensation. The solution would enable players to control their virtual assets and heirs to benefit from potentially valuable VW accounts and VAs.

It is also important to note that findings in this chapter will apply not only to VWs, defined more narrowly, but also to online games, widely played across the world and controlled by service providers. We will not consider video games only played locally at the user end, which excludes more meaningful interactivity online and a degree of permanence and stability.

(b) Conceptualisation of VWs and Games

From a linguistic perspective, VWs could be defined as states of human existence, which do not exist physically, are not real, but appear to be real from the program's point of view or that of the user.[13] From this definition, we could extract the most critical features that define VWs: computer-moderated; persistence; environmental attributes (immersive and persuasive worlds, mimicking the real world); interactivity; and the participation of multiple individuals.[14]

Developers use different business models for their VWs. Some of them are closed, used for military or business simulations, whereas others are open, commercial worlds, where users can join for free, for monthly fee payment (e.g. *World of Warcraft*), or operate on a freemium basis (e.g. *Second Life*), where the basic services are free and others have their price.[15]

The umbrella term for VWs is MMOPGs, but these can be divided into social and game worlds based on their player community and structure. In game VWs (massively multiplayer online role-playing games – MMORPGs), players take a specific role and compete to achieve certain predefined goals (e.g. *World of Warcraft*). In the social or unstructured worlds, the emphasis is on social interaction with other players and the environment (e.g. *Second Life*, *IMVU*). Therefore, these VWs are not games but platforms for social

[13] *Oxford English Dictionary* (*OED*) (online edn, Oxford University Press 2016) last accessed 1 August 2021.

[14] Erlank (n 1) 47–57.

[15] See J Fairfield, 'The end of the (virtual) world' (2009) 112(1) *West Virginia Law Review* 53; Riley (n 8).

interaction or 'mirror worlds'.[16] The third kind of VWs is kids' worlds, those targeting children as the main player base (e.g. Club Penguin).[17]

According to the technology employed to enable access to the worlds, the worlds are divided into client-based (e.g. *World of Warcraft*) and those where players can join simply online (e.g. *Second Life*). Some video games, including some VWs (e.g. *The Lord of the Rings Online, Dungeons & Dragons Online, EverQuest II, Diablo*), can also be accessed from intermediaries, the most prominent of which is an entertainment platform called Steam.[18]

This chapter will focus on two examples: *World of Warcraft* and *Second Life*. The reason for choosing the US-based VWs is that most of the successful Western VWs are indeed hosted in the US,[19] choice of law provisions usually points to US law, and most common law cases have been resolved there.[20] Also, these examples are chosen for their historical domination in the market, previous and retained user base, their impact and their 'cultural footprint'.[21] *Second Life* has been steadily declining in popularity, but it is still worth mentioning as most of the existing case law involves this VW and its historical and cultural significance and replicability to similar gaming models in the future.[22]

Before initiating the virtual property and contracts analysis, and in order to bring potential legal disputes closer to the reader, the following section will present some examples. These examples are actual US court cases, and they serve to illustrate legal issues appearing in VWs. Unfortunately, at the time of writing, there has not been a single UK case discussing the issues of VWs and VP.

16 KZero Worldswide, 'Radar charts Q2 2014 VWs and MMOs shown by genre, average user age and status' *KZero* (2004) <http://www.kzero.co.uk/blog/category/education-and-academia> last accessed 1 August 2021.

17 G Lastowka, *Virtual Justice: The New Laws of Online Worlds* (Yale University Press 2010) 58.

18 The platform distributes different video games and other software, from both independent and established software companies. It is also a communication, social networking and multiplayer platform, allowing different kinds of interactions between players (akin to social network sites). The further evolution of VWs includes innovative hardware (e.g. Oculus Rift), bringing even more reality to these worlds. See KZero Worldswide, 'Consumer virtual reality: State of the market report' *KZero* (2014) <http://www.kzero.co.uk/blog/category/education-and-academia> last accessed 1 August 2021.

19 B Edwards, 'The 11 most influential online worlds of all time' *PCWorld* (2011) <http://www.pcworld.com/article/228000/influentialonlineworlds.html> last accessed 1 August 2021.

20 Fairfield, 'Anti-social contracts' (n 8) 430.

21 Quinn (n 8).

22 Sporadic references will be made to other VWs and platforms, but the main analysis will be based on the examples of these two VWs.

5.2 Illustrations through Case Law

(a) *Bragg Case: Property and Jurisdiction in VWs*

The first and most famous VWs case is that of *Bragg* v *Linden Research, Inc.*[23] In this case, Marc Bragg sued the owner of *Second Life*, Linden Research, after it expelled him from the online community and reclaimed his VAs, 'effectively confiscating all of the virtual property and currency that he maintained on his account' (roughly $2,000 in real-world money on account).[24] Linden Lab expelled Marc Bragg, claiming that he had violated its terms of service by improperly buying land at an auction for approximately $300. *Second Life* moved to compel arbitration according to the terms of service agreement. Bragg, however, argued that the contractual terms between Bragg and *Second Life* were unconscionable because the service agreement assumed too much power and was unreasonably biased against the user. The court confirmed that the terms of service were unconscionable in relation to the mandatory arbitration clause and knocked it down.[25] More specifically, the court focused on the fact that there was a surprise due to hidden or missing terms because there was no notice of the serious expense and inconvenience to the plaintiff, having to spend ten to twenty thousand dollars to pay the arbitrators in addition to having to go to California from Pennsylvania in order to take part in the arbitration. The court said that the terms left the plaintiff with no effective remedy.[26] The court applied the Californian law in its analysis of the contract and noted that it must find both procedural and substantive unconscionability in California to find unconscionability.[27] It found both elements and concluded that the arbitration clause was unconscionable.[28]

This case has not decided on the issue of VP. Bragg initially brought up the property claim, asserting that his in-game assets are his property (his land,

[23] 487 F.Supp.2d 593, 612 (ED Pa 2007).

[24] Ibid. 611.

[25] Unconscionable terms are those 'so extreme as to appear unconscionable according to the mores and business practices' used at the time. See N Kutler, 'Protecting your online you: A new approach to handling your online persona after death' (2011) 26 *Berkeley Technology Law Journal* 1641; UCC § 302-2 (amended 2003); *Williams* v *Walker-Thomas Furniture Co*, 350 F.2d 445, 449 (DC Cir 1965); *Carnival Cruise Lines, Inc* v *Shute*, 499 US 585, 600–1 (1991).

[26] *Bragg* v *Linden Research, Inc* (n 23) 611. For more, see S Hetcher, 'User-generated content and the future of copyright: Part two – agreements between users and mega-sites' (2008) 24 *Santa Clara Computer & High Technology Law Journal* 829, 836.

[27] *Bragg* v *Linden Research, Inc* (n 23) 605, 606.

[28] Ibid. 611.

fireworks, and other items he possessed).[29] The court, unfortunately, did not discuss it, so VP, as demonstrated later, remains on the level of academic debates.

(b) Evans Case: Account Suspension and Settlement

The second case, involving *Second Life* and Linden, lost another chance to discuss VP by a court and provide us with some guidance on this issue. In *Evans et al.* v *Linden Research, Inc et al.*,[30] the central issue was fairness and validity of the contract (provisions about the suspension of accounts and users compensation). A group of users claimed to own their VAs[31] and complained that they had purchased virtual items and/or virtual land and later had their accounts unilaterally terminated or suspended by Linden. These players were not compensated for the value of the virtual land, items and/or currency in their accounts. In addition, the plaintiffs claimed that Linden made false representations about ownership of virtual land and virtual items and wrongfully confiscated these items from the class members they sought to represent.[32] Linden disputed the claimed ownership in VAs, recognising IP rights in users' creations, copyright in particular. It maintained that copyright in users' creations is indisputable; however, it has been licensed to Linden, and it is entitled to remove a licensed copy from its servers.[33]

Again, there was no decision in respect of VP. The case was settled,[34] and Linden agreed to do the following: return up to 100 per cent of the US dollar balances to the PayPal accounts of the plaintiffs; return up to 100 per cent of the Linden dollar balances in class members' accounts; pay two Linden dollars per square metre of virtual land held by class members; and regarding virtual items, to pay $15 per class member to their PayPal account or let the class members attempt to sell their virtual items on the *Second Life* Marketplace, at which point Linden will waive *Second Life*'s commission on the sales.[35] This example might illustrate Linden's attitude and concerns over VP and willingness to compensate the users instead of proceeding with the case, which might find some property in virtual items and land and have unwanted consequences for Linden (user's control, transfer, transmission and other incidents

[29] Ibid. 585.

[30] No C-11-01078 DMR (United States District Court, ND Cal 20 November 2012).

[31] Hearing Transcript 27:12–28:11.

[32] Ibid.

[33] Ibid. 37:7–10; 39:17–24; 53:15–24.

[34] *Evans et al., Plaintiffs,* v *Linden Research, Inc et al.*, No C-11-01078 DMR (United States District Court, ND Cal 25 October 2013).

[35] See the confirmation of settlement in *Evans et al.* v *Linden Research, Inc et al.* No C-11-01078 DMR (United States District Court, ND Cal 20 November 2012).

identified in Chapter 2). On the other hand, the fact that the court, as in the Bragg case, avoided a decision on VP and turned to contracts and IP, demonstrates again their reluctance to engage and make such a radical legal and policy decision. This reasoning is justifiable from a normative and doctrinal perspective, as suggested later in this chapter.

In addition to the Bragg and Evans cases, there have been two interesting virtual theft[36] cases in the Netherlands[37] and one in China.[38] However, these cases are examples specific to these civilian countries and should not be regarded as an indication of a general approach. In these jurisdictions' absence of relevant case law, it is uncertain whether the US or English criminal courts would recognise VP in theft cases. Moreover, even if, eventually, cases were prosecuted in the courts of the jurisdictions relevant to this book, the outcomes would not provide a firm argument for VP. This is because the rationale and definition of property in criminal cases are quite different from civil cases. Consequently, there is limited value in considering these cases and criminal law herein. In the lack of case law worldwide, the cases have been mentioned here to illustrate different outlooks on VP, rejecting their substantive relevance for this book.

To summarise, the scarce Western VWs case law illustrates the potential disputes that might arise in VWs, namely ownership, property claims and disputes over VW contract provisions. However, the cases have only opened up the floor to more debates and do not determine whether there is property in VWs. Furthermore, the disparate approaches in these cases are based on very different legal and cultural traditions. Finally, the cases focused on the second layer (see the classification in the section below, i.e. different items in *Second Life*, such as fireworks, avatars, weapons or land) and this layer, as demonstrated later in this chapter, is the most important, problematic and worth examining in detail. Also, it is interesting that Linden explicitly

[36] See more in JW Nelson, 'A virtual property solution: How privacy law can protect the citizens of virtual worlds' (2011) 36 *Oklahoma City University Law Review* 395, 413; Arias (n 9) 1306–7.

[37] Kerr (n 9) 422–3; BBC News, 'Virtual theft leads to arrest' (14 November 2007) <http://news.bbc.co.uk/1/hi/7094764.stm> last accessed 1 August 2021; Lodder (n 9) 3, 4, 8.

[38] W Knight, 'Gamer wins back virtual booty in court battle' *New Scientist* (23 December 2003) <http://www.newscientist.com/article/dn4510-gamer-wins-back-virtual-booty-in-courtbattle.Html> last accessed 1 August 2021; J Lyman, 'Gamer wins lawsuit in Chinese court over stolen virtual winnings' *TECHNEWSWORLD* (19 December 2003) <http://www.technewsworld.comystory/3244Lhtml> last accessed 1 August 2021; Shikowitz (n 8) 51; Glushko (n 8) 518; *Li v Beijing Arctic Ice Tech Dev Co* (Beijing Chaoyang Dist People's Ct 18 December 2003) <http://www.chinacourt.org/public/detail.php?id=143455> last accessed 1 August 2021.

admitted players' IP rights in the Evans case (the third layer, according to the classification below). Therefore, this layer is much less disputable and will not be discussed in detail.

Notwithstanding the vagueness left by these cases, this chapter will assess whether there is property in VWs, who owns this property and, finally, if existent, how this property transmits on death. Before discussing these issues, it is crucial to identify the potential objects of VP, that is, virtual assets. The following section will present a classification of VAs as possible objects of property in VWs and games more generally. This classification will be used as a basis for the analysis throughout this chapter.

5.3 Layers of Virtual Assets

Most virtual property theories tend to confuse different types of code and content in VWs, equating the underlying software (the building blocks of VWs) and the user-generated content (virtual assets). In this regard, Abramovitch offers a helpful theory and proposes three layers (or levels) where property or VAs can be identified within VWs.[39]

At the *first layer*, there is the developer's code, protected by IP as software. This level, therefore, represents software and code that determines properties, features of VWs, and users' actions and behaviours.

At the *second layer*, Abramovitch identifies objects or items inside the VW which resemble real-world items (objects like avatars, weapons, buildings, clothing, cars, spaceships, houses). This layer mimics real-world objects and includes a perception of physicality from a user's point of view.

At the *third layer*, she identifies in-game VAs that could be protected by IP (e.g. a book found lying on a table inside the VW, paintings, statues). This is essentially the user's creative work inside a VW, and it is different from the second layer in that it may lack physicality and does not mimic real-world objects. The difference between the two layers can be further analogised with the division of property rights in a physical object and copyright in a work embedded in that physical object.

The layer approach is helpful for the analysis in this book for two main reasons: first, it is more nuanced as an approach and does not represent a unified, rigid 'player-deserves-all' (VP should belong to the players) or 'the developer-deserves-all' perspective (property in servers or IP in software should extend to the virtual realm), usually found in the early 2000s literature. These two approaches fail to recognise, on the one hand, *constitutionalisation* of virtual

[39] SH Abramovitch, 'Virtual property in virtual worlds' *Gowlings.com* (2009) 1–2 <http://www.gowlings.com/knowledgecentre/publicationPDFs/TLI-2009-Susan-Abramovitch-Virtual-Property-in-Virtual-Worlds.pdf> last accessed 1 August 2021.

worlds and their significance for the player; and, on the other, the IP interests of the developer.

Second, this approach acknowledges the Internet architecture and the fact that significant investments are made by world owners, arguing simultaneously for assessing the rights of users at a different game level.

Third, this differentiation offers a possibility to discuss and suggest recognising various legal concepts at different code and virtual reality levels and offer some compromise and more widely acceptable legal solutions.[40] Protection for the different layers can be provided for by IP, property, limited real rights (rights on the property of another) or contracts, depending on the characteristics of an individual layer.[41]

The analysis in this chapter will accept and use this classification, focusing primarily on the second layer.[42] This layer has been discussed in the court cases illustrated earlier. Of course, the courts have not identified VAs using this classification, but the disputes in the Bragg and Evans cases concerned VAs such as land and other different items belonging to our second level.

The reason for excluding in-depth discussion of the first layer is that it is much less disputed, and the underlying code indeed belongs to the developer (protected by copyright or patent in software and property in physical servers).[43] The first layer will be discussed only to the extent it relates to or determines the second and third levels. Apart from having a more straightforward legal nature, the first level is beyond the scope of this chapter, as the book looks at the player's or user's ability to transmit their virtual assets on death. The first layer assets are a company's assets, and their succession is regulated differently, using company law rules.

The third layer will be mentioned sporadically, but IP issues will not be analysed in detail. This book considers novel issues in the transmission of

[40] Erlank (n 1) 182.

[41] Ibid.

[42] For more details about the copyright protection in VWs, see S Roncallo-Dow et al., 'Authorship in virtual worlds: Author's death to rights revival?' (2013) 6(3) *Journal of Virtual Worlds Research* 1; Miller (n 8).

[43] See for example cases such as *SAS Institute* v *World Programming* C-406/10 and *Nova Productions* v *Mazooma Games* [2007] RPC 25, which suggest that graphics in computer games could be regarded as artistic works and protected by copyright. In the US, the courts have developed the doctrine of 'cybertrespass' to companies' computer systems or servers, extending the tort of trespass to cyberworld. See *eBay* v *Bidder's Edge Inc*, 100 F.Supp.2d 1058 (ND Cal 2000); *Ticketmaster Corp, et al.* v *Tickets.com, Inc*, No CV 99-7654 (CD Cal 27 March 2000). For more, see M Carrier and G Lastowka, 'Against cyberproperty' (2007) 22 *Berkeley Technology Law Journal* 1485.

digital assets on death; transmission of IP rights to heirs is not in dispute if players' creations meet copyright requirements.

In order to emphasise the main distinction between VWs and games and other assets discussed in this book, property and proprietary rights in the second layer will be the focus. The main reason for this is the peculiar aspects of the assets, namely, physicality.

5.4 Virtual Property

Virtual property is a theoretical construct about property rights in the items and resources originating and existing in VWs and games. Much has been written *pro* and *contra* the recognition of virtual property. However, it still exists primarily in academic discussions, and courts or legislators have not recognised its importance. There have been some judicial attempts to address virtual property (see the Bragg and Evans cases, above), but there have not been any legislative efforts at all. This section aims to shed some more light on VP, exploring whether there should be property rights in VWs, and if not, what the potential alternatives are.

(a) The Legal Status of Virtual Property

This section will look at whether virtual property and virtual assets share the features of property and property objects identified in Chapter 2.

First, the discussion will assess whether Honoré's and Becker's incidents of property could be found in VP. Second, we will explore the leading analysis of VP and its features, that is, Fairfield's theory. He lists three major criteria: incidents of property, borrowing from the law, and economics literature. Coinciding with those identified in the second chapter, the main incidents are rivalrousness, permanence and interconnectedness. Castronova et al. use the same incidents as those inherent in physical objects, attempting to define and justify VP.[44] Some identify further incidents (such as scarcity,[45] secondary markets and 'value-added-by-users'[46]). The analysis in the following section will add tangibility to this list as an essential feature of property historically and still retained as such by some jurisdictions (e.g. England).[47]

[44] 'Virtual worlds are virtual because they are online, but they are worlds because there is some physicality to them.' See Castronova, 'On virtual economies' (n 5).

[45] Ibid. Some authors, however, claim that scarcity is artificially created and coded, and usually for the reasons of the provider's economic benefits. See Lastowka (n 17) 135; Erlank (n 1) 270, 271.

[46] Blazer (n 7) 139.

[47] Harbinja, 'Virtual worlds – a legal post-mortem account' (n 12) 273.

Honoré's Incidents

As discussed in Chapter 2, one of the most influential theories of property incidents has been offered by Honoré. His eleven exhaustive incidents (the right to possess, the right to use, the right to manage, the right to the income of the thing, the right to the capital, the right to security, the rights of transmissibility and absence of term, the prohibition of harmful use, the liability of execution, and the incident of residuarity) could be applied to our VP layers. For the first layer (owned by developers), all of the incidents are present.

Looking at the second level VP, only a few of these seem to be present, namely the right to possess, the right to use, the prohibition of harmful use, and the right to the income of the thing (to an extent, depending on the type of the VW). Most of the other incidents are in the hands of the providers (i.e. the right to the capital, the right to security, the rights of transmissibility and absence of term, the liability of execution, the incident of residuarity, and the right to manage). Ownership of the third level VP encounters similar difficulties, and this layer possesses the same incidents as the second one. In addition, it could be argued that it possesses the right to transmissibility (as IP does), but not the absence of term, since most contracts recognise IP in players' creations without recognising property at the same time. If we were to recognise VP, these incidents, according to Honoré, would need to be included for full ownership to exist.

Becker's Incidents

Building on Honoré's analysis, Becker proposes thirteen elements: the right (claim) to possess, the right (liberty) to use, the right (power) to manage, the right (claim) to the income, the right (liberty) to consume and destroy, the right (liberty) to modify, the right (power) to alienate, the right (power) to transmit, the right (claim) to security, the absence of term, the prohibition of harmful use, liability to execution, and residuary rules.[48] He further argues that anyone who has one of the first eight elements plus the right to security has a property right.

Again, there is no dispute about the first layer VAs. The second layer would lack the right (liberty) to consume and destroy (destroy in particular), the right (power) to alienate (for some VWs), the right (power) to transmit, the right (claim) to security, the absence of term, liability to execution, and residuary rules. Therefore, the bundle of eight rights is not present here, and VP would mean recognising these, according to this theory. Similarly, as

[48] L Becker, 'The moral basis of property rights' in JR Pennock and JW Chapman (eds), *Property* (New York University Press 1980) 190–1.

discussed above, third layer VAs would lack all of these, apart from the right to transmit. Consequently, the theory cannot justify the creation of VP.

Incidents of Property Objects vs Virtual Property Objects

A potential problem VP in the second and third layers would encounter is its alleged lack of tangibility. This problem would not be as significant for the civil law countries, as they recognise property in intangibles, either in the civil code, like France,[49] or by establishing a separate category of property, constitutional property, like Germany.[50] This could be more difficult for the English common law system, which refuses to consider intangibles property, at least in some cases (information), but decides to recognise it in others, for example IP. US law is more likely to recognise intangibles as property (see the relevant cases on propertisation of information in Chapter 6).[51]

Therefore, the intangibility of second layer VAs (intangible for the purpose of the classical legal definitions, i.e. lack of real-world tangibility and incorporeality, as it consists of code) would present an obstacle for recognising VP in English common law. Fewer issues would emerge in the US, and civil law systems would require legislative interventions. To develop this point further, it might be suggested that this layer does not have to be considered intangible, as it seems tangible to an avatar in a game, and if the level of immersion of a player is very high, then consequently, it could be tangible for the player as well.[52] At the moment, however, this line of thought is unlikely to be accepted by the English courts as a suitable legal test for tangibility, as demonstrated in Chapter 2.

Penner's analysis of property objects includes a requirement of 'separability' or 'thinghood', meaning that things, in order to be property, must not be conceived of as 'an aspect of ourselves or our on-going personality-rich

[49] J Bell et al. *Principles of French Law* (2nd edn, Oxford University Press 2008) 27.

[50] MJ Raff, *Private Property and Environmental Responsibility: A Comparative Study of German Real Property Law* (Kluwer Law International 2003).

[51] See important cases about the propertisation of information: *Exchange Telegraph Co Ltd* v *Gregory & Co* [1896] 1 QB 147; *Oxford* v *Moss* [1978] 68 Cr App R 181. Generally, see N Palmer and P Kohler, 'Information as property' in N Palmer and E McKendrick (eds), *Interests in Goods* (Lloyd's of London Press 1993) 187–206. The US common and statute law is readier to recognise property in different types of intangibles (e.g. fresh news). The doctrine of misappropriation is of a proprietary character, as established in *International News Service* v *Associated Press*, 248 US 215, 250 (1918). See commentary in RY Fujichaku, 'The misappropriation doctrine in cyberspace: Protecting the commercial value of "hot news" information' (1998) 20 *University of Hawai'i Law Review* 421.

[52] Erlank (n 1) 287–8.

relationships to others'.[53] This theory, for instance, would not consider personal data, body parts or blood as property, since they all lack the separability requirement and are aspects of ourselves. Applying this argument to our second layer, and immersion notwithstanding, it could be argued that avatars would lack these criteria whereas the rest of the VAs in this layer would not, as weapons, spaceships and clothes, for example, are separable both from the avatar and the player.

Similarly, the definition of property offered by Waldron focuses primarily on 'material resources', 'capable of satisfying some human need or want'.[54] This definition requires materiality and not tangibility, and it could be argued that second layer VAs are material resources within VWs, and they satisfy the player's need for entertainment, creation, competition, trade, education, and so on However, the third layer VAs are less likely to be considered material resources, and this layer encounters the same difficulties as IP.

The analyses will further be based on the features identified by Fairfield in his seminal work on virtual property. The first feature he analyses is rivalrousness, which means that consumption cannot be shared for a rivalrous resource; one person's possession and consumption physically excludes the other pretenders to the same resource.[55]

Fairfield thus discusses the possibility of applying the traditional concept of property, designed for chattels rather than IP, to virtual property that mimics the real, offline one (layer two VAs). He distinguishes between the computer, software code, designed as non-rivalrous (protected by IP, layer 1) and other types of code, rivalrous, 'designed to act more like land or chattel than ideas'[56] where if one person controls it, the others cannot.

Rivalrousness is, therefore, the physical quality of an object, different from exclusivity, which is an individual's power to control the use of an object.[57] Other commentators indeed use the term 'exclusivity' as a synonym for rivalrousness.[58] This is wrong, however, and Fairfield rightly notes that exclusivity is a function of rivalrousness, the quality that can be assigned to non-rivalrous objects by law or technology, for instance (e.g. IP creations and digital rights management). It is important to note that this code is rivalrous

[53] Ibid. 126.

[54] J Waldron, *The Right to Private Property* (Clarendon Press 1990).

[55] C Hess and E Ostrom, *Understanding Knowledge as a Commons from Theory to Practice* (MIT Press 2007) 352.

[56] Ibid. 1101.

[57] DL Weimer and AR Vining, *Policy Analysis* (5th edn, Longman 2011) 72.

[58] Westbrook (n 7).

because it is made that way and is a fundamental part of the Internet.[59] Examples of this code are domain names, URLs, websites, email accounts and VW items. Fairfield also warns of the confusion that occurs in trying to fit all intangibles into a category of non-rivalrous objects.[60] Other authors who support his stance concerning VP and rivalrousness are Horowitz,[61] Blazer[62] and Westbrook.[63]

Critics claim that VP and VAs are non-rivalrous. Nelson, for instance, disputes rivalrousness, or rather, exclusivity, of virtual goods using the same examples as Fairfield, that is, URLs and emails. He claims that the alleged owner cannot control this property to the exclusion of others because, according to the contract that a user concludes, the developer retains the ability to control these resources. Similarly, Glushko argues that the ease of copying code in the case of any digital property would undermine the exclusivity of virtual property as well.[64] These authors have again confused the notions of exclusivity, which is an economic and legal feature and relates to the rights conferred by contracts or property, and rivalrousness, which is a purely physical feature, so even if a provider retains the exclusive control over a virtual resource, the fact that only one user at a time can, arguably, physically experience it means that the resource is rivalrous.

In summary, rivalrousness is a feature of the second level virtual property. The problem with this feature incident is its unstable nature, as it only exists if created in that form by the developer. However, this should not be an issue since, ultimately, VWs are unstable too and would not exist if developers did not create them. Indeed, players and many theorists (e.g. Lastowka or Mayer-Schönberger), myself included, still accept VWs as such, claiming that however unstable and peculiar places they may be, VWs still represent replicas of the real world. In addition, even if we accept that VW items are not rivalrous, this is not a decisive point to discard their protection since IP resources are not rivalrous either and still are protected like, or similar to, property.

Permanence or persistence of VWs and in-game assets is another disputed feature, present in physical property and contested in the case of IP. Castronova defines persistence as the feature of VWs enabling them to

59 Fairfield, 'Virtual property' (n 7) 1053–4.

60 Ibid. 1063.

61 SJ Horowitz, 'Competing Lockean claims to virtual property' (2007) 20(2) *Harvard Journal of Law and Technology* 443.

62 Blazer (n 7).

63 Westbrook (n 7).

64 Glushko (n 8) 251–7.

'continue to run whether anyone is using [them] or not'.[65] Fairfield, like Castronova, argues that code is persistent too since 'it does not fade away after each use, and it does not run on one single computer'.[66] The code of a VW can be accessed from a variety of devices, and it persists on the servers of service providers. Thus, according to them, this quality of code makes it analogous to physical objects.[67]

However, this code can be accessed and modified at any given time by the developer, which is a critical weakness of this argument. Similarly, Erlank notes that permanence depends only on the cooperation of developers, who can make VP disappear at any time.[68] Chein warns that VWs are ephemeral and dynamic environments, and VP can be lost 'at the accidental flick of a power switch'.[69] Cifrino also notes this potential obsolescence of VW business models, giving the example of *City of Heroes*, a VW which ceased operation in 2012, after eight years.[70]

An issue related to the potential disappearance of VWs is the lack of interoperability between software in different VWs.[71] So, when a user's account has been restricted or terminated by one developer, the user cannot move it to another platform. There have been some efforts to make property in one VW compatible with the software in another VW, but until this is implemented, the quality of permanence remains rather dubious.[72]

Lastowka and Hunter claim that temporality is a weak argument against virtual property. They use the examples of lease or usufruct, which are property interests recognised in common law and are time-limited. Due to its time-limited protection (seventy years post-mortem in the EU and US), IP is another example of rejecting the objection of temporality.[73] Therefore, the lack of permanence in the second and third layer VAs could serve as a solid argument against VP in the classical conception of property and its

65 Castronova, 'On virtual economies' (n 5) 6.
66 Fairfield, 'Virtual property' (n 7) 1054.
67 Westbrook (n 7) 782–3.
68 Erlank (n 1) 275.
69 Chein (n 7) 1077.
70 Cifrino (n 7) 23–4.
71 Glushko (n 8) 512; Nelson, 'The virtual property problem' (n 7).
72 For more about these efforts, see Vacca (n 7) 22; D Terdiman, 'Tech titans seek virtual-world interoperability' *CNET News* (15 October 2007) <http://news.cnet.com/Tech-titans-seek-virtual-world-interoperability/2100-1043_3-6213148.html> last accessed 1 August 2021 (noting the status of converting VWs to interoperability); Virtual World Interoperability <http://Virtual Worldinterop.wikidot.com/start> last accessed 1 August 2021 (summarising the results of the 2007 Virtual Worlds Interoperability Community Summit).
73 Lastowka and Hunter, 'Virtual worlds' (n 1) 55–6.

permanence, and if one does not conceive of IP as property. On the other hand, notwithstanding the temporality of IP, the lack of this quality might exclude virtual property conceived in the traditional property sense but does not necessarily exclude proposing some other proprietary models for protecting virtual assets (like IP).

Fairfield argues that another physical quality of VW code is interconnectivity, analogous to the characteristic of objects in the real world (players can experience the connected world and interact with each other and the VW). Like Castronova,[74] Fairfield argues that 'code can be made interconnected, so that although one person may control it, others may experience it'.[75] As Erlank notes, if there were no interconnectivity in VWs, players would be able to experience only their own property, contrary to the whole idea of VWs.[76]

However, code is not necessarily interconnected since not all computer systems can run all code without necessary adjustments, and we have the problem of interoperability, as seen in the discussion on permanence in the section above.[77]

(b) Justifications of Virtual Property

The doctrinal question, that is, whether there *is* property in VWs, has been answered in the analysis above. VP does not share property concept incidents, and VAs do not possess characteristics of property objects. The following section will answer a normative question: whether there *ought to be* property in virtual worlds.

The key in recognising something as property is to identify the relevant theoretical justifications.[78] The next section will, therefore, refer to the leading Western justifications of *propertisation* (labour theory, utilitarianism and personhood theory), discussing the potential of their application to VAs and VWs. The analysis will use the layer classification explained above.

Labour Theory

Many authors contend that Locke's labour theory applies to virtual property. The main argument is that the time and effort users put in while creating

74 Castronova, 'On virtual economies' (n 5).

75 Fairfield, 'Virtual property' (n 7) 1054.

76 Erlank (n 1) 246.

77 Nelson, 'Fiber optic foxes' (n 7) 17.

78 Erlank argues that virtual property could be more easily recognised in common law systems, as these 'just require a good justification'. See Erlank (n 1) 252.

virtual assets should entitle them to claim property rights.[79] The time players spend in VWs is significant if we look at the empirical research conducted on this topic.

Relevant research has been ambiguous. Nevertheless, it could be argued that the time players spend in VWs is quite considerable. For instance, in 2020, research showed that online video games were in the UK's top ten online activities.[80] In 2010, Mayer-Schönberger and Crowley asserted that 9.4 million players are each 'in-world' for about 22 hours per week, claiming that 'subscribers to VWs could be devoting over 213 million hours per week to building their virtual lives'.[81] A global survey of 4,500 individuals in 2019 showed that those who play VWs or video games spend an average of 7 hours and 7 minutes each week playing and that the playing time had increased 19.3 per cent since 2018.[82] MMORPGs are still in the top seven types of games played. The research also demonstrates a significant amount of time spent watching others play games on platforms such as Twitch.

On the first obvious question of whether we could consider 'game playing' as labour, it is argued that labour in the form of 'grinding' can be deemed relevant for labour theory. Grinding is a series of repetitive menial actions in VWs, completed to level up one's character.[83] In addition, the quality of labour can be demonstrated by looking at the phenomenon of 'gold farming'. Gold farmers are a particular subset of users who dedicate their hours 'in game' specifically to creating assets of value for later sale on in-game or grey markets.[84] Gold farms or 'gaming workshops' might employ a few dozen such farmers who perform various tasks specific to a particular game to build up virtual currency for the farm owners.[85] Although the data is somewhat uneven, there were some quite staggering estimates of the value of this 'virtual

[79] Shikowitz (n 8) 1015–54.

[80] Statista, 'Internet activities performed in Great Britain (UK) 2020' (10 November 2020) <https://www.statista.com/statistics/275805/internet-activities-performed-in-great-britain/> last accessed 1 August 2021.

[81] Mayer-Schoenberger and Crowley (n 6) 1787; H Mahmassani et al., 'Time to play? Activity engagement in multiplayer online role-playing games' (2010) *Journal of the Transportation Research Board* 129–37.

[82] Limelight Network, 'The state of online gaming 2019' <https://www.limelight.com/resources/white-paper/state-of-online-gaming-2019/> last accessed 1 August 2021.

[83] AE Jankowich, 'Property and democracy in virtual worlds' (2005) 11 *Boston University Journal of Science and Technology Law* 173, 183.

[84] R Heeks, 'Understanding "gold farming" and real-money trading as the intersection of real and virtual economies' (2010) 2(4) *Virtual Economies, Virtual Goods and Service Delivery in Virtual Worlds* 1, 6.

[85] Ibid. 7.

economy'. Heeks, for instance, estimated in 2010 that approximately 400,000 people were employed in gold farming, of which perhaps 85 per cent were based in China. In 1999, Ryan estimated that one million gold farmers were working on a global trade worth more than $10 billion.[86] Therefore, the labour is already recognised as such in these black or grey markets. A more recent study demonstrates fluctuations in the virtual economy. According to the authors, the value of virtual currency in *World of Warcraft* 'plummeted heavily against real-world currencies across the world after the release of the game's newest expansion pack in August 2016'.[87]

The argument against applying labour theory to VWs is that most players play games for entertainment purposes and not gold farming or labouring in general. Therefore, the time spent playing a game cannot qualify as adequate labour for labour theory.[88] Erlank replies to this objection by noting that not all VWs are used for entertainment (some are indeed used for many other purposes, including education, business and politics), and that the real world also rewards individuals who play games there, giving the example of athletes (professional ones are paid). Second, he comments that some players do indeed 'labour' by 'painstakingly' repeating the same actions in order to reap a reward, like blacksmiths for instance (referring to grinding mentioned above).[89]

Advocates of applying Locke's theory to VP also argue that it is relatively easy to satisfy Locke's 'enough and as good' proviso in VWs (in short, that an individual can appropriate an object under the condition that there is enough and as good left for the others, the proviso subsequently revised by Locke[90]). In VWs, arguably, there is an infinite number of resources available to players to labour and create.[91] This does not have to be self-evident, however, as the abundance of the VW resources depends on the developers' will and actions, and for some of them, the users need to pay and do not labour on them (e.g. land in *Second Life*). The developers, therefore, artificially create a scarcity of resources in the VW. On the other hand, arguably, in-game resources are available to all players under the same conditions, and the developers

[86] Ibid.; ML Ryan, 'Immersion vs. interactivity: Virtual reality and literary theory' (1999) (28)2 *SubStance* 110.

[87] J Holm and E Mäkinen, 'The value of currency in World of Warcraft' (2018) *Journal of Internet Social Networking & Virtual Communities* article ID: 672253.

[88] Lastowka and Hunter, 'Virtual worlds' (n 1) 46; Erlank (n 1) 153.

[89] Erlank (n 1) 98.

[90] CB Macpherson, 'Editor's introduction' in J Locke *Second Treatise of Government: Essay Concerning the True Original Extent and End of Civil Government*, ed. with an intro. CB Macpherson (Hackett 1980) xvii.

[91] Ibid. 64–5.

can adjust the scarcity feature, making more resources available if needed. Consequently, looking at a VW as a self-contained entity, this proviso seems fulfilled.

According to the proponents of applying labour theory to virtual property, Locke's spoilage proviso is also satisfied (the argument that the labourer is limited to 'as much as anyone can make use of to any advantage of life before it spoils'[92]). The argument is that for the obvious reasons of the nature of VAs (underlying code that determines them), they cannot be spoilt, similar to money. Therefore, the limitation is unnecessary for VWs, since developers produce VAs and/or enable their creation by players and the limitation is embedded in the underlying code of the VW.

Lastowka and Hunter indicate that this justification for virtual property can be criticised based on Nozick's general objection to Locke's theory, namely, the labour which users embed in the VWs is insignificant compared with that of the owners of VWs.[93] Opponents of Nozick's argument argue that for some property, labour, no matter how insignificant it seems, adds value to a resource and recreates its essence.[94] Similarly, Lastowka and Hunter reply to this objection, arguing that this is correct in the sense that a player cannot claim property in the whole VW, but deserves property in the items where their labour makes up the most significant part of the value. They also assert that players do not claim property in the world itself but rather their items and avatars.[95]

The most commonly articulated objection to applying Locke's theory to virtual property is the same one used against propertisation of IP, that is, the absence of commons.[96] According to this argument, the commons, the initial stage from which appropriation occurs, does not exist here, and VWs are not common *ab initio* but are usually owned by the developers. Therefore, according to labour theory, they seem to have a better claim as they actually invest their labour and resources in creating VWs.[97] Cifrino shares this stance, noting that if any labour on the initial commons would create property rights, borrowing and sharing of any object would be a problem if someone

92 Ibid. 60.

93 Lastowka and Hunter, 'Virtual worlds' (n 1) 97; R Nozick, *Anarchy, State and Utopia* (Basil Blackwell 1974) 175.

94 GS Alexander and EM Peñalver, *An Introduction to Property Theory* (Cambridge University Press 2012) 48.

95 Lastowka and Hunter, 'Virtual worlds' (n 1) 63.

96 See SV Shiffrin, 'The incentives argument for intellectual property protection' (2009) 4 *Journal of Law, Philosophy and Culture* 49, 96; RP Merges, *Justifying Intellectual Property* (Harvard University Press 2011) 35–9.

97 Horowitz (n 61) 443–58.

later labours on that object and claims the title allegedly resulting from that labour.[98] Other authors reply to this, contending that the comparison could be made to Locke's commons created by God and VWs' commons created by their 'gods', or someone with godlike powers, the developers.[99] In addition, for those arguing that IP is property, in essence, the absence of commons can be bypassed and interpreted widely, as has happened practically.[100]

Prima facie, labour theory presents a reasonable justification for recognising property in the second level VW's code, as this code satisfies the labour requirement and the two provisos (spoilage and 'enough and as good'). In addition, a player's labour constitutes the most significant part of the value of the VAs. For the first level items, understandably, the developer's labour and investment constitute the most significant part of their value; therefore, the developer should be entitled to own this layer.

However, the lack of the commons here is problematic as one cannot argue that there is any common of ideas, facts or resources in VWs.[101] One way to neutralise this limitation would be to recognise the godlike powers of the developers and analogise them with God and Locke's commons. Alternatively, if the second layer is perceived separately and in relation to the other players and not the developer, then VWs features, which are open to all, can be seen as the commons. However, it is argued here that this argument is not plausible, mainly because labour put in by different individuals does not change the entire world, and the first layer remains developer-owned. Even if, arguably, there is a radical change in some instances (e.g. *Second Life* and similar worlds and games, where users do change the landscape significantly), this change does not defeat the property in the first layer. Locke's theory here thus serves better the interests of developers.

Personhood Theory

Personhood theories originate from Hegel's conception of property as an extension of personality,[102] and Radin's classifications of property as fungible and personal. For Radin, property is an essential vehicle for developing the personality, and therefore, property that is especially close to a

[98] Cifrino (n 7).

[99] Erlank (n 1) 156–7.

[100] See for example J Peterson, 'Lockean property and literary works' (2008) 14(4) *Legal Theory* 257.

[101] Apart from perhaps, open sources games, which are not the focus of this analysis.

[102] GWF Hegel, *The Philosophy of Right*, trans. TM Knox (Oxford University Press 1967) para 41.

person's self-definition deserves special legal protections and precedence over fungible property.[103]

This theory is, arguably, more applicable for justifying property interests in virtual assets than to justify traditional property.[104] In VWs, players are represented by a character, an avatar,[105] which is essentially a player's agent for interacting with the environment.[106] An avatar, and consequently a player, generally leads a more or less complete, rich and exciting life in VWs, often as a simulation of the real world. Using their avatars and offline, players communicate and socialise with others in the real world and gain reputation and social capital.

In most VWs, players usually establish substantial ties with their avatars, conceiving them as extensions of themselves, their psychological embodiments, *alter egos*.[107] A large body of research on VWs confirms this, referring to the concept of immersion.[108] Bartle, for instance, argues that VWs are all about 'the celebration of identity' and summarises the path players follow in the game in the phrase 'locate to discover to apply to internalise'. As the player develops, they travel from acquiring the skills for achieving something in the world, whatever that goal is, to exploring the world and applying the skills. The journey terminates with internalising the world and with complete immersion in it.[109] The concept of immersion in VWs is tied to presence and

[103] MJ Radin, 'Property and personhood' (1982) 34 *Stanford Law Review* 957.

[104] Lastowka and Hunter, 'Virtual worlds' (n 1).

[105] Castronova, 'On virtual economies' (n 5).

[106] For more about avatars, history and use in VWs, see Lastowka (n 17) 45–6; Dibble (n 3).

[107] Lastowka (n 17) 46; D Williams, T Kennedy and R Moore, 'Behind the avatar: The patterns, practices and functions of role playing in MMOs' (2011) *Games & Culture* 171.

[108] Y Lee and A Chen, 'Usability design and psychological ownership of a virtual world' (2011) 28(3) *Journal of Management Information Systems* 269; DA Bowman and RP McMahan, 'Virtual reality: How much immersion is enough?' (2007) 40(7) *Computer* 36–43; Ryan (n 86) 110; K Cheng and PA Cairns, 'Behaviour, realism and immersion in games' (in *Proceedings of the 2005 Conference on Human Factors in Computing Systems*, CHI 2005, Portland, Oregon, 2–7 April 2005 <http://www.uclic.ucl.ac.uk/paul/research/Cheng.pdf> last accessed 1 August 2021; L Ermi and F Mayra, 'Fundamental components of the gameplay experience: Analysing immersion' in S de Castell and J Jenson (eds), *Changing Views: Worlds in Play: Selected Papers of the 2005 Digital Games Research Association's Second International Conference*, 16–20 June 2005, Vancouver (DiGRA 2005) <http://www.uta.fi/~tlilma/gameplay_experience.pdf> last accessed 1 August 2021; P Sweetser and P Wyeth, 'GameFlow: A model for evaluating player enjoyment in games' (2005) 3(3) *ACM Computers in Entertainment* article 3A <http://www.itee.uq.edu.au/~penny/_papers/Sweetser-CIE.pdf> last accessed 1 August 2021.

[109] RA Bartle, 'Virtual worlds: Why people play' in T Alexander (ed.), *Massively Multiplayer Game Development 2* (Charles River Media 2005) 3–18 <http://www.mud.co.uk/richard/VIRTUALWORLDWPP.pdf> last accessed 1 August 2021; R Bartle, 'Presence and

an illusion that this computer-mediated environment is not mediated but real.[110] The result of this 'hill-climbing activity through identity space' is 'that players understand themselves more'.[111] Similarity, Lastowka shows immersion using the example of the use of language and the pronoun 'you' when referring to another person's avatar and 'I' for one's own avatar's actions.[112]

The argument against using this theory to justify VP is found in the inalienability of personal property, as suggested by Radin and achieved, for instance, in the case of moral rights on the Continent.[113] Therefore, this would result in proclaiming avatars and other second level VAs inalienable since they are so intrinsically related to a person. This is undesirable, however, since some users in VWs do want to trade their avatars, which often reach a considerable price on the markets.[114] Lastowka and Hunter maintain that even if avatars and other second level VAs were to be proclaimed inalienable, on the practical side it is not a certain outcome as the courts might conclude otherwise and permit virtual trade.[115] In addition, if classified as personal property, virtual assets would be better protected than fungible property, that is, the developers' property, raising more disputes rather than providing solutions.[116] On the other hand, something's being deemed non-transferable does not necessarily exclude its proprietary character (e.g. common, public property).

An objection to this theory in general, and its application to virtual assets in particular, can be found in the argument of 'separability' or 'thinghood', meaning that things, in order to be property, must not be conceived of as 'an aspect of ourselves or our on-going personality-rich relationships to others' (e.g. blood, body parts, personal data).[117] This objection is particularly applicable to avatars as property, considering the rich relationship between players

---

flow: Ill-fitting clothes for virtual worlds' (2007) 10(3) *Techné: Research in Philosophy and Technology* 39.

110 M Lombard and T Ditton, 'At the heart of it all: The concept of presence' (2004) 3(2) *Journal of Computer-Mediated Communication* <http://onlinelibrary.wiley.com/doi/10.1111/j.1083-6101.1997.tb00072.x/full> last accessed 1 August 2021.

111 Ibid. 15.

112 Lastowka (n 17) 46.

113 See J Hughes, 'The philosophy of intellectual property' (1988) 77 *Georgetown Law Journal* 287; B Hugenholtz, 'Copyright and freedom of expression in Europe' in N Elkin-Koren and N Netanel, *The Commodification of Information* (Kluwer Law International 2002) 239, 240–1; P Rigamonti, 'The conceptual transformation of moral rights' (2007) 55 *American Journal of Comparative Law* 67–122, 98.

114 Cifrino (n 7) 16; Lastowka (n 17) 176–7.

115 Lastowka and Hunter, 'Virtual worlds' (n 1) 65–6.

116 Erlank (n 1) 175–7.

117 See J Penner, *The Idea of Property in Law* (Oxford University Press 1997) 126.

and their avatars, but is less applicable to the other VWs items (swords, castles, houses, etc.).

Personhood theories could serve as a sound basis for justifying VP in the second and third level of code in VWs, those closely related to the player's personality, items and creations. The application of this theory, as demonstrated above, is not without difficulties and would not always serve players' interests (e.g. sale of avatars and other virtual assets).

Utilitarian Theory

Amongst the theories used in this chapter, the utilitarian theory is least applicable to justify virtual property in the second layer virtual assets. The main problem lies in the usefulness of VP for society, real-world non-players. It would potentially conflict with the felicific calculus principle of utilitarianism, looking for 'the greatest good for the greatest number'.[118] Lastowka and Hunter would disagree with this assertion, claiming that in-game assets, from the utilitarian perspective, do not need to be beneficial for society; however, they are undoubtedly helpful and valuable for the individuals engaging in creating and improving these assets. Therefore, if the society (VW) is perceived as an aggregation of individuals (players), the utilitarian concept could be used. According to these views, by recognising VP, users would be rewarded for their efforts and incentivised to create further and develop VWs.[119] An example of this is the exponential growth of *Second Life* users after Linden Lab changed its terms of service and promised ownership over players' creations.[120]

On the other hand, players are already incentivised to create, and one of the major factors why they choose to join a particular VW is creation; therefore, property in VAs would probably not make much difference. Being in VWs already potentially results in economic benefits for players. Players can exchange their VAs for real money in many VWs, which is known as real money trading (RMT). RMT includes two main components: primary, which occurs within the game and under the end user licence agreement

[118] J Bentham, *An Introduction to the Principles of Morals and Legislation*, ed. JH Burns and HLA Hart (Athlone Press 1970) 12–13.

[119] See WM Landes and RA Posner, *The Economic Structure of Intellectual Property Law* (Harvard University Press 2003); WM Landes and RA Posner, 'An economic analysis of copyright law' (1989) 18 *Journal of Legal Studies* 325, 326; S Leung, 'The commons and anticommons in intellectual property' (2010) *UCL Journal of Law and Jurisprudence* 16; S Kieff, 'Property rights and property rules for commercializing inventions' (2001) 85 *Minnesota Law Review* 697; EW Kitch, 'The law and economics of rights in valuable information' (1980) 9 *Journal of Legal Studies* 683.

[120] Vacca (n 7).

(EULA),[121] and secondary, which happens outside the game and beyond the EULA provisions. Players usually make money from selling VAs on online auctions within or outside the VW (some of the VWs expressly ban the use of external auctions, e.g. Blizzard's *World of Warcraft* EULA).[122] For instance, in 2006, Anshe Chung accumulated more than one million dollars in virtual assets, becoming the first millionaire of the popular VW *Second Life*.[123] In December 2009, a person known as 'Buss Erik Lightyear' paid $330,000 to own a virtual space station in *Planet Calypso*, an MMORPG.[124] The game allows exchanges between virtual currency and real dollars at a fixed exchange rate of 10 PED (virtual currency) to $1.[125] Wu estimates that the market for virtual goods in the US exceeded $3 billion in 2012 and it 'is expected to grow briskly in later years'.[126] In 2013, Linden Lab reported 1.2 million daily transactions for virtual goods and $3.2 billion worth of transactions in *Second Life* Economy.[127] However, it is still unclear whether there could be a further explosion in the numbers of VWs users and their transactions, provided that VP is recognised.

The incentives argument, therefore, works much better for developers. Creating and maintaining a VW can be a profitable business deal as they can earn from various sources, such as subscriptions, virtual sale commission,

[121] 'The EULA is a software license between the developer and the user (and generally drafted by the developer) that governs the relationship between these two parties. The EULA is generally presented as a graphical computer window that pops up when the [user] of the software begins running the program. The [user] is then presented with the terms of the license, and must click a button indicating that he/she has read and accepted those terms.' The software will only begin running if the user agrees to the EULA. See ibid. 43.

[122] An example of the existing auctions site is <https://www.playerauctions.com/wow-classic-tbc-items/> last accessed 1 August 2021.

[123] R Hof, 'Second Life's first millionaire' *Businessweek Online* (2006) <https://www.bloomberg.com/news/articles/2006-11-25/second-lifes-first-millionaire> last accessed 1 August 2021.

[124] M Schramm, 'Man buys virtual space station for 330k real dollars' *Joystiq* (2010) <http://www.joystiq.com/2010/01/02/man-buys-virtual-space-station-for-330k-real-dollars/> last accessed 1 August 2021.

[125] S Brennan, 'Crystal Palace space station auction tops 330,000 US dollars' *Joystiq* (2009) <http://massively.joystiq.com/2009/12/29/crystal-palace-space-station-auction-tops-330-000-us-dollars/> last accessed 1 August 2021.

[126] S Wu, 'Digital afterlife: What happens to your data when you die?' (2013) <http://dataedge.ischool.berkeley.edu/2013/pdf/digital-afterlife-white-paper.pdf> last accessed 1 August 2021.

[127] See *Second Life*, 'Second Life affiliate program' <http://secondlife.com/corporate/affiliate/?lang=it-IT> last accessed 1 August 2021.

purchase of land and other features.[128] In order to achieve this, understandably, they need to have a significant user base,[129] incentivised perhaps by VP rights. In addition, they need to have their rights in the first layer VAs to prevent free riding on their creations.

The free riding arguments (arguments against allowing an individual to obtain benefits from someone else's investment, preventing them from recouping costs) are also somewhat applicable to the second layer too, in the sense that VWs as a society take advantage of and become more attractive to new users with these creations, which developers profit from.[130] Another likely scenario is the free riding of other players, replicating and copying other players' creations (e.g. their original swords, houses, ships). However, as noted by Lemley for IP rights, free riding might even be desirable in VWs, as there is much less need to internalise negative externalities. As with IP, negative externalities are less prominent here than tangible property, as consumption by many players is desirable since it enriches the society and culture of VWs.[131] Also, the lack of scarcity in VWs means that free riding would not result in severe detriment, and the developers could make more resources available to players.

Conversely, one of the arguments *contra* using this justification for VP rights is the allocation reason. According to this view, utilitarian theories could be used to oppose the creation of property rights in VWs. They would decrease the welfare of VWs' owners and other users by giving property to individuals and creating, effectively, *the tragedy of anticommons*, where individuals would be able to prevent the use of VP, resulting in unwanted underuse

[128] For Blizzard profits, see for example E Makuch, 'Activision Blizzard profits hit $1.1 billion in 2012' *Gamespot* (2013) <http://www.gamespot.com/articles/activision-blizzard-profits-hit-11-billion-in-2012/1100-6403613/> last accessed 1 August 2021. For Linden Lab's, see J Reahard, 'Linden Lab's Second Life "extremely profitable" company looking to expand' *Massively by Joystiq* (2012) <http://massively.joystiq.com/2012/03/15/linden-labs-second-life-extremely-profitable-company-looking/> last accessed 1 August 2021.

[129] Statistics about the MMORPGs market show that in 2013 there were approximately 20 million subscribers, and that the peak in terms of numbers of subscribers was in 2011, close to 23 million. See TotalSubs, MMOData.net <http://users.telenet.be/mmodata/Charts/TotalSubs.png> last accessed 1 August 2021. The latest data still reports millions of *WoW* and other MMORPGs users worldwide (4.7 million). See Statista, 'In 2015, when Activision Blizzard last reported on World of Warcraft's subscriptions, the game had 5.5 million global subscribers. It is projected that the numbers will gradually decrease to hit 4.46 million in 2023' <https://www.statista.com/statistics/276601/number-of-world-of-warcraft-subscribers-by-quarter/> last accessed 1 August 2021.

[130] Landes and Posner, 'An economic analysis of copyright law' (n 119); MA Lemley, 'Property, intellectual property, and free riding' (2005) 83 *Texas Law Review* 1031, 1059–60.

[131] Lemley, 'Property' (n 130) 1059–60.

of VWs by players.[132] Lastowka and Hunter reply to these arguments, saying that they do not consider justifications for allocation but rather for creating property rights in virtual goods. According to them, this does not mean that property should not exist in VWs at all. The argument states that property is not allocated correctly, which can be corrected by the courts, for instance.[133] This response does not address the objection adequately. Instead, the nature of VWs and the layer approach would prevent underuse, as the first layer belongs to the developers and the rights in the second one are derived from this ownership.

5.5 Allocation of Ownership in Virtual Worlds

In this section, we assess the allocation of property in VWs, arguing that most developers curtail possibilities for players to assert any VP rights in second level VAs, even if theories of property justify this concept.[134] Moreover, where developers have envisaged some kind of player property rights in their EULAs (e.g. *Second Life*), these rights are minimal and can barely be categorised as property. The solution to rectify this imbalance, therefore, is potentially available in the form of consumer protection. However, due to the distinctive character of VWs and the areas these contracts aim to regulate, consumer protection laws do not prove very helpful.

Allocation of ownership, IP and other different rights in VWs is established through contracts. VW contracts come in the form of clickwrap licences (end user licence agreements – EULAs, terms of service – ToS, rules of conduct and other different policies).[135] The effects of these contracts are widely disputed, as they leave little or no freedom for the user, and no other choice apart from clicking 'I agree' or to decline, therefore refusing to take part in the game.[136] The most common model is that the developer claims all property and IP rights associated with the VW.[137]

[132] See MA Heller, 'The tragedy of the anticommons: Property in the transition from Marx to markets reviewed' (1998) 111(3) *Harvard Law Review* 621.

[133] Lastowka and Hunter, 'Virtual worlds' (n 1) 59–60.

[134] Harbinja, 'Virtual Worlds – a legal post-mortem account' (n 12).

[135] See for example Blizzard, 'World of Warcraft – end user license agreement' <https://www.blizzard.com/en-us/legal/fba4d00f-c7e4-4883-b8b9-1b4500a402ea/blizzard-end-user-license-agreement> last accessed 1 August 2021.

[136] Erlank (n 1); T Pistorius, 'Click-wrap and web-wrap agreements' (2004) 16 *SA Mercantile Law Journal* 568–76; MA Lemley, 'Terms of use' (2006) 91 *Minnesota Law Review* 459, 459–83.

[137] Jankowich conducted a survey of forty-eight VWs, confirming these assertions. See Jankowich, 'Property and democracy' (n 83).

Blizzard, the *World of Warcraft* and *Diablo III* developer, expressly excludes any property rights of users in assets created or traded in the game, in addition to forbidding the transfer of accounts (s 1 B iii of Blizzard EULA). Conversely, *Second Life* and Linden Lab give relatively extensive rights in content created by users. Initially, Linden labelled these rights as property, but in response to *Bragg* v *Linden Research, Inc*,[138] changed its terms to granting an IP right only.[139] It also denies property rights in virtual currency (Linden dollars), and land that users can buy in *Second Life*, reminding them of the limited licence they are granted.[140] Moringiello argues that Linden deceives its users as it effectively promises something resembling the bundle of land rights, that is, property, and then takes it back by way of service.[141] As Erlank rightly notes, even the recognised rights are somewhat illusory, as Linden limits them to the game and refuses any liability and compensation in the case of damage or loss of this property.[142] Nevertheless, he also reasonably opines that by insisting on regulating and limiting VP, the developer implicitly recognises its existence.[143]

On the other hand, Linden grants itself a non-exclusive licence in players' creations, the scope of which has been widened even more recently, leaving many players of *Second Life* displeased and embittered, wanting to leave.[144] Also, its EULAs caused Linden Lab to be involved in the most critical court cases about VWs and VP in the Western world.

[138] 487 F.Supp.2d 593, 612 (ED Pa 2007).

[139] Linden Lab, 'Second Life residents to own digital creations' *Press Release* (2003) <http://creativecommons.org/press-releases/entry/3906> last accessed 1 August 2021; 'Second Life terms of service' (15 December 2010) <https://secondlife.com/app/tos/tos.php> last accessed 1 August 2021, title 2; and see commentary in Vacca (n 7); AB Steinberg, 'For sale – one level 5 barbarian for 94,800 won: The international effects of virtual property and the legality of its ownership' (2009) 37 *Georgia Journal of International and Comparative Law* 381; J Gong, 'Defining and addressing virtual property in international treaties' (2011) 17 *Boston University Journal of Science and Technology Law* 101.

[140] See *Second Life*, 'Terms of Service' s 1.2 <http://lindenlab.com/tos> last accessed 1 August 2021.

[141] Moringiello (n 7).

[142] *Second Life* ToS part 9, or part XVII *WoW* EU ToS, or part 12 US. See Erlank (n 1) 102.

[143] Erlank (n 1) 112.

[144] M Korolov, 'Outrage grows over new Second Life terms' *Hypergrid Business* (30 September 2013) <http://www.hypergridbusiness.com/2013/09/outrage-grows-over-new-second-life-terms/> last accessed 1 August 2021; 'SecondLife® Content Creators Survey on Linden Lab TOS issue' <http://toytalks.weebly.com/1/archives/09-2013/1.html> last accessed 1 August 2021.

The case of *Bragg* v *Linden Research, Inc.*[145] was introduced in the above section 'Bragg Case: Property and Jurisdiction in VWs'. As noted there, the court confirmed that Linden's terms of service were unconscionable in relation to the mandatory arbitration clause and knocked the clause down. Importantly, the court said that the terms left the plaintiff with no effective remedy.[146]

More recently, in *Evans et al.* v *Linden Research, Inc et al.*, once again, there was no decision regarding virtual property. The case was settled, and even its relevance to the validity of the EULA is limited.

Even the 'liberal' VWs and games seem to be replicating these EULAs. An example of this is Steam, an entertainment platform distributing different games, including VWs. This very successful platform is considered user-friendly, open-source to an extent, and an alternative to the traditional business models.[147] Valve, the owner of Steam, created a very restrictive EULA (subscriber agreement), very much resembling those of other VWs. Therefore, apart from IP rights,[148] players' ownership over their creations and virtual money contained in their wallets[149] is limited and non-transferable, with an extended licence taken by the provider, Valve Corporation.[150] Valve has been criticised for banning a user who, contrary to the EULA, attempted to sell his Steam account.[151]

Following the above analysis, it could be argued, as many authors do, that the contracts are *prima facie* unfair.[152] The reasonable remedy would be challenging their unfair or unconscionable provisions in courts using consumer protection law.[153] One could argue that consumer protection law might be helpful to resolve these issues. At the level of the EU, Directive 2011/83/EU

[145] 487 F.Supp.2d 593, 612 (ED Pa 2007).

[146] Hetcher (n 26) 829, 836.

[147] 'The platform's record was from May 2021, peaking at 26.85 million concurrent users. Steam had approximately 120 million monthly active players in 2020.' See Statista, 'Number of peak concurrent Steam users 2013–2021' <https://www.statista.com/statistics/308330/number-stream-users/#:~:text=Steam%20had%20approximately%20120%20million,monthly%20active%20users%20in%202019> last accessed 1 August 2021.

[148] Steam, 'Subscriber agreement' s 6 <http://store.steampowered.com/subscriber_agreement/> last accessed 1 August 2021.

[149] Ibid. part C.

[150] Ibid. s 6 A.

[151] A Webster, 'Steam user violates subscriber agreement, loses $1,800 in games' *Ars Technica* (2011) <http://arstechnica.com/gaming/2011/03/steam-user-violates-subscriber-agreement-loses-1800-in-games/> last accessed 1 August 2021.

[152] Jankowich, 'Complex web of corporate rule-making' (n 8) 50.

[153] Riley (n 8) 907.

of the European Parliament and of the Council of 25 October 2011 on consumer rights would apply.[154] This Directive, implemented in the UK in the form of the Consumer Contracts (Information, Cancellation and Additional Charges) Regulations 2013 SI No 3134 and the Consumer Rights Act 2015, encompasses contracts regarding digital content, including games (see Recital 19 of the Directive).[155] According to the Act, terms that would potentially be deemed invalid are, for example, those limiting the developer's liability, reserving the right to terminate or modify terms discretionary and without notice, and arbitration clauses.[156]

Both the UK and EU legislation, however, apply to issues such as information to consumers, rights of withdrawal, liability, delivery and passing of risk, but do not address the issues of property rights, as subject matter cannot be considered unfair, and this is out of the scope of this legislation.[157] This law could apply to the parts of the contracts regulating the licence sale for using software (the first layer of VWs). However, the second and third layers are players' creations and would not fall within the definition of goods and services found in the consumer protection laws (as they are not goods or services sold by the developers). Similar, though much more limited protection can be found in California, mandated through the Consumers Legal Remedies Act (2006), including the prohibition of inclusion of previously discussed unconscionable provisions in the contract.[158]

So far, VW contracts have not been challenged much in the US and UK courts. In the UK, there is no such case at the time of writing. Most case law regarding online games has considered IP aspects of the game features, disputes between the developers, but rarely those between users and service

[154] OJ L 304, 22/11/2011 0064–0088. This Directive replaces, as of 13 June 2014, Directive 97/7/EC on the protection of consumers in respect of distance contracts OJ L 144/19 and Directive 85/577/EEC to protect consumers in respect of contracts negotiated away from business premises OJ L 372/31.

[155] Part 2 of the Act replaces the Unfair Terms in Consumer Contracts Regulations 1999. The Consumer Rights Act 2015, c 5 implements Directive 2011/83/EU of the European Parliament and of the Council of 25 October 2011 on consumer rights, amending Council Directive 93/13/EEC and Directive 1999/44/EC of the European Parliament and of the Council and repealing Council Directive 85/577/EEC and Directive 97/7/EC of the European Parliament and of the Council OJ L 304/64, 22/11/2011.

[156] Schedule 2 of the Act lists non-exhaustively terms that might be regarded as unfair.

[157] See the Consumer Rights Act 2015, s 64. See also Recital 51 of Directive 2011/83/EU of the European Parliament and of the Council of 25 October 2011 on consumer rights. Also, the EU does not interfere with property rights of member states. See Article 345 of the Treaty on the Functioning of the European Union (Consolidated version 2012) OJ C 326, 26/10/2012.

[158] California Civil Code §§ 1750 *et seq.*

providers when it comes to property. The US case law is more developed, and the Bragg and Evans courts found specific contract provisions unfair (jurisdiction, account suspension). Nevertheless, the courts' deliberations on property rights have been entirely accidental in discussing the main legal issues. Therefore, we should not rely on court cases to come in and resolve the issue of virtual property any time soon. Even if more cases were to appear, the outcome in the US might not be beneficial for players.[159]

To conclude, VW contracts, at the moment, deny players' virtual property rights in their creations and VW items. However, the courts have occasionally attempted to address the balance via doctrines of unfairness in contracts, which could be a potential solution. In principle, the question of creating and/or recognising proprietary rights and interests in VWs is not an issue that contracts can regulate but one of the general laws of property or IP. In addition, an attempt to apply consumer protection law to VWs' EULAs and allocation of property therein is contrary to the views of many authors mentioned in the subsequent section, namely, that VWs are not just games and their players are not just users but active participants, citizens, residents of the world. I too have argued this: I have analysed the constitutionalisation of VWs extensively in my earlier work and argued that VWs players possess characteristics of citizens of these worlds, and their statutes should be reconsidered accordingly.[160]

I have also argued that the present form of regulation, by contracts and code, is inadequate for protecting users' interests, especially their interest in autonomy. Relationships between players and providers often have arbitrary and *ad hoc* outcomes.[161] While this balance of power may promote commercial certainty and predictability for developers and significantly lower costs for users, the status quo is still unsatisfactory. The quasi-constitutional relationships are unfair and unsuitable, and there is a need for more accountability of service providers to their users. Recognising the features of VWs,

[159] See Gilbert (n 6) 242. Generally, see S Randall, 'Judicial attitudes toward arbitration and the resurgence of unconscionability' (2004) 52 *Buffalo Law Review* 185. On the unconscionability and Californian law, see Quinn (n 8). See also Chein (n 7).

[160] Harbinja, 'Virtual worlds – a legal post-mortem account' (n 12).

[161] Jankowich, 'Complex web of corporate rule-making' (n 8); Lastowka (n 17); Erlank (n 1); Fairfield, 'Virtual property' (n 7); Castronova, 'On virtual economies' (n 5); Castronova, 'Real products in imaginary worlds' (n 5); Castronova, 'The right to play' (n 5); Castronova, 'Virtual world economy' (n 5). I have followed their approach in Harbinja, 'Virtual worlds players – consumers or citizens?' (n 12).

their distinct character and place-like qualities, it is necessary to provide for a better legal and regulatory regime to protect their citizens.[162]

Such a system would recognise a service provider's interest and property or IP in the system and the software, but it would also consider the user's autonomy and choice over what happens to their VAs on death. The solution suggested in the section below is based on concepts drawn from private law, not public law, but it does consider the features of VWs (immersion, place-like features) and recognises the *constitutional* nature of VWs.[163]

5.6 Alternatives: Property Rights in the Property of Another

The analysis has so far been normative and theoretical with reference to the law. In the subsequent sections, however, the analysis will become more doctrinal to reflect legally on the specific nature of VWs. For the reasons identified when discussing virtual property above, it is argued here that full ownership of VP is not an adequate solution as it would be prejudicial to the interests of either the players or the developer of the VW. We therefore need more nuanced solutions that would serve as a compromise between these interests.

Some proposals have already experimented with property interests other than full ownership. These come in the form of limited real rights, derived from and subordinate to another person's full ownership. In civil law systems, these rights are known as servitudes: real (falling on immovable property) or personal (attached to a person, allowing them to enjoy the property of another).[164] In common law, these time-limited rights are usually only attached to immovables (real property) and are represented by notions such as easements, lease or life estate.[165] It is argued that such rights can serve usefully as models to consider the fact that the interests and rights of players are based on someone else's property (referred to above as the 'first layer', the developer's code and servers). Since VWs operate globally, these proposals need to experiment with both civil and common law concepts, trying to identify commonalities and to strike the best balance for VW players. I do not suggest in my earlier work that these common and civil law concepts should or can be merged and borrowed in either of the real-world jurisdictions, notwithstanding the

[162] Lastowka (n 17); Castronova, 'On virtual economies' (n 5); Castronova, 'Real products in imaginary worlds' (n 5); Castronova, 'The right to play' (n 5); Castronova, 'Virtual world economy' (n 5).

[163] Harbinja, 'Virtual worlds players – consumers or citizens?' (n 12).

[164] Bell et al. (n 49) 289–90; E Steiner, *French Law: A Comparative Approach* (Oxford University Press 2010) 389–90.

[165] M Dixon, *Modern Land Law* (7th edn, Routledge 2010) 267–8, 313.

arguments for legal transplants and borrowing in general.[166] As explained above, the proposal is a reform proposal, limited to VWs as the separate, peculiar places we consider them to be.

(a) Suggested Models: Virtual Easement

Slaughter proposes an exciting model, analysing the benefits and drawbacks of introducing a property or contractual regime for VWs. He introduces the concept of 'virtual easement'. According to him, this servitude would feature transferability (from one user to another, in life and on death); longevity (for as long as the user invests time and/or money and the VW exists); liability (no property remedies); *in rem* nature (except for the liability rule, which is *in personam*); and *numerus clausus* (finite number of iterations).[167] This theory appears as rather original and a good compromise between the rights of users and those of service providers. However, the flexibility it offers could be perceived as a possible source of uncertainty for players since different service providers could choose different terms also to their detriment, which is usually not the case with servitudes in the real world, especially in civil law systems, where the certainty of property rights is considered as an ultimate aim.[168]

Similarly, the system of easements (the common law counterpart of the civil law servitudes) has been argued for by Lastowka in his later work.[169] He sees it as the best solution since both the players and the VW owners are interested in something that depends on essentially one tangible thing, namely servers owned by the providers. Therefore, to enable rights on top of this ownership interest, it is necessary to introduce lesser rights for the benefit of VW inhabitants.[170] He does not suggest what features this model could have. A similar solution was offered by Fairfield in his later work.[171] Under the model he proposes, the licence agreement would also recognise covenant-style interests or servitude of users.[172] The problem with easements, covenants and leaseholds would be that, by definition, these interests are related to land,

[166] Harbinja, 'Virtual worlds – a legal post-mortem account' (n 12).

[167] Slaughter (n 7).

[168] This principle permeates legal writings referring to civilian systems, and their mandatory rules for property and rigidity, as van Erp notes: 'As a result, property law became a rather petrified legal area, rooted in a desire for legal certainty.' See S van Erp, 'Comparative property law' in M Reimann and R Zimmermann (eds), *The Oxford Handbook of Comparative Law* (Oxford University Press 2006) 1044.

[169] Lastowka (n 17) 127.

[170] Ibid.

[171] Fairfield, 'Anti-social contracts' (n 8).

[172] Ibid. 451–7.

immovable property.[173] In that case, we would have to use a somewhat weak analogy between land and developers' server systems.

(b) Suggested Models: Intangible Usufruct

Veloso introduces the concept of 'intangible usufruct'. He asserts that this is a good solution for the practical reason that it avoids one-sided arguments and aims to provide a way out of unfair contracts, while still respecting developers' interests.[174] He proposes three rules to govern the relations established by usufruct. First, that the developer should be considered the owner, under contract, and should provide for the right to use and the right to the fruits for the user; these rights are alienable and, when bundled together, should form a virtual property right.[175] Second, the developer may undertake any works and improvements or diminution on virtual property and/or the VW, but provided that such acts are not exercised arbitrarily, should they cause a diminution in the value of the usufruct or prejudice the right of the user.[176] Third, if the VW is terminated, the players are considered to have returned their virtual property to the developer thereby absolving the developer from any complaint that might arise. This approach appears reasonable, and the solution in this chapter will build upon this proposal, developing it in more detail, especially concerning the transmissibility and considering the different conceptions of servitudes (usufruct) between legal systems. I introduced the proposal in my earlier work, albeit tentatively and in less detail than in this book.[177]

(c) Proposal: VWs Usufruct

This chapter puts forward a reform proposal designed to balance the interests of the creators of VWs and the players or users in these worlds. Though not conceptually aligned with civilian usufruct and common law life estate (for reasons discussed in detail below), this model is inspired by it.[178]

As noted above, Veloso, Slaughter, Lastowka and I, in my previous work, suggest solutions in this domain modelled on civilian usufruct and common

173 See for example C van der Merwe and AL Verbeke (eds), *Time Limited Interests in Land* (Cambridge University Press 2012); Restatement (Third) of Property (Servitudes) (2000) §§ 4.6, 1.1 and 1.2.

174 Veloso (n 7).

175 Ibid. 73.

176 Ibid. 74.

177 Harbinja, 'Virtual worlds – a legal post-mortem account' (n 12).

178 Ibid.

law easement. Therefore, it is essential to review the implications of the models based on usufruct before introducing the new reform proposal.

Usufruct

Usufruct is a civil law concept that originates from Roman law, and it essentially entitles a person to the rights of use and fruits of another person's property. Under Roman law, the usufructuary had the right to use and enjoy the property and its fruits while preserving the substance of the property (i.e. the elements of *usus* – use, and *fructus* – fruits of one's property, but lacking *abusus* – alienation and transmission).[179] The common law concept of life estate has similar effects in relation to rights conferred to a life-tenant, particularly regarding the enjoyment of fruits.[180] In Scots law, a mixed legal system, a similar role is played by liferent. Usufruct does not have to pertain to immovable property; it can be created over movable and immovable property, although it is more commonly attached to the land.[181] The property owner retains nude ownership, that is, ownership burdened with a real right of enjoyment and use. The French and Belgian Civil Codes (FCC and BCC) employ a similar description, namely *usufruit* and *vruchtgebruik* respectively (FCC/BCC, Article 578).[182] In German law, the property may be similarly burdened with a *Niessbrauch* (BGB, §1030).

Usufruct is a real right, a right to the property itself and not merely a right against a person (the owner).[183] However, a key feature of usufruct is that it terminates on the death of the usufructuary (if not earlier).[184] This obvious temporal limitation does not prevent the right of usufruct from being alienated but only limits the time frame of the transferred usufruct to the life of

[179] Gaius, 2.30; D.7.1.1; D.6.1.33; D.7.1.72; D.7.4.2; D.23.37.8.3.S in P Scott (ed.), *Civil Law, Including The Twelve Tables, The Institutes of Gaius, The Rules of Ulpian, The Opinions of Paulus, The Enactments of Justinian, and The Constitutions of Leo* (Central Trust 1932) 286 <http://www.constitution.org/sps/sps.htm> last accessed 1 August 2021.

[180] J McClean, 'The common law life estate and the civil law usufruct: A comparative study' (1963) 12(2) *International & Comparative Law Quarterly* 649, 658.

[181] Ibid.

[182] The description in Old Dutch Civil Code, art. 803 (in force until 1992) was derived from Civil Code, art. 578. AL Verbeke, B Verdickt and DJ Maasland, 'The many faces of usufruct' in van der Merwe and Verbeke (n 173) 33–57, 37, citing C Asser, FHJ Mijnssen, AA van Velten and SE Bartels, *Mr. C. Asser's Handleiding tot de beoefening van het Nederlands burgerlijk recht 5, Zakenrecht, Eigendom en beperkte rechten* (5th edn, Kluwer 2008).

[183] Zenati-Castaing and Revet, *Les Biens*, 494 and de Page, *Traité élémentaire*, 153, cited in Verbeke et al. (n 182) 36.

[184] Cass. 3 July 1879; Pas. 1879 I 342; Borkowski and Du Plessis, *Roman Law*, 172; Baudry-Lacantinerie, *Précis de droit civil*, 770; de Page, *Traité élémentaire*, 258; Prutting, *Sachenrecht*, 364; Verbeke, 'Quasi-vruchtgebruik', 37, all cited in Verbeke and Maasland (n 182) 36.

the original usufructuary (FCC, Article 617). In principle, usufruct expires upon the death of the person on whose life the right was based, irrespective of any contracted term.[185] It is not possible to constitute a usufruct that is permanent or unlimited in time.[186] However, historically and nowadays, any fruits which the usufructuary has already gathered before death would pass to their heirs.[187] McClean finds that the common law concept of life estate and Scots law liferent have a similar effect to usufruct and confer almost the same rights.[188]

There are some problems with applying a solution based on the usufruct concept to VWs. Importantly, as noted above, usufruct in principle ends on the death of the usufructuary. Hence, nothing would persist in being transmitted to heirs on that person's death. Although some recent legal reforms in civil law countries such as the Netherlands demonstrate that there can be modifications to the usual rules of usufruct in the interests of policy,[189] no such reforms have affected the fundamental idea that the usufruct interest terminates on the death of the usufructuary.

A second problem relates to applying a solution based on usufruct to common law or other legal systems. Similar concepts (easements, leasehold or life estate in England) only apply to immovable property (or 'real property' in English law) and have very different legal nature and effects (regarding duration, use, transfer, etc.). It is not clear whether life estate in common law (the concept resembling usufruct most) applies to movables or relates only to land and immovable property.[190] As noted above, McClean argues that there is no actual difference in substance between usufruct and life estate and that in a mixed legal system, such as Scottish liferent, the right to use another's property (the fee) for life can extend to movables.[191] Notwithstanding these

[185] Verbeke et al. (n 182) 36n27.

[186] Ibid. 37n15. The temporal aspect also applies to the common law life interest. See McClean (n 180) 655; FH Lawson and B Rudden, *The Law of Property* (Oxford University Press 2002) 97.

[187] A Watson, *The Digest of Justinian, Volume 1* (University of Pennsylvania Press 1998) 242–3; W A Hunter, *A Systematic and Historical Exposition of Roman Law in the Order of a Code* (Sweet & Maxwell 1803) 388–9; Code civil, Articles 582–99.

[188] McClean (n 180).

[189] The Dutch Civil Code in Article 3:212, § 1 stipulates that if usufructuary assets are destined to be alienated, the usufructuary is entitled to alienate the assets in accordance with their intended purpose. See Verbeke et al. (n 182) 51–2.

[190] Ibid.

[191] GL Gretton and AJM Steven, *Property, Trusts and Succession* (2nd edn, Bloomsbury Professional 2013) 323; WJ Dobie, *Manual of the Law of Liferent and Fee in Scotland* (W. Green & Son 1941) 1–2.

differences between legal systems, the global uptake of VWs by players from many different jurisdictions means a solution based purely or mostly on one of these usufructuary or similar institutions may not scope well to VWs.

While usufruct has been an exciting inspiration in its original and pure form, it cannot be the foundation of a successful, multi-jurisdiction solution for providing rights to players to bequeath the value of their second layer VAs to their heirs. I have justified the need for such a solution earlier in this chapter and in my previous research, discussing constitutionalisation, the pervasive and immersive nature of the VWs environment, and time and labour players employ in VWs.

VWs Usufruct

The new model I suggest is 'VWs usufruct', an entirely new right, which could be introduced by domestic statutes or model law as in the US. VWs usufruct is a personal right of a player against a VW provider in second layer assets. The player has the right to use and transfer their second layer asset while playing the game. In addition, the player has a right to compensation in the form of monetary value for assets they have earned, acquired or purchased in the game, and such compensation belongs solely to their account and applies to their second layer assets.

With limitations explained in this section, the VWs usufruct transmits to heirs on death, which differs from the model suggested in my earlier work. Users who 'own' or create virtual assets acquire only contractual rights against the VW's owner through its ToS. Such personal contracts will be discharged on death unless there is an opposite provision in the contract.[192] As contracts rather routinely expressly exclude survivability, the transmission of virtual assets on death is impossible under the current VWs' ToS.

The right to transmit the VW's usufruct will only apply to the monetised value of assets that can be transferred. This differs from the only detailed post-mortem related proposal in VWs scholarship, introduced by Troung.[193]

[192] Principle '*Actio personalis moritur cum persona*' in *Beker* v *Bolton* (1808) 1 Camp 439; 170 ER 1033, revised by the Law Reform (Miscellaneous Provisions) Act 1934, c 41 (as amended), revised the rule mandating that all personal rights will survive against and for the benefit of the estate, with the only exception of defamation and claim for bereavement. For a commentary about the contracts and succession, see AR Mellows, *The Law of Succession* (4th edn, Butterworths 1983) 295–6; B Nicholas, *The French Law of Contract* (2nd edn, Clarendon Press; Oxford University Press 1992) 29–30; ML Levillard, 'France' in DJ Hayton (ed.), *European Succession Laws* (2nd edn, Jordans 2002) 219. For Germany, see K Kuhne et al., 'Germany' in Nicholas, *French Law of Contract* 244–57.

[193] OY Truong, 'Virtual inheritance: Assigning more virtual property rights' (2009) 21(3) *Syracuse Science and Technology Law Reporter* 57, 57–86.

She proposes that the courts honour players' wishes to bequeath the value of their virtual assets and, if the players fail to do so, and the VW contract has a non-survivorship policy, then it will operate to bar claims by heirs.[194] Troung suggests that players should be able to transfer the non-monetary value of their virtual property to their immediate family members,[195] but they would only be able to transfer the whole account, not an individual item or monetary value, due to the conflicting interests of the VW provider. This solution is quite contradictory, as it argues for the transfer of virtual assets alone, not their monetary value, to abide by the contract and avoid conflict with the VW owner. However, at the same time, it violates universal contractual provisions' non-transferability of the entire account.

By contrast, the VWs usufruct is designed to minimise disruption to the VW ecology and conflict with the VW owner's wishes while recognising the VW player's earned right to transmit assets they have worked for in-game (see further below). First, the right will only be transmissible as a monetary claim if VA exchanges are legal on recognised auction sites. If no such auction sites exist or ToS do not permit them, then monetisation is impossible, and so is the right to compensation. Thus, the VW owner is not faced with an unwarranted financial burden as they will be compensated at a market rate for the virtual assets the owner created and thus not have to reach into their own pockets. The VW owner will have received during life either subscriptions or revenue via other means (e.g. adverts), so allowing the VW to retain monetisable VAs after a player's death could be seen as an unfair windfall.

Second, unlike Troung's proposal, the VW user's right respects typical VW contractual provisions forbidding the transfer of accounts, as family members do not get access to the deceased's account and cannot play the game instead of the deceased player. This minimises disruption to the game and its rules and loss of new revenue from new players. In order to further minimise this disruption, the monetary compensation described above would ideally need to be claimed within a particular time, for example six months or a year maximum. Possibly the right might also only be claimed by family members, as Troung suggests as well, to minimise disruption and burden to the VW further, although there seems no prevailing reason to make an exception to standard rules of freedom of testation (as defined in each legal system) for VAs. All the other assets would return to the VW, and to the players who are immersed in the VW and interested in making further use of these assets.

[194] Ibid. 80.
[195] Ibid.

This solution is a law reform proposal, and it would need to be enacted by relevant legislation in the individual jurisdictions, notwithstanding the practical difficulties of such a reform (e.g. in the US, provisions from the Fiduciary Access to Digital Assets Act to be enacted by the state laws; relevant legislation in the UK and other European countries). Consequently, it would entail changes in EULAs.[196]

Advantages of VWs Usufruct

The first advantage of the VWs usufruct is that this model provides an acceptable compromise between the rights of the VW owner and those of the player. Practically, this is done in two ways: 1) recognising the respective contribution both of the capital to build the VW provided by the VW owner, as well as the money providers spend on maintenance and promotion of the world; and the labour as well as subscriptions and other monies provided by the players (e.g. money provided to purchase in-game assets); and 2) recognising the particular stake players have in ownership in VAs, even on death, which was explained above as relating to the constitutionalisation of VWs and the immersive environment in which players operate in-game.

The second significant advantage of this model is that it does not allow the heirs of a player to interfere with the operation of the VW after the player's death unless they pay to re-enter the game as new players with new accounts.

Third, the model does not interfere with standard provisions of VW contracts or EULAs forbidding the transfer of assets, accounts or passwords, except within recognised auction sites.

Fourth, this model does not provide for a general financial claim against the VW (either during the player's life or on death), which could be unduly burdensome if the VAs of the deceased could not be monetised.

Disadvantages of VWs Usufruct

First, the right suggested in principle operates only post-mortem. It does not require VWs to offer monetisation when a player leaves during life. Doing so might be seen as risky as potentially financially burdensome to existing VWs, thus discouraging growth and capital investment in future VWs. A compromise solution might be to apply the right during a lifetime to cases where the game is unjustifiably closed or destructively modified. This would not extend to justified improvements and developments of the VW, nor to bankruptcy

[196] It is worth noting, however, that it would be a matter for national legal systems to decide if the VW user's right could be excluded by contract. If this were allowed, it is likely the right would have little effect.

or similar where the VW owner had no choice but to close and assets are in any case likely to be seized by preferred creditors.

Second, the right might produce minimal and somewhat arbitrary benefits for players since many asset auction sites are illegal as they are unauthorised by the EULAs of the VWs. The issue then arises of whether VWs could be compelled by law to set up an authorised VA auction site, thus creating an additional burden on the provider. If the solution applies to the current state of play, the compromise would be reasonable from the VW owner's point of view, as they could effectively exclude it by not having an authorised auction site (and indeed, at present, there are few). Where there are recognised auction sites, service providers are already aware of this and approve of such a practice, so they can reasonably be expected to endorse the VW user's right. By corollary, players would have a reasonable expectation to realise and transfer the monetary value of their second layer VAs where authorised auction sites exist, so that value is something they would expect to transmit to their heirs as well.

Third, effective enforcement of the right may be difficult mainly when heirs and/or personal representatives are unaware of the VW in question or the game's environment in general. However, these difficulties have been overcome in relation to emails, as generally envisaged by the US Uniform Law Commission in the Uniform Fiduciary Access to Digital Assets Act (UFADAA).[197]

Finally, as noted above, an issue could be potential contractual waivers if (as is likely) EULAs of VWs attempt to exclude the new VWs usufruct. Again, and as suggested in the RUFADAA, this can be overcome by prohibiting such provisions. While some practical aspects may need to be fine-tuned, the idea is presented here as one of the principles to produce a fairer balance of outcomes between players and VW developers.

It is worth noting that the solution differs from those suggested in other case studies in that there I do not suggest any default transmission of assets in the email and social network examples. As explained in the introductory part of this chapter, the main reason for this is that privacy is not as essential here since VAs do not typically embody or carry personally identifiable data. VW players typically disguise their identity under chosen pseudonyms or even assigned names, so assets they acquire, such as gold or virtual 'magic swords', do not reveal personal data. The monetised value of the assets, which

[197] National Conference of Commissioners on Uniform State Laws, Draft Fiduciary Access to Digital Assets Act, s 3 (July 2014) Drafting Committee Meeting <http://www.uniformlaws.org/shared/docs/Fiduciary%20Access%20to%20Digital%20Assets/2014am_ufadaa_draft.pdf> last accessed 1 August 2021.

will transfer, reveals still less about the deceased. Therefore, the interest in PMP asserted in this book does not prevent the suggested default but limited transmission of second layer assets.

Finally, it is worth noting that the solution here is in the form of a principle, without going into the technical details of succession law, economics or bankruptcy law. Instead, this chapter aims to provide guidance, based on the analysis of the previous literature on virtual property, taking into account the EULA provisions and special features of VWs. Chapter 7 will suggest general solutions applicable to all the case studies. It is also worth emphasising that the findings and proposal in this chapter do not apply to all types of video games, including downloaded games, games played 'locally', at the end user's side, or streamed games on Twitch. The reason is that these lack the essential features discussed herein, that is, physicality, constitutionalisation and citizenship. The model does, however, apply to any future games that resemble VWs and include a degree of virtuality, immersion, citizenship and other qualities discussed in this chapter.

6

Emails

6.1 Conceptualisation and a Brief History of Emails

'Electronic mail' (email) is an electronic system for exchanging messages over the Internet. The common usage of the term 'email' refers to individual electronic messages, and usually only to the textual content of the messages and their attachments.[1] This chapter will adopt this terminology and refer to email messages (hereinafter email) in terms of their content. Email accounts (hereinafter accounts) enable access to emails, and an analogy usually used here is that of letters. Along this line, accounts are some form of 'physical' representation of emails, enabling and regulating access to their content, just as paper is a physical representation of letters and their content, defining access to this content. This analogy will be used and evaluated in more detail later in this chapter.

The history of emails started in 1965 when Van Vleck of MIT invented 'the first popular computer-based electronic mail service as a posting/delivery construct with addressing'.[2] In the subsequent twenty years, many other system components (e.g. transfer protocol, content or user feature) were developed to create the system as it is nowadays. The technical features of the system are as follows: flexible form (plain text, right format, attachments, pictures, videos); asynchronous character (people send and receive messages on their own time); broadcast (the ability to send messages to many

[1] See D Hansen, B Shneiderman and M Smith, *Analyzing Social Media Networks with NodeXL: Insights from a Connected World* (Morgan Kaufmann 2010) 106; J Shen et al., 'A comparison study of user behavior on Facebook and Gmail' (2013) 29 *Computers in Human Behavior* 2650, 2650–5.

[2] See EmailHistory.org, 'Email milestones timeline', ed. dcrocker (6 September 2012) <http://emailhistory.org/Email-Timeline.html> last accessed 1 August 2021; T Van Vleck, 'The history of electronic mail' (1 February 2010) <http://www.multicians.org/thvv/mail-history.html> last accessed 1 August 2021.

people simultaneously); push technology (the sender decides on the content and timing of a message); and threaded conversations.[3]

Email still represents the core of all online communications, along with social networking. Usage of emails is relatively evenly spread across different age groups, making it the most used activity online in the UK and US.[4] Today, communication is almost impossible to imagine without this quick, relatively reliable and convenient system used for various purposes, such as communication, task and contacts management, and sharing of documents, pictures, videos and other content as attachments, both for personal and business purposes.[5] One could argue that social media and instant messaging will gradually supplant emails in online communications. However, research has found that similarly to emails complementing telephone and face-to-face communication, the use of social networks has complemented the use of emails so far,[6] without resulting in a significant decrease in their use.

The consumer market is dominated by the email providers Google (Gmail), Microsoft (Outlook.com) and Yahoo! (Mail).[7] For this reason, these providers' terms will be the focus of the analysis in subsequent sections.

Notwithstanding the importance and the value of emails, the focus of this chapter will be on one particular aspect of emails, that is, whether an email is an asset capable of post-mortem transmission. Therefore, the analysis will mainly look at the nature of what might be most valuable for users: the content of emails and users' accounts. The chapter will not discuss communications and metadata ('data about data'[8]) or the email system and technical

3 Hansen et al. (n 1) 106–7.

4 For the US, see Statista, 'Popular digital activities among Internet users in the United States 2019' <https://www.statista.com/statistics/184559/typical-daily-online-activities-of-adult-internet-users-in-the-us/> last accessed 1 August 2021. For the UK, see Office for National Statistics, 'Internet access – households and individuals, 2020' (8 August 2020) <https://www.ons.gov.uk/peoplepopulationandcommunity/householdcharacteristics/homeinternetandsocialmediausage/datasets/internetaccesshouseholdsandindividualsreferencetables> last accessed 1 August 2021. Email is still the most popular activity online in general.

5 For more, see Hansen et al. (n 1) 105–25.

6 See Shen et al. (n 1) 2653; R Kraut et al., 'Internet paradox revisited' (2002) 58(1) *Journal of Social Issues* 49; B Wellman et al., 'Does the Internet increase, decrease, or supplement social capital? Social networks, participation, and community commitment' (2001) 45(3) *American Behavioral Scientist*436.

7 N Gilbert, 'Number of email users worldwide 2021/2022: Demographics & predictions' *FinancesOnline* <https://financesonline.com/number-of-email-users/> last accessed 1 August 2021.

8 See for example L Greenberg, 'Metadata and the world wide web' (2003) *Encyclopedia of Library and Information Science* 1876.

aspects. Instead, it will aim to question the legal nature of emails, represented by their content.

The analysis will focus on copyright (users' rights to control the original content of emails they create), property in information (whether users generally own information contained in their emails) and personal data (whether users control or own data relating to them as an identified or identifiable person).[9]

In addition to the first and essential question of the legal nature of emails, further problems around the transmission of emails on death identified in this chapter are the following: access to a user's account (regulated by service provider contracts, ToS); PMP (protection of the deceased's privacy); criminal legislation (laws on unauthorised access to computer systems); potential conflicts between wills, intestate succession laws and technological solutions to the transmission of emails (e.g. Google Inactive Account Manager); and jurisdiction and conflicts between the interests of the deceased, their family and friends. Most of these problems will be looked at in the respective sections below. However, the focus will be on the legal nature of emails, access and the conflicts between wills, succession laws and technology. The jurisdiction and criminal law issues will be mentioned only briefly to enable an in-depth analysis of the other issues, and because the focus of this book is mainly on civil law issues so criminal and conflicts of law issues are acknowledged but not dealt with in depth.

Therefore, the chapter will determine whether emails can be considered property or IP or if some other form of protection is better suited to them. The analysis will expand the findings in my earlier work.[10] Further, after exploring these issues, the analysis will touch upon the current allocation of ownership in emails by contracts and the issues surrounding potential post-mortem transmission. Eventually, the aim is to propose a solution for post-mortem transmission, notwithstanding legal issues and potential technological solutions.

6.2 Illustrations Through Case Law

In order to bring the problems around post-mortem transmission of emails closer to the reader and following the methodology established in the previous chapter, this section will first present the limited case law. The case law originates from the US and does not solve the issues identified in this chapter. Instead, these cases drew media and social attention to the issues of

[9] See the definition provided by the Article 4(1) of the General Data Protection Regulation.

[10] E Harbinja, 'Emails and death: Legal issues surrounding post-mortem transmission of emails' (2019) 43(7) *Death Studies* 435.

post-mortem transmission of digital assets generally, initiating further discussions in academic circles and some regulatory attempts (again, in the US).

US and European media widely reported the US case *In re Ellsworth*.[11] We have mentioned this case briefly in previous chapters, but as it concerns email primarily, we will present it here. In this case Yahoo!, as an email provider, initially refused to give the family of a US Marine, Justin Ellsworth, killed in action in Iraq, access to his account. It referred to its ToS, which, according to Yahoo!, were designed to protect the user's privacy by forbidding access to third parties on death.[12] Yahoo! also argued that the US Electronic Communications Privacy Act of 1986 prohibits it from disclosing users' personal communications without a court order.[13] The family claimed that as his heirs, they should have access to his emails and the entire account, his sent and received emails, as his last words. Yahoo!, on the other hand, had a non-survivorship policy, and there was a danger that Ellsworth's account could have been deleted. The judge in this case, however, allowed Yahoo! to enforce its privacy policy and did not order the transfer of the account login and password. Instead, he made an order requiring Yahoo! to enable access to the deceased's account by providing the family with a CD containing copies of the emails in the account.[14] As reported by the media, Yahoo! initially provided only the emails received by Justin Ellsworth on a CD, and after the family complained again, it allegedly subsequently provided paper copies of the sent emails.[15] This case clearly illustrates most of the issues in the post-mortem transmission of emails mentioned in the previous section (i.e. PMP, access, conflict of interests of the deceased and their family).

[11] *In re Ellsworth*, No 2005-296, 651-DE (Mich Prob Ct 2005). See for example BBC News, 'Who owns your e-mails?' (11 January 2005) <http://news.bbc.co.uk/1/hi/magazine/4164669.stm> last accessed 1 August 2021; P Sancya, 'Yahoo will give family slain Marine's e-mail account' *USA Today* (21 April 2005) <http://usatoday30.usatoday.com/tech/news/2005-04-21-marine-e-mail_x.htm?POE=TECISVA> last accessed 1 August 2021. See the discussion in T Baldas, 'Slain soldier's e-mail spurs legal debate: Ownership of deceased's messages at crux of issue' (2005) 27 *National Law Journal* 10, 10.

[12] Yahoo!, 'Terms of service' <http://info.yahoo.com/legal/uk/yahoo/utos-173.html> last accessed 1 August 2021.

[13] See A Kulesza, 'What happens to your Facebook account when you die?' *Blog* (3 February 2012) <http://blogs.lawyers.com/2012/02/what-happens-to-facebook-account-when-you-die/> last accessed 1 August 2021; Electronic Communications Privacy Act, 18 USC §§ 2510 *et seq*.

[14] See Associated Press release, *justinellsworth.net* (21 April 2005) <http://www.justinellsworth.net/email/ap-apr05.htm> last accessed 1 August 2021.

[15] See BBC News (n 11); Sancya (n 11).

Edwards and Harbinja provide a few possible interpretations of the case.[16] One interpretation is that Yahoo! owned the copies of the emails stored on its servers but was required by the court order to make the information in them available. For this option, justification can be found in the traditional division of rights in letters, where Yahoo! would own the emails (as a physical representation), but the deceased, as an author, owned the copyright, transferred subsequently to their heirs. The heir would have the rights of copyright holders. The second interpretation is to regard the deceased as the owner of the emails while alive, which then could be transmitted to the heirs of the deceased on death.[17] Edwards and Harbinja regard this option as less likely, as the court would then have considered the rights of the heirs as overriding the terms and conditions entered into by the deceased, ordering full access to the account. This did not happen, however, and the court only ordered the provision of the emails' content. It can be concluded that the court found Yahoo!'s ownership of the account and the heirs' right to access the content of emails. Therefore, the case left many questions open and provided little guidance and no principles that could be applied subsequently (concerning property, IP and privacy).[18]

A subsequent is case *Marianne Ajemian, Co-administrator & Another v Yahoo!, Inc.*[19] In this instance, the plaintiffs, co-administrators of their brother John Ajemian's estate, brought the action in the Probate and Family Court in Massachusetts, requesting, *inter alia*, a declaration that emails John had sent and received using a Yahoo! account were property of his estate. A probate judge dismissed the complaint, concluding that a forum selection clause required that suit be brought in California. The Appeals Court of Massachusetts reversed the first instance judgment, ordering further proceedings by the Probate Court, where the question of ownership of emails, amongst others, should be decided. Yahoo!, similarly to the Ellsworth case, contended that the Stored Communications Act[20] prohibited disclosure of the contents of the account to the administrators of Ajemian's estate. It remains to be seen whether the court will follow the Ellsworth case logic or be more

[16] L Edwards and E Harbinja, '"What happens to my Facebook profile when I die?": Legal issues around transmission of digital assets on death' in C Maciel and V Pereira (eds), *Digital Legacy and Interaction: Post-Mortem Issues* (Springer 2013) 115.

[17] See ibid. 121.

[18] See similarly J Darrow and G Ferrera, 'Who owns a decedent's e-mails: Inheritable probate assets or property of the network?' (2006) 10 *New York University Journal of Legislation and Public Policy* 281, 308; J Atwater, 'Who owns email? Do you have the right to decide the disposition of your private digital life?' (2006) *Utah Law Review* 397, 399.

[19] 2013 WL 1866907 (Mass App Ct 2013), No 12-P-178.

[20] 18 USC §§ 2701 *et seq.*

explicit and conclude that there are property rights in emails and whether they form a part of the account holder's estate.

There are currently no similar cases in the UK that would provide some guidance or even initiate discussions on the post-mortem issues. However, some more general guidance in relation to the legal nature of emails can be found in a recent English case that tackles the issue of property in emails. In *Fairstar Heavy Transport NV* v *Adkins*[21] Justice Edwards-Stuart concluded that emails could not be considered property. The case concerned a commercial dispute between Mr Adkins, the company's ex-employee, and the company's new owners. The dispute involved important emails sent to Mr Adkins, which had been forwarded to his private email address and deleted from the company server. The company claimed that the emails should be declared the property of the company. Referring to previous case law relating to the status of information as property in the context of letters,[22] Justice Edwards-Stuart identified a distinction between a physical medium and the information it carried, noting that only a physical object (paper) can be owned.[23] Justice Edwards-Stuart's analysis illustrates five different scenarios that would be the likely results if an email were considered capable of being property. The sensible conclusion the judge made was that, due to practical reasons, and the fact that the misuse of information contained in emails is otherwise protected (confidential information, contracts, copyright), 'There are no compelling practical reasons that support the existence of a proprietary right – indeed, practical considerations militate against it.'[24] Subsequently, the Court of Appeal recognised the difficulties that property in information encounters conceptually. The court wisely avoided this discussion and decided that the real issue in the case was that of agency. Therefore, the first instance decision provides some guidance and an indication that emails are not considered property in black-letter English law. At first glance, this makes it clear that we need to consider some other legal mechanisms to define the nature of emails, such as copyright, contracts and privacy. This chapter will discuss all these issues and provide a black-letter and normative analyses of property in information (i.e. email content).

21 [2012] EWHC 2952 (TCC). See the detailed analyses in Edwards and Harbinja (n 16).

22 See for example *Philip* v *Pennell* [1907] 2 Ch 577; *Boardman* v *Phipps* [1967] 2 AC 46; *Coogan* v *News Group Newspapers Ltd and Mulcaire* [2012] EWCA Civ 48; *Force India Formula One Team* v *1 Malaysian Racing Team* [2012] EWHC 616 (Ch).

23 *Fairstar Heavy Transport NV* v *Adkins* [2012] EWHC 2952 (TCC) para 58. See also Lord Upjohn in *Boardman* v *Phipps* [1967] 2 AC 46, 127, 275; Lord Walker of Gestingthorpe in *Douglas* v *Hello! Ltd* [2008] 1 AC 1; *Force India Formula One Team* v *1 Malaysian Racing Team* [2012] EWHC 616 (Ch).

24 *Fairstar Heavy Transport NV* v *Adkins* [2012] EWHC 2952 (TCC) para 69.

6.3 Legal Nature of Emails

In order to answer the main research question, whether emails are transmissible on death, the chapter will consider two alternative paradigms as to the nature of emails: 1) emails are protected by copyright as literary or artistic works; and 2) they are property. *Prima facie*, emails are perceived mainly as literary works created by their authors, the email senders. Therefore, copyright appears to be one of the most obvious answers when determining the legal nature of emails. The following section will thus discuss copyright in emails, concerning transmission on death. Subsequently, the analysis will embark on property issues in information and personal data (a type of email content not susceptible to copyright protection).[25]

(a) Copyright in Emails and Post-Mortem Transmission

Emails contain a lot of potentially or actually copyrighted materials that users share with different recipients. These works can be protected by copyright as literary or musical works.[26] Although the attachments potentially have enormous value for the users, both economically and emotionally, the focus of this chapter is not on the copyrightable or copyrighted works in the form of attachments that have already been published elsewhere. These works may include books (published or not), stories, videos, photographs and music, among others. The reason behind this decision is that, whereas some attachments may not be available anywhere else but only as emails (unpublished works), a majority of authored works will probably be available and published elsewhere (offline and online).[27] In addition, if they are available elsewhere offline and/or online, these works do not represent digital assets *stricto sensu*, as defined in the Introduction to this book. They will then represent the physical manifestation of a part of a digital asset. For instance, there is the possibility that emails can be printed or saved on the recipient's or sender's computer. Again, these materials are either a physical manifestation of digital assets or a fraction of an asset saved and stored in a digital form. For these materials, the transmission is clear, and there is no need to discuss it in this book (copyright lasts for seventy years after the author's death and transmits

[25] These findings develop my earlier work in Harbinja, 'Emails and death' (n 10).

[26] Copyright, Designs and Patents Act 1988, s 3; US Copyright Code 17 USC § 101.

[27] Published works encompass Internet publications as well. For definitions of publication, see for example UK Copyright, Designs and Patents Act 1988, c 48, s 175; US Copyright Code 17 USC § 101; Article 3 of the Berne Convention for the Protection of Literary and Artistic Works of 9 September 1886, revised at Paris 24 July 1971, 25 UST 1341, 828 UNTS 221. See also generally D McCallig, 'Private but eventually public: Why copyright in unpublished works matters in the digital age' (2013) 10:1 *SCRIPTed* 39, 43–4.

to their next of kin). The focus, therefore, will be on the unpublished content of emails, either in the form of an attachment or as text, and what happens to copyright in this work post-mortem. Therefore, an email as a digital asset will be looked at holistically, meaning as part of all of the emails included in a user's account. Also, photographs will not be discussed in depth here. This type of content is much more associated with social networks and therefore is analysed in Chapter 4.

Copyright in the EU, UK and the US subsists in unpublished works for a duration equal to copyright in published works, that is, seventy years after the author's death.[28] Historically, at some point, copyright protection of unpublished work was perpetual in the common law jurisdictions, the UK and US.[29] This has changed, and the duration has been harmonised at the EU level and with US law.[30] Additionally, a fundamental shift in the EU copyright law resulted in incentivising the publication of unpublished works. The Copyright Term Directive, and consequently UK law,[31] awarded twenty-five years of copyright protection for the first lawful publication of work previously unpublished after its copyright protection of seventy years had expired.[32]

Emails and attachments unpublished elsewhere and not existing in the physical form defined by the courts, therefore, could potentially qualify for copyright protection as literary works primarily.[33] Publishing to a limited number of people is not making the content available to the public, and therefore emails would not meet the requirement of publication in the UK

[28] Article 1 of Directive 2006/116/EC of the European Parliament and the Council of 12 December 2006 on the term of protection of copyright and certain related rights (codified version) [2006] OJ L372/12.

[29] In the UK, until the adoption of the Duration of Copyright and Rights in Performances Regulations 1995 SI No 3297; in the US until the 1976 Copyright Act, when unpublished works were brought under federal jurisdiction. See for example ET Gard, 'January 1, 2003: The birth of the unpublished public domain and its international consequences' (2006) 24 *Cardozo Arts & Entertainment Law Journal* 687, 697–702. On the other hand, Scots law, for instance, historically did not recognise copyright in unpublished works and interestingly, for letters in particular, the courts drew on the civilian *actio iniuriarum* and the common law idea of literary property to protect privacy in correspondence. See HL MacQueen, 'Ae fond kiss: A private matter?' in A Burrows, D Johnston and R Zimmermann (eds), *Judge and Jurist: Essays in Memory of Lord Rodger of Earlsferry* (Oxford University Press 2013).

[30] Council Directive 93/98/EEC of 29 October 1993 harmonizing the term of protection of copyright and certain related rights [1993] OJ L290/9; 1976 Copyright Act 17 USC § 302.

[31] Copyright and Related Rights Regulations 1996 SI No 2967 reg 16.

[32] Article 4 of Council Directive 93/98/EEC (n 30).

[33] Copyright, Designs and Patents Act 1988, s 3(1); US Copyright Code 17 USC § 101.

and US.[34] The content will have to meet the general copyright requirements of originality and fixation (recording in the UK).

Fixation or recording would not create a significant obstacle, as electronic fixation has been recognised as meeting the requirements.[35] US law mandates that work is fixed only 'when its embodiment in a copy . . . is sufficiently permanent or stable to permit it to be perceived, reproduced, or otherwise communicated for more than transitory duration'.[36] The focus of this definition is on the notion of 'a period of more than transitory duration'. The US courts have interpreted this in several cases, including *MAI Systems* v *Peak Computers*,[37] where the court confirmed that reproductions in random access memory (RAM) are copies fixed according to the Act. This finding is significant as RAM copies are not permanent and are present only while a computer is turned on.[38] In the UK, CDPA 1988 mandates that 'Copyright does not subsist in a literary, dramatic or musical work unless and until it is recorded, in writing or otherwise.'[39] Writing is further defined as 'any form of notation or code, whether by hand or otherwise and regardless of the method by which, or medium in or on which, it is recorded'.[40] The UK definition appears more straightforward than the US one, referring to any medium, therefore including digital recording. Accordingly, case law provides that 'an artistic work may be fixed in the source code of a computer program'.[41] Consequently, the fixation requirement is satisfied in the case of emails. Emails are stored 'more

[34] See the US case *Getaped.com, Inc* v *Cangemi*, 188 F.Supp.2d 398, 62 USPQ.2d (BNA) 1030 (SDNY 2002), where publication on the website, available to all, constituted publication for the purpose of US Copyright Code 17 USC § 101. This interpretation would arguably comply with the UK Copyright, Designs and Patents Act 1988, c 48, s 175.

[35] The Berne Convention (n 27) in Article 2 does not require fixation, but allows member states to use this requirement in their national law. The US and the UK both utilised this option. For the requirements set in the US, see the definition in Copyright Code 17 USC § 101. For the UK, see Copyright, Designs and Patents Act 1988, ss 3(2) and 178.

[36] US Copyright Code 17 USC § 101.

[37] 911 F.2d 511 (9th Cir 1993).

[38] Other cases following this line of argument are *Triad Systems* v *Southeastern Express Co*, 64 F.3d 1330 (9th Cir 1995); *Stenograph LLC* v *Bossard Associates, Inc*, 144 F.3d 96 (DC Cir 1998); *Advanced Computer Servs* v *MAI Systems*, 845 F.Supp.356 (ED Va 1994); *Intellectual Reserve, Inc* v *Utah Lighthouse Ministry, Inc*, 53 USPQ.2d 1425 (D Utah 1999); *Lowry's Reports, Inc* v *Legg Mason, Inc*, 271 F.Supp.2d 737 (D Md 2003); *Storage Technology Corp* v *Custom Hardware Engineering & Consulting, Inc*, 2004 US Dist LEXIS 12391 (D Mass 2004).

[39] Copyright, Designs and Patents Act 1988, s 3(2).

[40] Copyright, Designs and Patents Act 1988, s 178.

[41] *SAS Institute Inc* v *World Programming Ltd* [2013] RPC 17 para 29.

than transiently' on service providers' servers, 'in the cloud', and are more permanent than in RAM.

Originality would, arguably, create a more significant issue since many emails contain mere information, such as facts and personal data, and probably would not pass the threshold of originality developed by the UK and US courts (no matter how, admittedly, low the threshold is).[42] If we look at the cases involving copyright in letters, it is clear that business correspondence[43] or a solicitor's letter to a client[44] and personal letters[45] pass this threshold. This can mean that emails that consist of personal or professional correspondence and are of some length (even a few sentences) could satisfy the requirement of originality. A bigger problem would be, for instance, emails containing one sentence (e.g. 'I'll meet you at 9, OK'), data indicating time and place ('My address is: 256 Wonderland Lanes, Neverland, NL1 0PP'), or a single word ('Deal', 'Fine', 'Perfect'). Data protection laws clearly protect the address and other personal data examples. In the UK, single words are refused copyright protection (e.g. Exxon).[46] The courts, however, had different views in awarding copyright protection to titles and headlines. For instance, 'Splendid Misery', a book title, was denied copyright in *Dick* v *Yates*,[47] as was 'the Lawyer's Diary'

[42] For the US see *Burrow-Giles Lithographic Co* v *Sarony*, 111 US 53 (1884); *Feist Publications* v *Rural Telephone Service Company, Inc*, 499 US 340, 363 (1991). The most important UK cases are *Walter* v *Lane* [1900] AC 539; *Univ of London Press, Ltd* v *Univ Tutorial Press, Ltd* [1916] 2 Ch 601; *Interlego AG* v *Tyco Industries Inc* [1989] AC 217; *Express Newspapers Plc* v *News (UK) Ltd* [1990] FSR 359 (Ch D); *Newspaper Licensing Agency Ltd* v *Marks & Spencer plc* [2001] UKHL 38; [2002] RPC 4. See for example DJ Gervais, 'Feist goes global: A comparative analysis of the notion of originality in copyright law' (2002) 49 (4) *Journal of the Copyright Society of the U.S.A.* 949; P Samuelson, 'Originality standard for literary works under U.S. copyright law' (2001–2) 42 *American Journal of Comparative Law* Supplement 393; A Rahmatian, 'Originality in UK copyright law: The old "skill and labour" doctrine under pressure' (2013) 44(4) *International Review of Intellectual Property and Competition Law* 4; A Waisman, 'Revisiting originality' (2009) 31(7) *European Intellectual Property Review* 370–6.

[43] *Cembrit Blunn Ltd, Dansk Eternit Holding A/S* v *Apex Roofing Services LLP, Roy Alexander Leader* [2007] EWHC 111 (Ch). In *Tett Bros Ltd* v *Drake & Gorham Ltd* [1928–1935] MacG Cop Cas 492 (Ch, 1934), copyright in the following text (omitting 'Dear Sir' and 'Yours' etc.) was held to be infringed: 'Further to the writer's conversation with you of today's date, we shall be obliged if you will let us have full particulars and characteristics of "Chrystalite" or "Barex."'

[44] *Musical Fidelity Ltd* v *Vickers* [2002] EWCA Civ 1989; [2003] FSR 50.

[45] *Pope* v *Curl* (1741) 2 Atk 342; *Lord and Lady Perceval* v *Phipps* 2 V & B 19; *Macmillan & Co* v *Dent* [1907] 1 Ch 107.

[46] See the word 'Exxon' in *Exxon Corp* v *Exxon Insurance Consultants International Ltd* [1982] Ch 119.

[47] [1881] Ch 6.

in *Rose* v *Information Services Ltd.*[48] In other cases, however, headings were given the status of a literary work and were protected by copyright.[49] The European Court of Justice has subsequently provided some guidance on this issue in *Infopaq International A/S* v *Danske Dagblades Forening.*[50] The court opined that specific sentences or even parts of them could be copyrightable, depending on the originality of a respective sentence.[51] This decision has been followed by the English High Court and the Court of Appeal in *Newspaper Licensing Agency Ltd & Ors* v *Meltwater Holding BV & Ors.*[52] In the High Court, Proudman J applied the *Infopaq* test and concluded that 'headlines are capable of being literary works'.[53] The judge went even further, holding that 'it appears that a mere 11 word extract may now be sufficient in quantity provided it includes an expression of the intellectual creation of the author'.[54] The US Copyright Office, conversely, denies registration of copyright in names, titles and short phrases.[55]

It is interesting to look briefly at whether a string of emails would constitute a work of joint authorship. This has not been tested in courts, however, and as in the case of social networks, the conversation would lack an essential element of a high degree of integrity, so that the contributions of individual authors are 'inseparable or interdependent parts of a unitary whole'[56] or 'not distinct'.[57] Here, the contributions are easily distinguishable and separable, as they are all tagged by an author's name and can be edited or deleted at any time.[58]

48 [1978] FSR 254.

49 *Shetland Times Ltd* v *Wills* [1997] FSR 604. For more, see HL MacQueen, '"My tongue is mine ain": Copyright, the spoken word and privacy' (2005) 68 *Modern Law Review* 349.

50 [2009] EUECJ C-5/08 (16 July 2009).

51 See ibid. para 47.

52 [2010] EWHC 3099 (Ch); [2011] EWCA Civ 890.

53 Ibid. para 71.

54 Ibid. para 77.

55 See US Copyright Office, Circular 34, 'Copyright protection not available for names, titles, or short phrases' (reviewed January 2012) <http://copyright.gov/circs/circ34.pdf> last accessed 1 August 2021; *Becker* v *Loew's, Inc*, 133 F.2d 889 – Circuit Court of Appeals (7th Cir 1943); *Glaser v St Elmo*, CC, 175 F.276, 278; *Corbett v Purdy*, CC, 80 F.901; *Osgood v Allen*, 18 Fed Cas No 10,603, 871. See *Warner Bros Pictures v Majestic Pictures Corp*, 70 F.2d 310, 311 (2d Cir 1934); *Harper v Ranous*, CC, 67 F.904, 905; *Patten* v *Superior Talking Pictures*, DC, 8 F.Supp.196, 197.

56 US Copyright Code 17 USC § 101.

57 UK Copyright, Designs and Patents Act 1988, c 48, s 10.

58 S Hetcher, 'User-generated content and the future of copyright: Part two – agreements between users and mega-sites' (2008) 24 *Santa Clara Computer & High Technology Law Journal* 829, 888.

In summary, UK and EU law would be more likely to protect by copyright short-length email content than the US, where emails in the forms of single words and short phrases would not be protected. For the emails that would pass these requirements (e.g. longer private or business letters), copyright in unpublished works would be applicable because the exchange of communication privately between senders and recipients cannot be considered a publication.[59]

Furthermore, authors of literary or artistic works would be entitled to moral rights, in addition to the copyright as an economic right. In the UK, moral rights include the right to be identified as the author (CDPA, s 77), the right to object to derogatory treatment of work (CDPA, s 80) and the right against the false attribution of work (CDPA, s 84). The first two rights subsist as long as copyright lasts (seventy years post-mortem), and the third lasts until twenty years after a person's death (CDPA, s 86). Unless a person waives their moral rights (CDPA, s 87), the right to be identified as the author and the right to object to derogatory treatment of work transmit on death, passing on to the person as directed by will or to a person to whom the copyright passes, or they sit exercisable by a personal representative (CDPA, s 95). The right against false attribution is only exercisable by a personal representative under the same provision of CDPA.

The US Copyright Act contains a similar provision for the types of moral rights conferred to authors. However, these rights expire on the author's death and therefore do not apply to our issue of post-mortem transmission of copyright in email content.[60]

In the UK, therefore, users would have moral rights for seventy or twenty years post-mortem, depending on the type of right, unless waived. Moral rights in the UK, in principle, transmit on death, but there are further relevant issues concerning the limited access of a user's heirs to this content. Since we focus on unpublished work in this chapter (as published works can be accessed elsewhere), the problems with passing them on are identified below.

Analysis

Authors who argue that copyright is the right approach to protecting emails, especially from the post-mortem perspective, analogise emails with letters, claiming that as authors, users should have property in copies and copyright, and the heirs should be able to inherit these just as they would physical letter

[59] As it is private communication and not publication according to the statutory definitions.

[60] § 106A.

boxes.[61] Regarding letters, English law has a long-established principle that the physical medium, paper, can be owned, whereas information contained therein cannot.[62] Similarly, in the US, the law provides that an author retains copyright in the letter, irrespective of the physical possession of the letter.[63]

It is suggested in this chapter that the letter analogy is unsuitable. The problem with it is that there is no physicality in emails (at least not as traditionally conceived by the courts, requiring tangibility or corporeality). Unlike letters, in emails there is only the content, information, and account owned by the service provider; the underlying electrons travelling through the Internet and eventually, the object code, 1s and 0s. The possession of emails is not exclusive (as in letters), and there is a lack of control required for property in the physical medium. Therefore, as rightly remarked by Justice Edwards-Stuart, property and the letter analogy is misplaced here. Perhaps a more acceptable analogy would be metaphorical when discussing the personal value of emails comparable to the value that the family and next of kin attach to letters. Again, the real problem is in the 'letter box', which is an account here. Thus, we face problems of ownership and access since the deceased's emails will probably only exist in an online webmail account that the heirs do not control.

Looking at the content only, copyright in emails would imply that the heirs can control the publication and have copyright in the unpublished works.[64] However, as seen in the following sections, access to emails is not a simple question, and it is often denied to the heirs of a deceased user. Consequently, the potential publication of an unpublished work contained in an email might not be lawful (as required by UK and EU law, see section above), as it would be contrary to the terms and conditions agreed upon by

[61] See J Mazzone, 'Facebook's afterlife' (2012) 90 *North Carolina Law Review* 143, 10, referring to *Grigsby* v *Breckenridge* 65 Ky (2 Bush) 480 (1867). See also US Copyright Code 17 USC § 202.

[62] *Boardman* v *Phipps* [1967] 2 AC 46, 89, 102 and 127. See for example The nineteenth-century case of *Grigsby* v *Breckenridge* (n 61). Under the law, 'the recipient of a private letter, sent without any reservation' acquired 'the general property, qualified only by the incidental right in the author to publish and prevent publication by the recipient, or any other person'. This 'general property', the court added, 'implies the right in the recipient to keep the letter or to destroy it, or to dispose of it in any other way than by publication'.

[63] See for example *Salinger* v *Random House*, 811 F.2d 90 (2d Cir 1987); *New Era Publications* v *Henry Holt & Co*, 873 F.2d 576 (2d Cir 1989); US Copyright Code 17 USC § 202. See WM Landes, 'Copyright protection of letters, diaries and other unpublished works: An economic approach' (1992) 21 *Journal of Legal Studies* 79.

[64] See Copyright, Designs and Patents Act 1988, s 93 ('Copyright to pass under will with unpublished work').

the user. It would, therefore, be unlikely that the heirs, under the current terms and conditions, would be able to lawfully access and publish this work if their access to the account is unlawful.

One could counter-argue that the contract with the service provider ends on death, and since this is not applicable any more, the heirs would be able to publish the work lawfully. This is quite debatable, however. The contract ends, and after a period of inactivity, the account is deleted, so there can be no access regardless. Even if the heirs or personal representatives were to request access before this time expires, the providers would most likely refuse to grant it, allowing access in exceptional circumstances and invoking PMP. This scenario would be similar to an offline one where an heir inherited copyright in letters but had to steal them from the house of the dead person's former lover or publish them against the wishes of the deceased (e.g. Max Brod famously published Franz Kafka's manuscripts, contrary to his expressly stated wish).[65] Would this publication be equally 'unlawful'? In theory, arguably it would, but considerable differences render this analogy inadequate. The publication against an author's wishes is weighted against the interests of the public to gain access to these works in the second scenario. These are, however, comparatively exceptional cases and most content would not belong to this category. The first example is inapplicable to the online world, as it would be harder to gain access to emails, both for practical reasons (it would require a level of technical skills to break into an account) and because the providers would disable access, contractually and using technological restrictions.

Moreover, according to CDPA 1988, s 93, another requirement is that a bequest entitles the beneficiary to 'an original document or other material thing recording or embodying a literary, dramatic, musical or artistic work which was not published before the death of the testator' and consequently to copyright embodied in such a medium. The problem with applying this provision to unpublished email content is that accounts are not being bequeathed and probably cannot be considered material things or property for this definition. It would be complicated to interpret this provision to permit the transmission of unpublished social network works. Even if the will says 'I leave my whole estate to x' or 'the residue', an 'estate' will not be sufficiently wide to include these works. Emails, as suggested in the following section, are not property, nor are the underlying accounts. The requirement of materiality is lacking, and there is a problem of accessing this copyrightable material due to the contractual limitations. The provision would need to be changed or the

[65] See LJ Strahilievitz, 'The right to destroy' (2005) 114 *Yale Law Journal* 781, 830–1.

technology solutions (as proposed in the final section of this chapter) would need to be recognised as an 'entitlement' for CDPA 1988, s 93.

US federal copyright law does not include similar limitations to the UK ones set out above. The US Copyright Code equates the transmission of copyright with the transmission of personal property.[66] There are, however, similar issues of accessing this content and privacy interests of the deceased that might prevent the default transmission of copyright in email content.

McCallig has put forward a different argument against using copyright to address digital remains. He argues that this would jeopardise the PMP of the deceased as, after the expiration of copyright, these digital remains would fall into the public domain and the service providers could use the content as they wished, like the rest of society.[67] McCallig argues that this would discourage people from leaving emails behind, and instead, in fear of public disclosure, they would delete them and leave nothing to their friends, family, historians and society at large.[68] This needs to be treated with caution, however, since the deceased's decision would not be the same in every case imaginable. All this leads to the solutions suggested later in this chapter.

The problem with copyright is that not all emails would meet the requirement of originality, and consequently, we would have a regulatory vacuum for a considerable number of emails. For those emails that satisfy copyright requirements, the problem is that terms and conditions and PMP might clash with this as the heirs might decide to publish something that was not intended to be disclosed by the deceased and is highly personal. This eventually would limit the deceased's autonomy, usually respected for offline assets (through testamentary freedom in this case).[69] Therefore, while copyright protection of emails could be helpful for a fraction of emails that would meet copyright requirements, it does not seem to be a useful solution for the issues surrounding their post-mortem transmission in general. In order to tackle emails as digital assets holistically, an alternative model of protection is required.

[66] US Copyright Code 17 US Code § 201, (1)(d)(1).

[67] McCallig (n 27) 55.

[68] Ibid. 56.

[69] The concept is generally considered to be wider and more significant in common law countries. See for example F du Toit, 'The limits imposed upon freedom of testation by the boni mores: Lessons from common law and civil law (continental) legal systems' (2000) 11 *Stellenbosch Law Review* 358, 360; MJ de Waal, 'A comparative overview' in KGC Reid, MJ de Waal and R Zimmermann (eds), *Exploring the Law of Succession: Studies National, Historical and Comparative* (Edinburgh University Press 2007) 1–27, 14; RA Trevisani and W Breen, '1. USA', KFC Baker, '4. England' and A Steiner, '5. Germany' in International Legal Practitioner, 'Restrictions on testamentary freedom: A comparative study and transnational implications' (1990) 15 *International Legal Practitioner*, 14–16, 20–4 and 24–6.

(b) Property in Emails

As indicated earlier in this chapter, the emails of an average user will contain information, personal data and copyrightable content. Therefore, the following sections will focus on information and personal data, representing a high proportion of email content.

This chapter subsequently demonstrates that the courts use the same analogy as this analysis and primarily discuss the informational character of emails, as their predominant content. 'Information' as understood here (as in most of the analysed and referred to legal scholarship) encompasses data, ideas, facts, news, and so on, and should be taken as an umbrella term for all the diverse types of data and information, not necessarily used in the same manner as in the information science literature.[70] For instance, in the case of emails, information would include non-copyrightable material, such as short phrases, single words and jokes.

Compared with the other case studies in this book, the legal implications of emails have at least initially been addressed by the courts (see the Fairstar case). Nevertheless, the case law in England and the US about the nature of emails, as seen above, is scarce, hard to interpret, decided by lower courts and often contradictory.

The following section will explore black-letter law regarding property in information and personal data. Along with the normative background discussed subsequently, the black-letter law analysis will serve as a basis to explore whether some of the email content represented by information can be considered property.

Information as Property

PERSONAL DATA

In this section, personal data is discussed at the outset because its non-proprietary character is evident. Information, in general, is a less straightforward example, so the discussion will start with this relatively settled issue, at least in terms of black-letter law and the majority of legal scholarship.

Personal data, as noted earlier, forms a very significant part of an email's contents. Therefore, the legal nature of personal data protection will be explored here briefly. Personal data belongs to the broad category of information. This data, however, has some distinctive features as well, as it is

[70] For instance, amongst other criteria they use, Nimmer and Krauthaus distinguish information products by the form of information (summarised data, analysed data, unorganised and organised raw data). See RT Nimmer and PA Krauthaus, 'Information as a commodity: New imperatives of commercial law' (1992) 55 *Law and Contemporary Problems* 103, 110.

intrinsically tied to a person and is the focus of so-called information privacy. Therefore, privacy regimes employ different instruments to award protection to personal data. Models based on human rights, torts or contracts have been widely discussed or applied. European countries mainly perceive privacy and control over personal data as a human right, establishing the EU-wide data protection regime.[71] The United States has been using a tort law model.[72] The tort model has recently penetrated English law in *Google Inc* v *Vidal-Hall & Ors*,[73] where the Court of Appeal recognised the 'tort of misuse of private information'. This decision has the potential to revolutionise English law on the protection of personal data. However, the actual effects of the decision will be tested over time in subsequent cases.

Personal data has not traditionally been considered a type of property. Therefore, the question is purely theoretical, and scholars contemplate it when trying to identify the best regime for protecting personal data.

The property rights model is based on a presumption that personal data in practice already is or should be considered as an asset or commodity.[74] The property rights model for the protection of privacy has been the subject of an extensive debate within the US legal and economic scholarship. Most arguments that the proponents of this system use focus around the main goals of enabling individuals to control the collection, use and transfer of personal data better, to participate in sharing the profit resulting from the use and processing of personal data, and forcing companies to internalise these new costs and make better decisions on investing in the collection and use of personal data.[75] In addition, since property rights are rights *in rem* and have *erga omnes* effect, that is, they can be enforced against anyone, proponents argue that property in personal data could help individuals protect their rights not

[71] Charter of Fundamental Rights of the European Union 2007/C 303/01, Article 8, 7 December 2000. See for example C Prins, 'Privacy and property: European perspectives and the commodification of our identity' in L Guibault and B Hugenholtz (eds), *The Future of the Public Domain* (Kluwer Law International 2006) 223–57, 223; Regulation (EU) 2016/679 of the European Parliament and of the Council of 27 April 2016 on the protection of natural persons with regard to the processing of personal data and on the free movement of such data, and repealing Directive 95/46/EC (General Data Protection Regulation) OJ L 119, 04.05.2016; cor OJ L 127, 23.5.2018.

[72] Restatement (Second) of Torts (1977) §§ 652A–652E; AJ McClurg, 'A thousand words are worth a picture: A privacy tort response to consumer data profiling' (2003) 98 *Northwestern University Law Review* 63.

[73] [2015] EWCA Civ 311.

[74] See for example World Economic Forum, 'Personal data: The emergence of a new asset class 5' 7 <http://www3.weforum.org/docs/WEF_ITTC_PersonalDataNewAsset_Report_2011.pdf> last accessed 1 August 2021.

[75] P Samuelson, 'Privacy as intellectual property?' (1999) 52 *Stanford Law Review* 1125, 1128.

only against data controllers[76] but against third parties as well.[77] A further significant benefit of property over torts privacy regime is the principle that there is no need for individuals to demonstrate harm in order to be able to protect their property. Ownership entails the right to control one's property, irrespective of any actual harm potentially caused. Tort regime is based upon the right to restitution for harm. This is true both for the European and the US legal contexts.[78]

There are, nevertheless, significant disadvantages of the property model. Thus, for example, Litman forcefully argues that the property model would promote transactions in personal data, which should be discouraged. Also, alienability as a property feature would vest control in the data miner, rather than the individual, resulting in less privacy eventually.[79] Thus, propertisation would allow the purchaser of personal data to sell it further and, therefore, lessen the owner's control.[80] These arguments, however, are based on a presumption of full alienability of property. This does not have to be the case.[81] To overcome this unwanted consequence of propertisation, some authors propose 'hybrid alienability'[82] or a model resembling the limited rights granted under copyright law rather than a 'traditional "property" right, a right against all comers and all uses'.[83]

Propertisation of personal data arguments originate from the United States. There are some examples of authors discussing the phenomenon in the European context, too. Prins, for instance, characterises the EU regime as utilitarian, as it aims to promote the free flow of personal data, and rather

[76] Article 4(7) of the General Data Protection Regulation.

[77] See BJ Koops, 'Forgetting footprints, shunning shadows: A critical analysis of the "right to be forgotten" in big data practice' (2011) 8:3 *SCRIPTed* 256–8, 256. Or for the US perspective, see C Conley, 'The right to delete' (2010) <https://www.aaai.org/ocs/index.php/SSS/SSS10/paper/view/1158 1 August 2021.

[78] Ibid. 247.

[79] J Litman, 'Information privacy/information property' (2000) 52 *Stanford Law Review* 1283, 1304. See also JE Cohen, 'Examined lives: Informational privacy and the subject as object' (2000) 52 *Stanford Law Review* 1373, 1391.

[80] Samuelson, 'Privacy as intellectual property?' (n 75) 1136.

[81] See for example JB Baron, 'Property as control: The case of information' (2012) 18 *Michigan Telecommunications and Technology Law Review* 367, 382–3; PM Schwartz, 'Property, privacy, and personal data' (2004) 117 *Harvard Law Review* 2055, 2093; S Rose-Ackerman, 'Inalienability and the theory of property rights' (1985) 85 *Columbia Law Review* 931 (arguing that 'alienability is not a binary switch to be turned on or off, but rather a dimension of property ownership that can be adjusted in many different ways'); LA Fennell, 'Adjusting alienability' (2009) 122 *Harvard Law Review* 1403, 1408.

[82] Schwartz (n 81) 2094–8.

[83] Cohen (n 79) 1428–9.

controversially argues that the EU regime is more receptive to a property regime than that of the United States.[84] Similarly, discussing the property model, Purtova argues that it could provide a useful framework, which would enable better control of personal data, even within the EU, notwithstanding the differences in property concepts in both common and civil law countries. She argues primarily for introducing the protective feature of property, its *erga omnes* effect, rather than its alienability feature.[85] In my earlier work, I have argued that due to the introduction of the right to be forgotten and data portability rights, the GDPR is moving towards the propertisation of personal data.[86]

In summary, personal data has never been legally protected as property. Propertisation arguments remained at the theoretical level, without influence on the legislation or case law.[87] Protection of personal data has been provided through data protection legislation, by breach of confidence or as torts. Evidence presented suggests many problems in conceiving personal data as property, the majority of the arguments originating from the general discussion on propertisation of information. The arguments refer to the problem of incidents, that is, information does not share the incidents of physical objects of property. In addition, propertisation may produce monopolisation of information and personal data and clash with freedom of speech. Finally, as demonstrated above, propertisation would contradict the human rights nature of privacy. Propertisation of personal data remains a theoretical construct and, fortunately, a rather unsuccessful one so far.

LAW ON INFORMATION AS PROPERTY

In black-letter law, the general approach is that information is indeed not regarded property. English common law has repeatedly refused to recognise property in information, with some sporadic counter-examples. This section follows the main black-letter arguments against propertising information, focusing on the nature of the civil law protection of information, for the reason that this book has adopted a civil law perspective as a central focal point, which is consistent with the latter exploration of post-mortem ownership of

[84] Prins (n 71) 245.

[85] See N Purtova, 'Property in personal data: Second life of an old idea in the age of cloud computing, chain informatisation, and ambient intelligence' in S Gutwirth et al. (eds), *Computers, Privacy and Data Protection: An Element of Choice* (Springer Science Business Media 2011) 61.

[86] E Harbinja, 'Does the EU data protection regime protect post-mortem privacy and what could be the potential alternatives?' (2013) 10:1 *SCRIPTed* 19.

[87] Ibid. 21.

emails. Succession and property and copyright are predominantly civil law issues, so the criminal law discussions are outside the scope of this book. In addition, the courts have traditionally applied different rationales in assessing property for criminal and civil cases.

English common law, in a majority of cases, has not been ready to recognise information as property. For instance, in *Boardman* v *Phipps*,[88] Lord Upjohn maintained 'it is not property in any normal sense, but equity will restrain its transmission to another if in breach of some confidential relationship'.[89] There are some earlier authorities in English common law conferring a proprietary character to particular kinds of information: *Jeffrey* v *Rolls-Royce Ltd*,[90] where Lord Redcliffe treated 'know-how' as an asset distinct from the physical records in which it was contained;[91] *Herbert Morris Ltd* v *Saxelby*,[92] where Lord Shaw of Dunfermline held that trade secrets are 'his master's property';[93] and *Dean* v *MacDowell*,[94] where Judge Cotton held that information constitutes property of the partnership.[95] Nevertheless, Palmer and Kohler state that these authorities do not establish 'a universal characterisation of information as property'.[96] Instead, other areas of law (like contract, tort and breach of confidence) are desired.[97]

The infamous case where an English court found property in information is *Exchange Telegraph Co* v *Gregory & Co*.[98] There, the Court of Appeal upheld an injunction to restrain the defendant broker from publishing information, quotations in stocks and shares from the Stock Exchange, because the information was the plaintiff's property.[99] However, this stance has not been supported by most of the subsequent case law.

In the United States, information as property authorities vary significantly among the individual states, but courts are more willing to recognise certain information status as property. As demonstrated below, examples include the 'fresh news' doctrine found in misappropriation and trade secret law.

88 [1967] 2 AC 46 (HL).
89 Ibid. 128.
90 [1962] 1 AER 801.
91 Ibid. 805.
92 [1916] 1 AC 688 (HL).
93 Ibid. 714.
94 (1878) 8 Ch D 345.
95 Ibid. 354.
96 N Palmer and P Kohler, 'Information as property' in N Palmer and E McKendrick (eds), *Interests in Goods* (Lloyd's of London Press 1993) 7.
97 Ibid. 4–5.
98 [1896] 1 QB 147.
99 Ibid. 152–3 (Lord Esher MR).

In the US case *International News Service* v *Associated Press*,[100] the Supreme Court held that fresh news could be regarded as quasi-property, provided that misappropriation by a competitor constitutes unfair competition.[101] There, the Court used a classical Lockean justification for establishing quasi-property in the news, invoking the pains and labour that were taken advantage of by the plaintiff's competitor. The case was a base for developing the doctrine of misappropriation in the United States 'as a general common law property right against some takings of information of commercial value'. Moreover, while both state and federal courts have adopted the doctrine as a general rule of unfair competition (thus granting protection to objects outside the reach of IP protection), it has been widely criticised for its lack of analysis and superficiality.[102] For example, reputable judges maintain that this doctrine awards protection to objects that the conventional body of IP law refuses to protect,[103] thus potentially restricting access to the public domain while upsetting the balance that IP law attempts to achieve.[104] The doctrine has been a subject of wide controversy in American academic writing.[105] Nonetheless, lower courts have followed the rule of misappropriation outlined in the case of International News Service.[106]

In contrast to the US misappropriation doctrine announced in the case of International News Service, England established the doctrine of breach

[100] 284 US 215 (1918).

[101] Ibid. 236.

[102] SM Besen and LJ Raskind, 'An introduction to the law and economics of intellectual property' (Winter 1991) 5(1) *Journal of Economic Perspectives* 3, 25.

[103] Such as fact, for instance. See *International News Service* v *Assoc Press*, 248 US 215, 250 (1918) (Brandeis, J, dissenting).

[104] This is the balance between incentivising inventions and creativity and rewarding labour, on the one hand, and freedom of expression and access to knowledge and public domain, on the other.

[105] See for example DG Baird, 'Common law intellectual property and the legacy of International News Service v Associated Press' (1983) 50 *University of Chicago Law Review* 411; EJ Sease, 'Misappropriation is seventy-five years old; should we bury it or revive it?' (1994) 70 *North Dakota Law Review* 781; RA Be, 'Dead or alive?: The misappropriation doctrine resurrected in Texas' (1996) 33 *Houston Law Review* 447, 449.

[106] RY Fujichaku, 'The misappropriation doctrine in cyberspace: Protecting the commercial value of "hot news" information' (1998) 20 *University of Hawai'i Law Review* 421, 447. Most of the cases where courts did recognise a misappropriation action involved either appropriation of breaking news or sports performances, likely because that information was a source of revenue for media companies. See for example *Associated Press* v *KVOS, Inc*, 80 F.2d 575 (9th Cir 1935), *rev'd on other grounds*, 299 US 269 (1936); *Pottstown Daily News Publishing Co* v *Pottstown Broad Co*, 192 A.2d 657 (Pa 1963) 202; *Pittsburgh Athletic Co* v *KQV Broad Co*, 24 F.Supp.490 (WD Pa 1938); *Twentieth Century Sporting Club* v *Transradio Press Service, Inc*, 300 NYS 159 (NY Sup Ct 1937).

of confidence to protect valuable information.[107] Breach of confidence is an equitable doctrine that possesses a primary purpose similar to the American 'trade secret law' doctrine.[108] Regarding breach of confidence, English courts seem to agree that information cannot be considered property[109] and, arguably, that protection instead lies in tort law. For example, in *OBG Ltd* v *Allan*, Lord Walker stated, 'Information, even if it is confidential, cannot properly be regarded as a form of property.'[110] Similarly, in *Moorgate Tobacco* v *Philip Morris*, Judge Deane, writing about the breach of confidence, declared that confidence's 'rational basis does not lie in proprietary right'; instead, 'it lies in the notion of an obligation of conscience arising from the circumstances in or through which the information was communicated or obtained'.[111] However, a recent Court of Appeal case tied breach of confidence to IP, deciding that confidential information should be regarded as a type of IP.[112] This is an unusual decision, however, and it does not follow the principles established in the previous and applied in the subsequent case law.[113]

The doctrine of trade secrets is the American counterpart to the breach of confidence in England. The Uniform Trade Secrets Act broadly defines trade secrets as any information that is secret, derives economic value from secrecy, and is the subject of reasonable measures to maintain its secrecy.[114] Generally, trade secrets can include various types of information, such as chemical formulas, source code, methods, prototypes, pre-release pricing, financials, budgets, contract terms, business plans, market analyses, salaries, information about suppliers and customers, experiments, positive and negative

[107] C Waelde et al., *Contemporary Intellectual Property: Law and Policy* (3rd edn, Oxford University Press 2013) 774.

[108] Ibid. 775–6.

[109] See for example M Conaglen, 'Thinking about proprietary remedies for breach of confidence' (2008) 1 *Intellectual Property Quarterly* 82, 84; W Cornish and D Llewelyn, *Intellectual Property: Patents, Copyright, Trade Marks and Allied Rights* (Sweet & Maxwell 2007) 8, 50–4.

[110] *OBG Ltd* v *Allan* [2007] UKHL 21, 275.

[111] *Moorgate Tobacco Co Ltd* v *Philip Morris Ltd* (No 2) [1984] 156 CLR 414, 438. See also *Boardman* v *Phipps* [1967] 2 AC 46, 89–90, 102, 127–8; *Breen* v *Williams* [1996] 186 CLR 71, 81, 91, 111–12, 129; *Cadbury Schweppes Inc* v *FBI Foods Ltd* [1999] 167 DLR (4th) 577, 48; *Douglas* v *Hello! Ltd* (No 3) [2005] EWCA Civ 595 (Eng); [2006] QB 125, 119, 126.

[112] *Coogan* v *News Group Newspapers Ltd and Mulcaire* [2012] EWCA Civ 48.

[113] See the discussion in the following section.

[114] Uniform Trade Secrets Act, 14 ULA 529 § 1(4) (2005). However, US courts tend instead to use the negative definition, defining trade secrets 'by what [they are] not'. See DS Almeling, 'Seven reasons why trade secrets are increasingly important' (2012) 27 *Berkeley Technology Law Journal* 1091, 1107.

experimental results, engineering specifications, laboratory notebooks and recipes.[115] Exploring the evolution of the doctrine in the US, Lemley and Weiser[116] demonstrate the shift from referring to trade secrets as property in the nineteenth century to a combination of contracts, torts and property, and eventually to the unfair competition approach adopted by the Restatement of Torts in 1939.[117] In England, that shift never happened, and trade secrets remain protected by the breach of confidence doctrine.

Nevertheless, the US courts have never really decided whether confidential information or trade secrets are property. Some have held that this inquiry is not essential and that what matters is that the information is protected.[118] Academic debate continues. Similarly, American academics debate whether trade secrets are primarily property, contractual, IP rights, torts, or something that belongs in the criminal law domain.[119] For commentators, trade secret law involves elements of different areas: property, contract, tort, fiduciary duty and criminal law.[120] Other authors and courts describe trade secrets as property.[121] One of the earliest cases deeming trade secrets to be property

[115] See ibid.

[116] MA Lemley and PJ Weiser, 'Should property or liability rules govern information?' (2007) 85 *Texas Law Review* 783, 789.

[117] Restatement of Torts § 757 (1939).

[118] See AE Turner, *The Law of Trade Secrets* (Sweet & Maxwell 1962) 12; *EI du Pont de Nemours Co* v *Masland*, 244 US 100, 102 (1917). See also AE Turner, 'Nature of trade secrets and their protection' (1928) 42 *Harvard Law Review* 254.

[119] See for example WB Barton, 'A study in the law of trade secrets' (1939) 13 *University of Cincinnati Law Review* 507, 558; J Chally, 'The law of trade secrets: Toward a more efficient approach' (2004) 57 *Vanderbilt Law Review* 1269; V Chiappetta, 'Myth, chameleon, or intellectual property Olympian? A normative framework supporting trade secret law' (1999) 8 *George Mason Law Review* 69; DD Friedman et al., 'Some economics of trade secret law' (1991) 5 *Journal of Economic Perspectives* 6; CT Graves, 'Trade secrets as property: Theory and consequences' (2007) 15 *Journal of Intellectual Property Law* 39; JW Hill, 'Trade secrets, unjust enrichment, and the classification of obligations' (1999) 4 *Virginia Journal of Law and Technology* 2; EW Kitch, 'The law and economics of rights in valuable information' (1980) 9 *Journal of Legal Studies* 683; C Montville, 'Reforming the law of proprietary information' (2007) 56 *Duke Law Journal* 1159; CJR Pace, 'The case for a federal Trade Secrets Act' (1995) 8 *Harvard Journal of Law and Technology* 427, 435–42; GR Peterson, 'Trade secrets in an information age' (1995) 32 *Houston Law Review* 385; M Risch, 'Why do we have trade secrets?' (2007) 11 *Marquette Intellectual Property Law Review* 1; MP Simpson, 'Trade secrets, property rights, and protectionism – an age-old tale' (2005) 70 *Brooklyn Law Review* 1121.

[120] Hill (n 119).

[121] See for example Restatement (Third) of Unfair Competition § 39 cmt b (1993) (describing early trade secret theory as based on property rights); *Carpenter* v *United States*, 484 US 19,

is *Peabody* v *Norfolk*.[122] There, the Massachusetts Supreme Judicial Court defined a principle applicable to property law in general. Regarding trade secrets, the court said that the inventor or discoverer of secret information does not have exclusive rights against the public or the good faith acquirer, 'but he has a property in it, which a court of chancery will protect against one who in violation of contract and breach of confidence undertakes to apply it to his own use, or to disclose it to third persons'.[123] Later, the courts continued to connect trade secrets to property. In 1984, the Supreme Court held that trade secrets are property for purposes of the Fifth Amendment's Takings Clause.[124] Additionally, since trade secrets are intangible, the court stated that the existence of a property right depends on the extent to which the trade secret is protected from disclosure.[125] However, despite these references, American trade secret law is still a fusion of tort and unjust enrichment law.[126] Nevertheless, it is worth noting that many authors still argue that trade secrets are IP rights.[127]

These contrasting views of the doctrine demonstrate that US courts and legislators have been more willing to recognise information as property despite the problems discussed earlier in this book. In principle, however, the property paradigm cannot be used for all kinds of information and cases because it mainly relates to commercially valuable information.

Palmer and Kohler note that information might be deemed property in the future, which would provide the courts with an additional instrument.[128] At the moment, if it is recorded in a tangible form, then information can be vindicated using an action for trespass or conversion, that is, property

26 (1987); *Electro-Craft Corp* v *Controlled Motion, Inc*, 332 NW.2d 890, 897 (Minn 1983); *IMED Corp* v *Systems Engineering Associates Corp*, 602 So.2d (Ala 1992).

122 98 Mass 452, 457–8 (1868).

123 Ibid. 458.

124 *Ruckelshaus* v *Monsanto Co*, 467 US 986, 1002–3 (1984) (citing Locke's Second Treatise and other sources to support the finding that trade secrets can be property). See also Hill (n 119).

125 *Ruckelshaus* v *Monsanto Co*, 467 US 986, 1002. See also *Kewanee Oil Co* v *Bicron Corp*, 416 US 470, 474–6 (1974).

126 See Hill (n 119). The legislation of trade secrets has been quite a recent phenomenon in the US. Before 1980, there was no legislation on this matter. The initial effort to codify and harmonise trade secrets law was that of the Uniform Law Commission, which in 1979 adopted the uniform Trade Secrets Act. In 1996, Congress passed a federal statute criminalising trade secret misappropriation, the Economic Espionage Act 18 USC 55 1831-9. See Uniform Trade Secrets Act, 14 ULA § 529 (2005); DS Almeling et al., 'A statistical analysis of trade secret litigation in state courts' (2011) 46 *Gonzaga Law Review* 57, 67–8.

127 Lemley and Weiser (n 116).

128 Palmer and Kohler (n 96) 206.

remedies. Thus there is a contradiction in not awarding protection when information is intangible.[129]

THE FAIRSTAR CASE

The question of whether new, intangible information such as emails should be regarded as property arose in the recent English case *Fairstar Heavy Transport NV* v *Adkins*. This section will examine the scenarios identified by the court in more detail. Justice Edwards-Stuart's analysis of property in emails illustrates five different scenarios: 1) the title remains with the creator; 2) the title passes to the recipient (analogous to a letter); 3) the recipient had a licence to use the content of the email; 4) the sender has a licence to retain the content and use it; and 5) the title is shared between the sender and the recipient, as well as any subsequent recipient.[130]

In each of these scenarios, Judge Edwards-Stuart focused on the unwanted consequences that would follow if the information in emails were to be recognised as property. Under the first scenario (the *creator* of the email content retains property in it), he noted that the *in rem* nature of property[131] would entitle the sender to request deletion of the email. The judge pointed out that this 'would be very strange – and far-reaching'.[132] Under the second scenario (the *recipient* has the property right), he pointed out, similarly, that the recipient would instead be entitled to request deletion. In addition to that 'strange outcome', he noted that further complications would arise if the email were forwarded to many recipients, who in turn might forward it to even more recipients. There, 'the question of who had the title in its contents at any one time would become hopelessly confused'.[133] Under the third and fourth scenarios, Justice Edwards-Stuart discussed the difference between cases of illegitimate use of information where the email was considered property, whereby one side was given a licence to use it, and cases where there was a misuse of confidential information. He noted that the only difference is that if emails were considered property, it would not be necessary to show that the information was confidential. However, if the information was not confidential, he argued that there would be few situations where people would want to limit its use. Therefore, he concluded that 'there is no compelling need or logic for adopting either of options (3) or (4) and so in relation to

[129] Ibid. 188.
[130] Ibid. 61.
[131] The sender has a claim against the whole world.
[132] *Fairstar Heavy Transport NV* v *Adkins* [2012] EWHC 2952 (TCC) para 64.
[133] Ibid. para 66.

these options I would reject a plea that the law is out of line with the state of technology in the 21st century'.[134]

Under the fifth scenario (shared proprietary interests in email contents), Justice Edwards-Stuart discussed several possible consequences of losing information in emails due to technical issues. He argued that, in such cases, the affected party could not gain access to the parties' servers with whom they shared property in emails. He concluded that 'the ramifications would be considerable and, I would have thought, by no means beneficial'.[135] Accordingly, he found that emails are not to be considered property.[136]

Subsequently, the Court of Appeal has recognised the same conceptual difficulties that property in information would encounter as those that Justice Edwards-Stuart identified.[137] However, the court further asserted that this does not mean that there can never be property in any kind of information. The inquiry depends on the quality of the information in question.[138] This would mean that information such as 'know-how' might be susceptible to property instead of personal data.[139] Accordingly, the court wisely avoided this discussion and decided that the real issue in the case was that of agency and that Mr Adkins, as a former agent of Fairstar, had a duty to allow Fairstar to inspect emails sent to or received by him and relating to its business.[140] In another recent case, the Court of Appeal confirmed this long-standing position and, concerning the customer data contained in a database, maintained restated that information is not regarded as property in English law.[141] Conversely, the medium carrying the information is an object of property.[142] The position is still evolving, and questions around propertisation of intangibles, namely, virtual assets in the form of virtual currencies, are subject to the Law Commission's inquiry at the time of writing.[143]

[134] Ibid. para 67.

[135] Ibid. para 68.

[136] Ibid. para 69.

[137] *Fairstar Heavy Transport NV* v *Adkins* [2013] EWCA Civ 886 para 47.

[138] Ibid. para 48.

[139] Ibid.

[140] Ibid. para 46.

[141] See *OBG Ltd* v *Allan* [2007] UKHL 21; [2008] 1 AC 1, 275, and the discussion of this topic in S Green and J Randall, *The Tort of Conversion* (Hart 2009) 141–4. See also *Your Response Ltd v Datateam Business Media Ltd* [2014] EWCA Civ 281, 42 (Lord Justice Floyd).

[142] *Fairstar Heavy Transport NV* v *Adkins* [2013] EWCA Civ 886.

[143] Law Commission, 'Digital assets: Call for evidence' (April 2021) <https://www.lawcom.gov.uk/project/digital-assets/> last accessed 1 August 2021.

In conclusion, it can generally be argued that English courts do not consider information to be property, whereas US law has done so more readily.

Theoretical Considerations of Property in Information

FEATURES OF PROPERTY AND INFORMATION

The analysis in this section will consider whether the legal stances in the United Kingdom and the United States should be reconsidered to recognise property in information. The particular framework used to examine these stances is the most widely accepted conception of property in common law systems: the 'bundle of sticks' theory. In the information context, this theory encompasses the following 'sticks': 1) the control of copying, 2) access, modification, use, and 3) disclosure of data and information.[144]

Providing for all the sticks in the bundle in the information context is usually a complex task, if possible, due to the characteristics that differentiate information from traditional property. The primary differences between tangible and intangible property objects and rights are the following:

- Information is non-rivalrous, and therefore more than one individual can experience it at the same time.[145] This creates the problem of possession, as possession can be concurrent and cannot be transferred as in the case of tangible property.[146]
- Information is often non-separable, acting as a part of an individual right holder.[147]
- As opposed to most of the traditional property objects, copying information is accessible and not very costly.[148] This adds to the difficulty of excluding others from using information.

[144] See Nimmer and Krauthaus (n 70) 113.

[145] See J Boyle, 'The second enclosure movement and the construction of the public domain' (2003) 66(1) *Law and Contemporary Problems* 33, 41; RG Hammond, 'Quantum physics, econometric models and property rights to information' (1981) 27 *McGill Law Journal* 47, 54; MA Lemley, 'Property, intellectual property, and free riding' (2005) 83 *Texas Law Review* 1031, 1032, 1059–60.

[146] See Nimmer and Krauthaus (n 70) 105.

[147] 'Separability' or 'thinghood' means that a thing, in order to be property, must not be conceived as 'an aspect of ourselves or our ongoing personality-rich relationships to others'. See J Penner, *The Idea of Property in Law* (Oxford University Press 1997) 126.

[148] See Hammond (n 145) 54. Usually, with the exception of highly confidential and protected information, where it could be considerably harder and costlier.

- Information is often time-limited, erasable and more fluid, while tangible property arguably has a quality of persistence and permanence.[149]
- Information is not easily excludable and therefore requires legal measures to mandate its excludability.[150]
- Information does not depreciate with use, and some of it sometimes even gains additional value with use, which is not the case with tangible property that devaluates with use.[151]
- The abundance of information is inconsistent with the requirement of scarcity for traditional property.[152]

Therefore, information incidents differ significantly from the incidents of traditional tangible property, identified in Chapter 2. Therefore, applying the traditional property 'sticks' or incidents (such as use, control, exclusion, possession, destruction) to information is difficult. Courts frequently use these arguments to deny the information status of property (as in the Fairstar case and other cases cited in the previous section).

Theories of Property as Justifications for Propertising Information

LABOUR THEORY

This section will continue to explore the potential normative justification for property in information. This analysis will use the significant Western theories for justifying property, examined in Chapter 2, to establish whether these arguments could be used for establishing property rights in information.

This discussion will borrow from the normative justifications for the recognition of IP. This is because the same major property theories have been used to justify both IP rights and propertisation. In addition to the same rationale, IP variants of these theories are even better suited to the information context, given that IP resources share many of the same features as information identified in the section above (they too are intangible, non-rivalrous and non-permanent).

We will first look at labour theory and its applicability to justify the propertisation of information. Lockean arguments are widely used to justify

[149] TJ Westbrook, 'Owned: Finding a place for virtual world property rights' (2006) *Michigan State Law Review* 779, 782–3.

[150] For more on excludability, see Boyle, 'Second enclosure movement' (n 145) 42. For Hammond, public goods are separated from private goods by a principle of exclusion and for information to have this feature, a considerable cost would need to occur. See Hammond (n 145) 54.

[151] See Boyle, 'Second enclosure movement' (n 145) 44.

[152] See Hammond (n 145) 53.

property and IP in common law systems.[153] According to Locke, a creator owns their person and labour, and inventions and intellectual creations are products of labour. Consequently, a creator owns their creations thus generated. However, when applying this to information generally, one encounters problems of labour and creation. Information may be simple facts, news, or other things that could not qualify as IP and would not entail labour being employed, though perhaps this is not true for certain types of information, such as trade secrets or fresh news.[154]

Further, apart from the questionable quality of labour for information generally, Locke's limitation on appropriation (e.g. 'the enough and as good' and spoilage provisos)[155] must be considered. In the case of IP, the 'enough and as good' proviso is likely to be satisfied since information as a resource is not at least theoretically scarce (but if, for instance, it were monopolised, artificial scarcity would be created), and there is no risk of depletion.

Additionally, like IP,[156] some information (knowledge, facts, ideas) is arguably so essential and influential to the public that appropriation harms people.[157] Some information could be necessary for self-preservation and subsistence, as required by Locke; its appropriation would harm the welfare of others, and there would not be enough and as good left for others in the commons if the access to it were to be limited by property rights.[158] This is particularly the case if propertisation would, as suggested by many prominent commentators, jeopardise free speech, expression, sharing of knowledge, and keeping archives and accurate historical records.[159]

For Locke's second proviso, the spoilage principle, IP and information are less subject to waste due to spoilage, at least in the material sense. Furthermore, it is easier to isolate the value of human work than it is for real property, as

[153] See for example J Hughes, 'The philosophy of intellectual property' (1988) 77 *Georgetown Law Journal* 287; W Fisher, 'Theories of intellectual property' in SR Munzer (ed.), *New Essays in the Legal and Political Theory of Property* (Cambridge University Press 2001) 168–201; SV Shiffrin, 'Lockean arguments for private intellectual property' in Munzer (ed.), *New Essays in the Legal and Political Theory of Property* 138–68, 138–9.

[154] See the case law and discussion in the previous section.

[155] CB Macpherson, 'Editor's introduction' in J Locke *Second Treatise of Government: Essay Concerning the True Original Extent and End of Civil Government*, ed. with an intro. CB Macpherson (Hackett 1980) xxi.

[156] WJ Gordon, 'A property right in self-expression: Equality and individualism in the natural law of intellectual property' (1993) 102 *Yale Law Journal* 1533, 1540–78, 1567–70.

[157] See Shiffrin, 'Lockean arguments' (n 153).

[158] J Peterson, 'Lockean property and literary works' (2008) 14(4) *Legal Theory* 385, 387–90, 399.

[159] See Lemley (n 145); Samuelson, 'Privacy as intellectual property?' (n 75); Litman (n 79); Shiffrin, 'Lockean arguments' (n 153); L Lessig, *Code: Version 2.0* (Basic Books 2006).

there is no labouring on independent physical materials.[160] Other authors reject this as a sound explanation, noting that due to the non-rivalrous nature of intangible assets, unlimited production is possible and, consequently, there is a problem with spoilage when the creator is unable or unwilling to use all of these assets (creations) or convert them to money (which does not spoil).[161] In contrast, others claim this is not necessarily correct, asserting that only the complete non-usage of works would qualify for this limitation. Otherwise, creations, even if used in a limited manner, would not spoil in the sense of the Lockean waste proviso.[162] Moreover, many argue that most information would be better shared, contemplated, discussed and developed.[163] Although these arguments apply to information, some types of information (e.g. trade secrets or personal data) may lose their usefulness and function if not used at the right time and exploited properly, a scenario that relates to the tragedy of the commons arguments.

Another potential issue would be the commons, which is very difficult to define abstractly in information. We could borrow from IP theory and consider the commons equivalent to the IP public domain. However, this approach would encounter similar difficulties to those that the public domain faces. The main objection is that the Lockean commons referred to the original appropriation at an earlier stage of societal development and to tangible assets only, thus it is inapplicable to the public domain and, consequently, to the case of information commons.[164]

In summary, labour theory could be employed to justify property in certain kinds of information, where labour that could qualify as adequate for labour theory (e.g. trade secrets) is present. However, its general application to all kinds of information is unsuitable. First, there is a problem with the quality of labour deployed. It is doubtful that 'labouring on information' commons could be analogous with labouring on tangible property resources in Lockean terms. There is also a problem with applying Locke's provisos ('enough and as good' and spoilage), as propertisation of many types of information would not leave enough and as good for others and would face issues of undesirable commodification of information.

[160] Hughes (n 153) 51. For a more detailed discussion, see Shiffrin, 'Lockean arguments' (n 153) 140, 141; GS Alexander and EM Peñalver, *An Introduction to Property Theory* (Cambridge University Press 2012) 191–2.

[161] BG Damstedt, 'Limiting Locke: A natural law justification for the fair use doctrine' (2003) 112 *Yale Law Journal* 1179, 1182–3.

[162] RP Merges, *Justifying Intellectual Property* (Harvard University Press 2011) 58.

[163] Shiffrin, 'Lockean arguments' (n 153) 166–7.

[164] See ibid. See also Merges (n 162) 35–9.

Further, propertisation would restrict the availability of resources for further creation, may result in restriction of freedom of speech and autonomy, and jeopardise historical records and knowledge sharing. Another problem is the features of the commons. In the case of IP and information, the commons could be seen as the public domain, a concept very different from the Lockean notion of the commons in the initial stage of human development. Further, many would argue that 'labouring' on the public domain and appropriating resources from it would jeopardise further creation, innovation, development and access to valuable resources. Finally, the commons is even more problematic in personal data, as such data is, by definition, tied to an individual and does not belong to everyone. Accordingly, labour theory is even less applicable to personal data.

UTILITARIAN CASE

This section will first explain the utilitarian theories used to justify IP and draw parallels with applying the theory to propertising information. Inspired by Bentham, utilitarians and the neoclassical law and economics school argue that the primary purpose of awarding intellectual IP protection is incentivising innovation.

Utilitarian theory often develops on the notion of free riding and the theory known as the 'tragedy of the commons'.[165] These arguments claim that treating all IP as commons poses the threat of free riding. Free riding disables the owner from internalising the costs of investment in their creations and then recouping them in the market. Landes and Posner maintain that 'the nature of public goods renders them vulnerable for replication and use by free riders, thereby creating the risk of not recovering the production costs'.[166] If IP protection were not awarded, those who did not create could still enjoy the benefits.

On the other hand, the creators would be unable to recover the investment, efforts and costs they incur in the process of creating and innovating.[167] According to the theory set forth by Demsetz, this phenomenon should be eliminated as it represents the negative externalities that should be internalised, as free riders obtain benefits from someone else's investment.[168] Thus,

[165] H Demsetz, 'Toward a theory of property rights' (1967) 57 *American Economic Review* 347, 347–59; S Kieff, 'Property rights and property rules for commercializing inventions' (2001) 85 *Minnesota Law Review* 697; Kitch (n 119) 683; WM Landes and RA Posner, 'An economic analysis of copyright law' (1989) 18 *Journal of Legal Studies* 325, 326.

[166] Landes and Posner (n 165).

[167] Ibid. 353–4.

[168] For a commentary, see Lemley (n 145) 12.

according to Landes and Posner, IP protection increases socially valuable IP production.[169]

Landes and Posner, however, do recognise the need to strike a balance between public and private interests as the central problem of copyright law.[170] The most important indicator is the net welfare approach, which seeks 'the greatest good for the greatest number'.[171] For example, in the context of copyright, this means that IP rules should be geared to 'maximize the benefits from creating additional works minus both the losses from limiting access and the costs of administering copyright protection'.[172]

Lemley offers an excellent critique of this theory, arguing that it is based on a 'fundamental misapplication of the economic framework set out by Harold Demsetz'.[173] He explains the difference between IP and tangible property, which does confer negative externalities, and costs for owners and non-rivalrous resources.[174] IP, unlike tangible property, presents an issue of internalising positive externalities.[175] This is because the consumption of creative output by many is desirable, as it enriches society and culture.[176] Lemley maintains that positive externalities are impossible to internalise, and there is no reason to do that; therefore, 'if "free riding" means merely obtaining a benefit from another's investment, the law does not, cannot, and should not prohibit it'.[177] Alexander also supports this stance.[178]

Other opponents of this line of reasoning find that the goal of striking an appropriate balance between private and public in the copyright context cannot be entirely realised under utilitarian justifications.[179] The problem in these justifications for copyright, as Boyle or Zemer would argue, is that they emphasise the property component as a precondition for incentivising creation,

169 Ibid.

170 Landes and Posner (n 165) 326.

171 J Bentham, *An Introduction to the Principles of Morals and Legislation*, ed. JH Burns and HLA Hart (Athlone Press 1970) 12–13.

172 Landes and Posner (n 165) 184.

173 Ibid. 18.

174 Lemley (n 145) 2.

175 This issue prevents the positive externalities from being enjoyed by the public. Ibid

176 Ibid. 56

177 Ibid. 24.

178 See Alexander and Peñalver (n 160) 184.

179 L Zemer, 'On the value of copyright theory' (2006) *Intellectual Property Quarterly* 1, 55–71; Lemley (n 145) 1066–7.

thus disregarding the role of the public domain[180] or the self-interested motivation for creation without legal incentives.[181]

In addition, critics of this approach claim that it is not true that IP protection is always necessary to recover the cost of innovation.[182] This claim mainly relates to patents, as they are understood to require the highest level of investment compared with other IP rights.[183] To support this argument, critics present examples of hard-to-copy or reverse engineer innovations (e.g. integrated circuits and hardware protected by obfuscation techniques). In addition, some innovators recoup profits by keeping their innovations secret, or other inventors may distribute products in a way that is expensive to replicate (e.g. motion pictures on film stock or encrypting data). Finally, in a constant circle of innovation, there is a phenomenon where first movers can recoup costs (e.g. the news, fashion and trade secrets).[184]

Applying this theory to information, utilitarian arguments, especially the free riding concept, could be used to justify propertisation of some kinds of information (e.g. trade secrets). Nevertheless, the notion of free riding does not apply to all information and personal data, and it cannot be used as an argument for propertising either of these. The reason for this is that information and personal data, at least those included in digital assets, do not require investment as IP usually does, and free riders, therefore, would not prevent anyone from recouping the non-existent investment. Also, the incentivising innovation and creation of information arguments might not work perfectly, especially in the case of online, digital information where the phenomenon of information overload is considered. Many authors argue that there is no need to incentivise information that is already over-produced.[185] It is also self-evident that incentivising the production of personal data is unnecessary,

[180] J Boyle, *Shamans, Software and Spleens: Law and the Construction of the Information Society* (Harvard University Press 1996) 244.

[181] SV Shiffrin, 'The incentives argument for intellectual property protection' (2009) 4 *Journal of Law, Philosophy and Culture* 45, 49.

[182] Ibid. 51, 57.

[183] See Landes and Posner (n 165) 350.

[184] See Alexander and Peñalver (n 160) 188; WM Cohen, RR Nelson and JP Walsh, 'Protecting their intellectual assets: Appropriability conditions and why U.S. manufacturing firms patent (or not)' National Bureau of Economic Research, Working Paper No 7552, 2000) 13.

[185] See MJ Eppler and J Mengis, 'The concept of information overload: A review of literature from organization science, accounting, marketing, MIS, and related disciplines' (2004) 20(5) *The Information Society: An International Journal* 325; MS Oppenheimer, 'Cybertrash' (2011–12) 90 *Oregon Law Review* 1; TA Peredes, 'Blinded by the light: Information overload and its consequences for securities regulation' (2003) 81(25) *Washington University Law Quarterly* 417.

as it has already been shared and used on a large scale online, and digital assets contain a vast amount of such data. Instead, there are generally more significant concerns over how to control and share less personal data online. In addition, all the utilitarian arguments face the same objections as IP, that is, they should be non-rivalrous and, as is the case with information sharing and enriching culture in the IP context, internalising positive externalities as should be avoided. Moreover, the tragedy of the commons objection is not applicable either, especially to personal data, since there is no commons to start with and such data is intrinsically related to a person. Utilitarian arguments are therefore weak justifications for the propertisation of information.

PERSONHOOD THEORIES

Personhood theories of personal and IP represent a solid alternative to the previous theories. They emphasise a personal, non-pecuniary version of IP, concluding that intellectual creation is an expression of one's self.[186] Discussing whether ideas and creations can be considered things and property, Hegel notes that they can be contracted but are inward and mental. It is hard to describe such a possession in legal terms 'because its field of vision is as limited to the dilemma that this is "either a thing or not a thing" as to the dilemma "either finite or infinite"'.[187] Further, Hegel concludes that even though talents and accomplishments are internal and are owned by the mind, 'by expressing them it may embody them and this way they are put in the category of "things"'.[188] Hughes finds this theory appealing, noting that 'the Hegelian personality theory applies more easily because intellectual products, even the most technical, seem to result from the individual's mental processes'.[189]

As noted in Chapter 2, one of the most prominent contemporary theories based on Hegelian arguments is Radin's personhood theory. Radin divides property into fungible and personal categories and asserts that 'the more closely connected with personhood, the stronger the entitlement'.[190] Therefore, according to this theory, there are powerful grounds for strong IP protection. However, the problem here is whether this theory justifies the alienability of creative works or limits it. Fisher, for instance, wonders if an author can restrict further communication of her work once she has revealed

[186] See Hughes (n 153) 330 ('An idea belongs to its creator because the idea is a manifestation of the creator's personality or self.').

[187] GWF Hegel, *The Philosophy of Right*, trans. TM Knox (Oxford University Press 1967).

[188] Ibid.

[189] Hughes (n 153) 365.

[190] MJ Radin, 'Property and personhood' (1982) 34 *Stanford Law Review* 957, 986.

it and whether it 'nevertheless continues to fall within the zone of her "personhood"'.[191] Netanel replies that 'authors in fact have a strong interest in continuing sovereignty over their expression'.[192] Weinreb, conversely, maintains that the expression, after having been communicated, takes a life of its own and would 'come down to an economic interest, the author herself commodifying what was declared uncommodifiable'.[193] A similar objection could be applied to personal data in particular. Thus, even though personal data is intrinsically tied to a person, propertisation, even in the form of personal property, might not be the best solution, as it would commodify such data and disable users' control over it.

Other critics note that Hegel's theory lacks a romantic view of a creator and, under this theory, IP is just like other species of property in that it is strictly formal and abstract.[194] Furthermore, according to Schroeder and Alexander, Hegel says nothing about whether IP should be protected. They assert that Hegel just claims that if society adopts such a regime, it is coherent to formulate it in terms of actual property, rather than some *sui generis* rights.[195]

Personhood theory applies to information to an extent. However, because of their non-personal, commercial character, some kinds of information (such as trade secrets and fresh news) cannot be justified under this theory. In contrast, other information (such as personal data that is intrinsically tied to an individual) can perhaps find better support under this approach. Nevertheless, this suggestion is not free from problems either, and as identified above, it can lead to the commodification of information and personal data.

In summary, even if the normative obstacles were overcome and either the labour or personhood theories were to be applied, propertisation would face the problem of the undesirable commodification and monopolisation of information and personal data. There, property would not provide any desirable protections and would arguably jeopardise free speech.[196]

To conclude, the non-copyrightable content of emails, information and personal data is not (doctrinal argument) and should not be (normative

[191] Fisher (n 153) 190.

[192] See NW Netanel, 'Copyright alienability restrictions and the enhancement of author autonomy: A normative evaluation' (1993) 24 *Rutgers Law Journal* 347, 400.

[193] L Weinreb, 'Copyright for functional expression' (1998) 111 *Harvard Law Review* 1149, 1222.

[194] See Alexander and Peñalver (n 160) 199.

[195] Ibid. 189.

[196] See Baron (n 81); Radin (n 190); A Rahmatian, 'Copyright and commodification' (2005) 27(10) *European Intellectual Property Review* 371, 371–8; C May, 'Between commodification and "openness": The information society and the ownership of knowledge' 2005 (2) *Journal of Information Law & Technology*.

argument) considered property. Other safeguards established for information and personal data should be utilised to protect emails (breach of confidence, trade secrets, data protection). This, tentatively, means that the non-proprietary character of emails to a large extent precludes their post-mortem transmission. Further analysis in this chapter will demonstrate some problems with this one-size-fits-all conclusion.

6.4 Allocation of Ownership in Emails

This section will analyse the allocation of ownership/property/copyright (these terms are to be taken provisionally, and they reflect how providers refer to users' content and not the analysis above, which concluded differently) and access to users' email contents as established by service provider contracts. After discussing whether emails are property, this section will aim to answer the question of who gets these property rights or copyright according to the contracts users conclude before starting to use emails. The allocation and access are essential as they prevent or, rarely, allow the deceased users' personal representatives or next of kin access to the content.[197]

Unlike the previous case study (virtual worlds), where providers refuse to recognise any right in users' content, the question of ownership of the content users 'upload, submit, store, send or receive' is much clearer in this case study. Service providers recognise users' ownership of their content, and they claim a worldwide, royalty-free and non-exclusive licence to use and perform other actions with the content. This is, in principle, valid for all three leading service providers analysed in this chapter.[198] There are some minor differences, however. When stating ownership, Google refers to all content, whereas Microsoft mentions email explicitly as content that users own.[199] The other difference is that Google and Microsoft ToS apply to all content, whereas in Yahoo!'s ToS, for instance, the corresponding provision and the licence apply only to 'photos, graphics, audio or video'.[200] For all other content that users 'submit or make available for inclusion on publicly accessible areas of the Yahoo Services',[201] Yahoo! retains 'the worldwide, royalty-free, non-exclusive,

[197] Harbinja, 'Emails and death' (n 10).

[198] Google, 'Terms of service' (effective 31 March 2020) <http://www.google.com/intl/en-GB/policies/terms/> last accessed 1 August 2021; Yahoo!, 'Terms of service' <https://policies.yahoo.com/ie/en/yahoo/terms/utos/index.htm> (legacy terms that still apply to those who have accepted them) last accessed 1 August 2021.

[199] Microsoft, 'Services agreement, Outlook 3.1' <http://windows.microsoft.com/en-gb/windows-live/microsoft-services-agreement> last accessed 1 August 2021.

[200] Yahoo!, 'Terms of service' (n 198) para 9.2.

[201] Ibid.

perpetual, irrevocable, and fully sub-licensable licence'.[202] Emails do not seem to belong to any of the categories, and the only provision applicable is the general one, where users generally retain ownership over the content. Notwithstanding the discussion about information and personal data in the previous section, this general provision is misleading and is potentially applicable to copyrightable content only.

The issue appears clear: content is copyrightable if it fulfils the requirements of, and/or it can be protected by, the tort of misuse of confidential information, trade secrets, data protection or publicity rights, depending on the qualities of the actual content, and it is 'owned' by the user according to the ToS. The account, however, is not the property of an individual. The individual has a right to use it by contract but does not have a right to transfer it,[203] and the account remains the service provider's property.[204] It could be argued that the username and/or password could also be owned by an individual (like a key to one's property, an accessory), but the actual underlying system that enables the functioning of the account is the IP of the service provider. In summary, it is unclear what these ToS describe, but it is probably access to emails and their retention on the service providers' servers.

Even if we set aside the difficulties in proclaiming intangible objects as property, the fact here is that a service provider owns the account and email servers, and the user only uses these facilities under terms and conditions. Therefore, the account cannot be transferred as the sender of an email does not own the account in the first place.[205]

(a) Intermediary Contracts and Transmission of Emails on Death

The current terms of service of the leading webmail providers offer different and contradictory options for transmitting emails on death. This section will canvas the policies relating to deceased users of the major email providers chosen as case studies in this chapter.

[202] Ibid. para 8.

[203] Microsoft, 'Services agreement' (n 199).

[204] See Google, 'Terms of service' (n 198). See similarly J Lamm, 'Planning ahead for access to contents of a decedent's online accounts' *Digital Passing Blog* (9 February 2012) <http://www.digitalpassing.com/2012/02/09/planning-ahead-access-contents-decedent-online-accounts/> last accessed 1 August 2021.

[205] In accordance with the legal principle of *nemo dat*. See *Henderson & Co* v *Williams* [1895] 1 QB 521; *Shaw* v *Commissioner of Metropolitan Police* [1987] 1 WLR 1332; *Farquharson Bros* v *C King & Co Ltd* [1902] AC 325; *Mercantile Bank of India Ltd* v *Central Bank of India* [1938] AC 287, upholding *Farquharson*; *Central Newbury Car Auctions Ltd* v *Unity Finance Ltd* [1957] 1 QB 371.

Yahoo!, as seen in the Ellsworth case, refuses to pass on logins, passwords and the content of the messages to heirs.[206] In its deceased user policy, it expressly refers to privacy of the deceased and the non-transferable nature of the account ('Pursuant to the TOS, neither the Yahoo account nor any of the content therein are transferable, even when the account owner is deceased').[207] A personal representative or an executor can only request an account to be closed, billing and premium services suspended, and 'any contents permanently deleted for privacy'.[208]

Google permits passing on the contents of a Gmail account to the deceased's heirs but only in exceptional circumstances.[209] Google explicitly protects the deceased's privacy, mentioning this on multiple occasions in the relevant section on its help page.[210] However, in addition to this general policy, Google has recently launched a pioneering 'code' solution for post-mortem transmission of emails and other services. Its Inactive Account Manager (IAM) introduced in April 2013 enables users to share 'parts of their account data or to notify someone if they've been inactive for a certain period of time'.[211] Via this procedure, the user can nominate trusted contacts to receive data if they have been inactive for the time chosen (three to eighteen months). After their identity has been verified, the trusted contacts are entitled to download the data the user has left them. The user can also decide only to notify these contacts of the inactivity and delete all their data. There is a link directly from the user's account settings (in the data tools section) to IAM.

A fundamental problem with IAM is the verification of trusted contacts. Text messages are sent to trusted contacts (mandatory), and in addition, the user can choose to be notified of their timeout by email. This could prove problematic as a phone number is not an official way of proving identity. Furthermore, people tend to change their mobile phone providers and numbers, and some of them may never be able to be notified, so the user's wish will not be honoured in these cases. This problem has been recognised by Google,

[206] See the discussion above of Yahoo!'s terms of service (n 198) and the Ellsworth case. See also Yahoo!, 'Options available when a Yahoo account owner passes away' <https://help.yahoo.com/kb/mobile/SLN9112.html?impressions=true> last accessed 1 August 2021.

[207] Ibid.

[208] Ibid.

[209] Google, 'Submit a request regarding a deceased user's account' <https://support.google.com/accounts/contact/deceased?hl=en&ref_topic=3075532&rd=1> last accessed 1 August 2021.

[210] Ibid.

[211] Google, 'About Inactive Account Manager' <https://support.google.com/accounts/answer/3036546?hl=en> last accessed 1 August 2021.

too, but the company considers the two-factor authentication suitable for the time being before better ways of identification are employed (e.g. identity tokens, fingerprint identification).[212]

A second problem is a transfer of content via IAM to trusted contacts, which would provide for different beneficiaries than the offline ones. It would, perhaps, include friends and a digital community that would not be considered in an offline distribution of property. This further leads us to the connected problem of conflicts between the interests of the deceased (expressed in their digital will or traditional will), family (as heirs) and friends (with whom the deceased might have firmer ties online than with their heirs offline, as research suggests).[213] This issue becomes more complex in the different jurisdictions where Google's users are based worldwide. Google, however, considers itself bound primarily by Californian probate law in this and other similar cases (e.g. requesting a US court order in the access procedure described earlier).[214] This is understandable, especially as the service was designed and developed initially by Google's developers and 'techies' (staff working on the development of technology mainly), without significant input from the legal and policy departments.[215] Their input came later, and Google is still contemplating the viability and scalability of the service. Google argues that the legislation should be technologically neutral, allowing for the development of similar technologies that appropriately tackle post-mortem issues.[216] Overall, this could be welcomed as a good development that respects autonomy and allows users much more control over their data on death. This is especially important as Google stores an enormous amount of users' data through all of its services (Gmail, YouTube, Google+, Google Drive, Photos).

In line with the other providers, Microsoft offers no rights of login or access to the representatives of deceased users.[217] Its 'Next of Kin Process' provides the release of Outlook.com content (all emails and their attachments, address book, and Messenger contact list) to the next of kin of a deceased or incapacitated user and/or closure of the Microsoft account. Microsoft refuses to provide the password and to transfer ownership of the account to the next of kin. Instead, in an earlier version of its terms, it offered to release

212 Interview transcript, Google employee (on file with the author).

213 See E Kasket, 'Access to the digital self in life and death: Privacy in the context of posthumously persistent Facebook profiles' (2013) 10:1 *SCRIPTed* 7.

214 Ibid.

215 Interview (n 212).

216 Ibid.

217 See Mazzone (n 61) n98.

the content on a DVD, shipped to the next of kin.[218] It has slightly revised these terms to include explicit information advising users to seek legal help to access the deceased's account.[219]

(b) Analysis

First, the above discussion has demonstrated that email service providers expressly recognise users' ownership of their email content. The service providers claim a worldwide, royalty-free and non-exclusive licence to use and perform other actions with the content.

Second, among email service providers, a norm has emerged of allowing heirs discretionary access to content in the accounts of deceased users, but no formal property right is recognised or transmitted. There is usually an express prohibition of transfer of account login details and the account itself. This is inconsistent with the declaratory recognition of users' ownership. Google provides, exceptionally, for users' control over their content post-mortem through IAM. *Prima facie*, the prohibition on accessing the deceased user's account is not an issue, as the licence to use the account ends with the user's death and, clearly, the account owner (the service provider) could stop others from accessing it. Nevertheless, this contradicts the service providers' explicit provisions on users owning their content because this ownership excludes transmission on death, which is one of the main features of property and ownership.

Third, none of the providers allows access to the full account itself, invoking privacy protection and the Stored Communications Act. The Act, however, does not prevent disclosure in the cases when there is consent from the user or if they wish to disclose the data voluntarily.[220] This is the argument used by Google to justify its approach in IAM. In addition, a court might order access to the account, as attempted in the Ellsworth case.

[218] Microsoft, 'My family member died recently/is in coma, what do I need to do to access their Microsoft account?' (Ael_G. asked on 15 March 2012) <http://answers.microsoft.com/en-us/outlook_com/forum/oaccount-omyinfo/my-family-member-died-recently-is-in-coma-what-do/308cedce-5444-4185-82e8-0623ecc1d3d6> last accessed 1 August 2021.

[219] Microsoft, 'Accessing Outlook.com, OneDrive and other Microsoft services when someone has died' <https://support.microsoft.com/en-us/office/accessing-outlook-com-onedrive-and-other-microsoft-services-when-someone-has-died-ebbd2860-917e-4b39-9913-212362da6b2f?ui=en-us&rs=en-us&ad=us> last accessed 1 August 2021.

[220] See 18 USC § 2701 – Unlawful access to stored communications; § 2702 – Voluntary disclosure of customer communications or records.

6.5 Post-Mortem Privacy

An important phenomenon that arises from considering the transmission of emails is post-mortem privacy. It will be discussed herein because it is one of the features affecting rules on the transmission of assets on death. As seen in the previous section, service providers refer to PMP (without using the term itself) when refusing to transfer a deceased's account. In addition, as argued in Chapter 3, this notion deserves legal recognition beyond the piecemeal and patchy approach that is dominant at the moment. The theoretical and doctrinal analysis from Chapter 3 and my earlier findings applies to this chapter.[221]

Concerning the main topic of this chapter, PMP serves as a basis for arguing against the general transmission of emails on death without the deceased's consent, that is, by default, through the laws of intestacy or by requiring the intermediaries to provide access to the deceased's emails. PMP is recognised explicitly in the court's decision in the Ellsworth case and the service providers' ToS. Therefore, recognition of PMP questions the default position of using transmission by way of the laws of succession for some kinds of digital assets (those containing a vast amount of personal data, such as emails and social networks).

Rather than using the current offline defaults, it is argued that more nuanced solutions for the transmission of emails are needed. These solutions will be explored in the following section. It will aim to account for the privacy interest of the deceased, thus upholding the user's autonomy and expression of their wishes regarding what happens to their emails after their death. Although not prioritised currently, these interests should be considered when suggesting solutions for the transmission of digital assets in general. This proposition is in line with the underlying principle of this book, autonomy, which should be extended on death in the form of PMP, analogous to its extension in the form of testamentary freedom.

In the case of emails, which consist predominantly of personal data, this book recommends protecting autonomy and privacy by setting up and recognising the in-service options for PMP protection (e.g. Inactive Account Manager) legally. Theories of autonomy discussed in Chapter 3 support the in-service solutions. Autonomy, or free will, practically translates into privacy interests and the user's control of what happens to the personal data in their accounts. These privacy interests should be extended post-mortem, analogous to the post-mortem extension of autonomy reflected in respect of testamentary freedom. For emails, such an extension could be achieved via technological, in-service solutions, which would be recognised by the law of succession

[221] Harbinja, 'Emails and death' (n 10).

(e.g. Inactive Account Manager; see the section below). This way, effect could be given to the autonomous wishes expressed by a user of the technology, enabling the protection of the user's PMP. The following section explains how this would be technologically viable and how the law could effect it.

6.6 Solutions for the Transmission of Emails on Death

This section will offer some tentative solutions concerning the transmission of emails on death. More general solutions will be offered in the last chapter.

As noted in the previous section, email accounts contain much more personal data and information relating to the deceased than could be imaginable offline in the case of letters, for instance. Users' online lives are stored and controlled by service providers. It is argued here that any solution should shift the control to users. The old rules of succession, aiming to account for individuals' wishes and balancing these interests with the interests of their heirs, are not applicable *per se*, mainly because of the highly personal and individualistic nature of these digital assets.

It is argued here that the best solution to the problems identified in this chapter is to respect and foster the user's autonomy and create technological solutions that would implement this endeavour. The solutions could resemble Google's IAM, but there is also scope for further technological and policy innovation. In addition, adequate legislation is necessary for this, aiming to neutralise the potential conflicts between the laws and the code solutions. In this respect, the US Uniform Law Commission work is a good start, but as noted further in the Conclusion, the outcome of this work is still uncertain, and its influence would be significant only if the provisions of the Uniform Act were adopted as laws of the individual states. There is also a need for legislation to recognise these services and remove the obstacles for transmission created by copyright law at the UK level.

Along with the probate reforms, an ideal solution would recognise PMP and protect the deceased's personal data. In Europe, this could be done at the EU level by envisaging the deceased's personal data protection in future data protection reforms. This protection could be time-limited (e.g. fifty or seventy years post-mortem like copyright) and again, recognise the user's autonomy and pre-mortem choice (e.g. mandating service providers to require the choice to be expressed during the registration process, or on some other appropriate occasion).

7
Conclusion

Possible solutions for the issues identified in previous chapters will be grouped loosely into technology and market solutions, followed by legal and policy solutions, reflecting Lessig's taxonomy of the four regulatory modalities of cyberspace: 'code' (i.e. technology and architecture), market, law and norms.[1]

The main idea advanced in this book is that the interests of individual users to decide what happens to their data on death should be recognised and protected. In other words, the book promotes user autonomy, privacy, identity and technological options that correspond with the offline, traditional ones (i.e. freedom of testation). The solutions also recognise novel phenomena of immortality, considered under the concept of postmortal privacy. This is not to say that some other legitimate interests should be disregarded, such as public interest, the need to maintain archives and historical records, freedom of expression or the freedom to conduct business. However, due to the scope of this book, an in-depth examination and balancing of these interests is not viable.

All these solutions are tentative. They originate from the analysis in this book, and I will aim to develop further the principles established here in future research projects and publications. The ambition of this book was to set the scene, introduce and explore critical theoretical and legal issues, and offer a framework for future thinking, rather than to offer precise solutions for each issue.

7.1 'Code' and Market Solutions

'Code' or technology solutions, using Lessig's taxonomy mentioned above, are online services aiming to assist in the disposition of digital assets on death, digital estate planning, succession and remembrance. A significant category of stakeholders is online services, which aim to help with the disposition of digital assets on death. They aim to shift the control of digital assets to users

[1] L Lessig, *Code: Version 2.0* (Basic Books 2006).

by enabling the designation of beneficiaries who will receive the passwords and content of digital asset accounts. This way, the services impliedly recognise user property in digital assets and attempt to bypass restrictions imposed by the terms of service discussed in this book. Understandably, they also see a growing market and an opportunity for investment and profit.

These services, still primarily US-based but increasingly hosted in the UK, are categorised in this book as follows:

- *Digital wills*, for example Legacy Locker, now part of the True Key service,[2] Cirrus Legacy,[3] Beyond Life[4] or SecureSafe[5]. This kind of service works on the principle that a user stores their account information and passwords, and nominates a 'digital heir' or a beneficiary who will get access to this information. The beneficiary or someone else (e.g. Account Activator in SecureSafe) reports their death and provides a death certificate, and after a validation process the digital heir gets access to the account information. The SecureSafe service has now changed its business model entirely, focusing on password management for businesses.
- *Messaging services*, for example ifidie, a Facebook application that allows users to leave messages to Facebook friends on death.[6]
- *Memorial and legacy websites*, for example BCelebrated, an autobiographical legacy website that offers a personalised memorial website, protected private messages and emails, activated by chosen activators.[7]
- *Combined solutions*, combining offline and online services. For example, My Digital Executor, which involves two solicitors who keep email accounts, passwords and a list of digital assets. Assets are then transferred in the form of codicil;[8] MyWishes, which offers a comprehensive list of services, including digital estate planning, will writing, bucket list and advance care planning;[9] and Final Fling, which provides advice on living

[2] Password Box, 'Legacy Locker' (now True Key) <https://www.passwordbox.com/legacy-locker> last accessed 1 August 2021.
[3] Cirrus Legacy, 'Making it easy for your guardians' <http://www.cirruslegacy.com/139-guardians.html> last accessed 15 June 2019 (no longer available).
[4] Beyond Life <https://beyond.life/make-will-online> last accessed 1 August 2021.
[5] SecureSafe, 'Questions about data inheritance' <http://www.securesafe.com/en/faq/inheritance/> last accessed 1 August 2021 (now changed its business model).
[6] ifidie, 'What happens to your Facebook profile if you die?' <http://ifidie.net> last accessed 1 August 2021.
[7] BCelebrated <http://www.bcelebrated.com/> last accessed 1 August 2021.
[8] My Digital Executor <http://www.mydigitalexecutor.co.uk/the-solution-2/> last accessed 1 August 2021.
[9] MyWishes <https://www.mywishes.co.uk/how-it-works> last accessed 1 August 2021.

and dying well (funerals, celebrations, bereavement, treasure trove, wills, advance decision, safe deposit box and essential documents; wills printed out, signed and witnessed).[10]

Lamm et al. categorise these solutions differently, focusing on the character of actions they promise to undertake on death. Accordingly, they find four categories: services offering to store passwords; services facilitating the administration of digital assets; services performing specific actions (e.g. removing all the data on behalf of a deceased person); and services that currently do not exist, but hypothetically provide their services through partnerships with the service providers of the deceased's accounts.[11] This categorisation is very similar to the one used in this book, with the slight difference that it focuses on actions rather than on business models.

In our earlier work, Edwards and I evaluated some of the 'code' solutions and concluded that 'these are not themselves a foolproof solution'[12] for five main reasons:

- They could cause a breach of terms of service (due to the non-transferable nature of most assets, as suggested in the previous chapters).
- There is a danger of committing a criminal offence (according to the provisions of the anti-interception and privacy laws; see previous chapters).
- The services are inconsistent with the law of succession and executry (they do not fulfil the requirements of will formalities; conflicts may arise with the interests of heirs under wills or laws of intestacy; there are jurisdiction issues, etc.).
- There are concerns over the business viability and longevity of the market (this has proven correct for many services, as indicated above).
- The issues of security and identity theft (the services store passwords and keys to valuable assets and personal data).[13]

Similarly, Beyer and Cahn, and Lamm et al. identify most of these problems.[14]

[10] Final Fling <http://blog.finalfling.com/> last accessed 1 August 2021.

[11] J Lamm et al., 'The digital death conundrum: how federal and state laws prevent fiduciaries from managing digital property' (2014) 68 *University of Miami Law Review* 385, 408.

[12] L Edwards and E Harbinja, '"What happens to my Facebook profile when I die?": Legal issues around transmission of digital assets on death' in C Maciel and V Pereira (eds), *Digital Legacy and Interaction: Post-Mortem Issues* (Springer 2013) 144.

[13] Ibid.

[14] N Cahn, 'Probate law meets the digital age' (2014) 67 *Vanderbilt Law Review* 1697, 1706; Lamm et al. (n 11) 400–1.

The issues are significant, and it is not recommended that the services be used in their current form and with the law as it stands. However, with improvements and provided that the law recognises them, they may be suitable for broader use in the future. In principle, the services are more suitable for the online environment; they recognise the technological features of digital assets and enable an automated transmission on death. Conversely, the issues surrounding them are numerous and complex, so I do not envisage their legitimate reception soon, at least not outside the US, where the RUFADAA might encourage their use.

In addition to these more established code solutions, a recent phenomenon of the deceased's deepfakes and chatbots or ghostbots deserves some consideration. For instance, a MyHeritage service called DeepNostalgia allows users to animate photographs of late relatives and share them across various platforms.[15] The service uses technology licensed from a deep-learning start-up company called D-ID,[16] in which video re-enactment, fixed sequences of movements and gestures are applied to uploaded photos, allowing individuals in the photo to smile and blink.[17] The technology is still in quite a rudimentary form, but it nevertheless raises questions of consent, reputation, personality and identity post-mortem, the issues discussed in this book.

A more advanced version is a chatbot created using AI and the deceased's data. Recently, Jason Rohrer, an indie games developer, created Samantha, a chatbot built using OpenAI's GPT-3 application programming interface (API). The software was then used by thousands of people, including a man who used the program to simulate his late fiancée. Due to a public outcry and the alleged violations of its rules, OpenAI discontinued Rohrer's access to its GPT-3 API.[18] These technologies add to the number of problems identified for code solutions. Currently, these problems are predominantly ethical and revolve around big questions of immortality, recreation and existence, but will soon become more relevant for the law. For example, the EU's recent Proposal for AI Regulations in Article 52 requires users of AI systems that generate or manipulate 'image, audio or video content that appreciably resembles existing persons, objects, places or other entities or events and would falsely appear to a person to be authentic or truthful ("deep fake")' to 'disclose that

15 MyHeritage <https://www.myheritage.com/deep-nostalgia> last accessed 1 August 2021.

16 D-ID <https://www.d-id.com/> last accessed 1 August 2021.

17 MyHeritage, 'FAQ' in MyHeritage (n 15).

18 K Quach, 'A developer built an AI chatbot using GPT-3 that helped a man speak again to his late fiancée. OpenAI shut it down' *The Register* (8 September 2021) <https://www.theregister.com/2021/09/08/project_december_openai_gpt_3/> last accessed 8 September 2021.

the content has been artificially generated or manipulated'.[19] This provision merely requires transparency and does not answer questions specific to the creation of the deceased's deepfakes and chatbots, such as whether this 'content' infringes the deceased's rights of privacy, autonomy and dignity; who has the right to use such a system and create deepfakes; what dataset is being used; and whether consent is necessary. Understandably, the proposal does not aim to address all these issues either, so a more holistic law reform is necessary. This is a developing area that goes beyond the questions examined in this book, and I will continue exploring it in my future research.[20] I have mentioned it here for completeness.

(c) In-Service Solutions

For the purpose of this book, in-service solutions include technology and service features that enable the transmission of a digital asset or part of the deceased's content to beneficiaries in a service internally. I have analysed Google Inactive Account Manager and Facebook Legacy Contact extensively in Chapters 4 and 6. These solutions have been implemented mainly in response to pressure placed on service providers by the media and families of deceased users, rather than as a result of pressure from users themselves or being initiated by providers. The likely reason is the general reluctance of individuals to contemplate their death, and providers' fear that reminders of it would damage their reputations. However, the market is moving towards providing answers, and these efforts should be recognised and supported by policy and the law.

Notably, the existing solutions for the transmission of digital assets within service providers should evolve. Service providers need to make them more visible because they are barely used and not advertised. Service providers should amend their terms of service and make them more coherent with their post-mortem solutions. For instance, they should recognise the transferability of content on death explicitly in their terms of service.

In virtual worlds, these terms will allow personal representatives of a deceased user to access and recoup any benefits arising from virtual world usufruct. Thus, a personal representative could sell valuable items a user left behind, for example through online auctions, and pass the monetary value to the user's heirs or beneficiaries.

[19] Proposal for a Regulation of the European Parliament and of the Council laying down harmonised rules on artificial intelligence (Artificial Intelligence act) and amending certain union legislative acts, Brussels, 21.4.2021, COM(2021) 206 final, 2021/0106(COD).

[20] E Harbinja, L Edwards and M McVey, 'Governing ghostbots' (forthcoming).

Email providers should aim to make the provisions of their contracts with users more coherent (those relating to ownership and the transfer of a user's content). In addition, given the prevalence of post-mortem privacy, they should recognise this phenomenon more clearly in their terms of service. The user should decide on the deletion of the content or leaving some of it to a beneficiary. The visibility of these options is vital, and the user should be adequately informed through terms of service and a 'wizard' or a pop-up window that would facilitate a user's choice.

Facebook's terms of service should explicitly state that a user's choice of Legacy Contact trumps the option of memorialisation and requests submitted by the next of kin or friends. Other social networks, including Facebook's own Instagram, should follow Facebook's lead, in principle, enabling their users to decide whether they wish their account to be deleted on death or if they would like to leave some of their content to a beneficiary. This option should be visible, and users could, for instance, be required to go through a 'wizard' to check their post-mortem choice. At the moment, users are advised to use available post-mortem options, but they should be aware of conflicts that these may cause between the in-service beneficiaries and heirs. For instance, if they leave a piece of content protected by copyright to someone other than their heir, the heir would have a claim against that person. I have explored this in more detail in Chapter 4.

Concerning the suggested deletion of a user's content, it is worth noting that it does not mean deletion of all personal data and content associated with the deceased person, as this is, arguably, impossible. Instead, the deletion would be limited to a particular service and the user's account. Thus, in order to respect the rights of other users in their content, the deletion would not include, for instance, emails in another user's inbox or private messages sent on Facebook. That would be impractical and unfair to the recipient of the communication or content.

In the future, it would be helpful to consider the implementation of Schafer's idea of ZombAI, whereby an intelligent agent (AI) would be used to interpret the deceased's wishes and continue their existence in some form.[21] For example, the agent could learn from an individual and provide a contextual interpretation of their wishes after death. It could include a tool for the technologically appropriate disposition of digital assets and the post-mortem protection of the deceased's personality and privacy interests. The agent could serve as a 'defender' of the deceased's personality and identity-related interests

[21] B Schafer, 'On living and undead wills: ZombAIs, technology and the future of inheritance law' in L Edwards, B Schafer and E Harbinja (eds), *Future Law: Emerging Technology, Regulation and Ethics* (Edinburgh University Press 2020).

for a limited time (thirty or fifty years), and it could even adapt to changed circumstances after the individual's death.

The AI agent, developed with ethical, social and legal concerns in mind, would have the capacity to protect postmortal privacy, a novel concept developed in this book. Ideally, this protection would include the totality of the deceased's post-mortem persona, their informational body and digital remains. It would have the potential to address novel concerns around ghost-bots and digital resurrection mentioned above. This solution would challenge some core paradigms of succession law, legal personhood, and other traditional areas of law and ethics, so it requires in-depth research and law reform that may not happen very soon.

7.2 Law and Policy Solutions

I reject the proposition that we should leave the regulation of the transmission of digital assets on death to the market. The analysis in this book demonstrates problems for users and society created by new technologies and service providers' contractual conditions. It is argued that legal intervention is required.

We have analysed most of the existing laws that regulate digital assets and post-mortem privacy in Chapter 3. We have identified their deficiencies and argued for a law that would recognise the technological, social and economic reality. No existing law is sufficient *per se*. To be successful, a legislator needs to consider succession law, probate, personality, privacy, data protection, IP, contract, criminal law and other areas considered in this book. Holistic law reform is vital for a phenomenon that goes beyond just assets and wealth and includes digital remains that are highly personal and sensitive. I also agree with Morse and Birnhack, who maintain that users need to be empowered to make decisions about their digital remains, and as such 'a top-down, one-size-fits-all law will frustrate the wishes of large segments of the user population'.[22]

An acceptable legal solution should aim to recognise technology as a way of disposing of digital assets, as a more efficient and immediate solution online, one that recognises technological limitations, autonomy and the changing landscape of relationships there (co-constructed profiles and sharing). Succession laws applicable to a traditional estate should not apply to digital assets by default. As concluded in the previous chapters, the content in digital assets is not always property, it is potentially protected by copyright as unpublished works, and it consists mainly of personal data and information.

[22] T Morse and M Birnhack, 'The posthumous privacy paradox: Privacy preferences and behavior regarding digital remains' (2020) *New Media and Society* 1, 19.

Further, it includes digital remains that go beyond personal data and privacy and result in immortality, which the law should consider in a comprehensive approach. Therefore, the law should recognise these novel features and enable user choice and transmission of copyrighted material and other content, where applicable. An example of this is the US RUFADAA, analysed in Chapter 3.

In a written submission to the NSW Law Reform Commission, Edwards and I made specific proposals of what the law should ideally include.[23] We argued that access to digital assets should always be exercised after death only by personal representatives (PRs) of the deceased, and there should be no default access for families or friends of the deceased to digital assets. We also maintained that there is a need to balance the heirs' interests in remembering the deceased and receiving economic benefits from them with the privacy interests of the deceased, as well as a need to consider the practical issues for platforms that host these assets. We concluded that the PR is best equipped legally and practically to strike this balance and be a single point of contact for the platform, so it has certainty when giving access to the deceased's assets.

We have identified an issue in jurisdictions that allow automatic access by a PR on death, namely transferring highly private digital content (e.g. intimate blog posts) to family members after death, which may not be what the deceased would have preferred. Accordingly, we suggested that the PR's access rights be amended slightly in relation to certain digital assets to provide for the most nuanced legislative solution to date. Those assets that are intrinsically likely to be highly personal (e.g. friends-locked social media accounts) should be treated differently from those that are likely to be non-private or principally of monetary value (e.g. virtual worlds and games accounts, financial domain names, Amazon or eBay accounts).

For personal assets, we suggest a hierarchy of instructions to be followed by PRs: (a) in-service tools, (b) will, (c) failing this, distribution of assets falls to be governed by any terms of service relevant and only the deceased's catalogue of communications is accessible by default. For monetary assets, unfettered access should be allowed to the PR, and there should be an explicit provision for clarity that this access right trumps platforms' terms of service even if they provide to the contrary. The document required by the PR to secure access should be the same as that required to access typical non-digital assets of the estate, for example a grant of probate of the will or letters of administration.

[23] L Edwards and E Harbinja, 'Written submission', NSW Law Reform Commission: Access to digital assets upon death or incapacity (2019).

These principles should be implemented through amendments to the probate and succession laws in England. This could be effected through a regulation, which would primarily amend the Wills Act 1837 and the Administrations of Estates Act 1925, recognising digital assets as a specific part of the deceased's estate. The Law Commission commenced revising the law of wills in 2017 and this process is expected to last for another few years. Unfortunately, the reform does not include digital assets as the Commission considers these to fall outside its scope.[24] Another reform is looking at digital assets, but only considering their property and contract aspects and in so far as they include blockchain and similar technologies.[25]

Recently, Ian Paisley, a member of the UK Parliament, introduced the Digital Devices (Access for Next of Kin) Bill, proposing to give the next of kin of a dead or incapacitated person default access to devices. It includes access to content a person has bought online and personal data like photographs, emails and messages.[26] This *ad hoc*, ill-conceived bill fails to acknowledge all the nuances and complexity discussed in this book. The proposal completely disregards the need to consider various relevant areas of law and construct a holistic law reform, as discussed here. It is to be hoped that Parliament will recognise this and reject the proposal.

A reasonable idea would be to negotiate and recognise these principles at the EU level to harmonise the practice and the law. Recent events suggest some development in this area. In January 2022, the European Commission introduced the European Declaration on Digital Rights and Principles, which reads, 'Everyone should be able to determine their digital legacy, and decide what happens with the publicly available information that concerns them, after their death.'[27] The proposal introduces digital legacy more formally in the EU for the first time. However, there are difficulties, as the EU cannot impose solutions on matters of property and substantive succession law, so

[24] Law Commission, 'Making a will' (Consultation paper 231, 2017) <https://www.s3-eu-west-2.amazonaws.com/lawcom-prod-storage-11jsxou24uy7q/uploads/2017/07/Making-a-will-consultation.pdf> last accessed 1 August 2021.

[25] Law Commission, 'Digital assets: Call for evidence' (April 2021) <https://www.lawcom.gov.uk/project/digital-assets/> last accessed 1 August 2021.

[26] R Bradbury, 'A proposed UK law would automatically hand loved ones access to your messages, photos, and emails after you die' *Business Insider* (31 January 2022) <https://www.businessinsider.com/uk-law-proposed-for-family-get-devices-deceased-2022-1?utmSource=twitter&utmContent=referral&utmTerm=topbar&referrer=twitter> last accessed 31 January 2022.

[27] European Commission, 'European Declaration on Digital Rights and Principles for the Digital Decade' Brussels, 26.1.2022 COM(2022) 28 final, 5.

the Declaration is likely to remain just a good idea.[28] The EU could decide to extend data protection or privacy protections post-mortem, but even that would be a partial solution that disregards a holistic law reform. Even if we ignore this major obstacle, the document includes imprecise terms in its current form, such as 'determine' and 'publicly available information'. The word 'determine' should be replaced with 'control', and the decision should extend to digital assets and remains, as suggested in this book. Otherwise, the Declaration risks being reductionist and imprecise.

In addition to these general principles for law reform, Chapter 5 introduced a solution distinct from the ones in the other case study chapters. Recognising the conflicting interests of developers and players, in line with the doctrinal and normative analyses of virtual property and the phenomenon of *constitutionalisation* of VWs, the chapter proposes a novel compromise solution in the form of virtual usufruct. This concept pertains to the second level virtual assets and it transmits on death. It is a law reform proposal and could be introduced by terms of service, that is, internally to a VW, or could generally be mandated by the law.

Chapter 6 identified difficulties around the transmission of copyright in unpublished works stored in digital assets. These difficulties can be resolved by explicitly allowing access to a user's account to a personal representative through the provider's terms of service, as long as the user has not requested deletion of the account. In addition, copyright law that requires unpublished works to be stored on a medium that would form a part of an estate should be amended and clarified. One of the ways to clarify this is by inserting a provision into the UK Copyright, Designs and Patents Act 1988, which mandates that this provision applies to digital assets and copyright in unpublished works is transmissible (as these are not tangible media or part of an offline estate), provided that the user has not expressed a contrary wish pre-mortem.

It is also suggested that the data protection regime in the UK and the EU should recognise PMP. This can be done, for instance, by envisaging protection of the deceased's personal data in the member states' legislation across the EU (akin to what many member states have done; see Chapter 3 for

[28] The EU does not interfere with property rights of member states. See Article 345 of the Treaty on the Functioning of the European Union (Consolidated version 2012) OJ C 326, 26.10.2012; Regulation (EU) No 650/2012 of the European Parliament and of the Council of 4 July 2012 on jurisdiction, applicable law, recognition and enforcement of decisions and acceptance and enforcement of authentic instruments in matters of succession and on the creation of a European Certificate of Succession L 201/107. The Regulation deals with cross-border issues in succession and does not interfere with the substantive national succession laws. See for example Recital 15.

more detail). The GDPR permits member states to provide for such protection, but does not protect the deceased's data itself.[29] This protection could be time-limited (e.g. thirty or fifty years post-mortem), and it could recognise a user's autonomy and pre-mortem choice (e.g. mandating service providers to require the choice to be expressed during the registration process or on some other appropriate occasion). This suggestion needs to be developed in more detail to address some prominent issues, such as who would consent on behalf of the deceased to process their personal data. Ideally, the EU would pass amendments to the GDPR to this effect, but this is unrealistic given legislative processes and the EU's priorities at the moment. Harmonising this aspect of data protection would contribute to the legislative aim of maximum harmonisation, which has not been achieved concerning the deceased's data. It is also unlikely that the UK Data Protection Act 2018 will be amended to this effect soon. It is something to be considered for the future, hopefully.

Legal professionals working in this field play a crucial role since they are able to discuss these issues with their clients in the process of will drafting and estate planning. Therefore, efforts of professional organisations and associations, such as STEP (an association of professionals working in family planning, including probate and succession laws),[30] should be recognised, as they aim to harmonise the practice and raise awareness within the legal profession.[31]

7.3 Concluding Remarks

This book does not aim to encompass all the necessary reforms, changes and challenges in this complex and broad area. Instead, it offers a thorough legal examination of the theoretical and doctrinal issues surrounding online death and digital assets. It discusses and links different areas of the law, humanities and social sciences to provide critical answers and suggestions about what happens to the individual's digital assets and online identity after they die.

[29] Recital 27 of Regulation (EU) 2016/679 of the European Parliament and of the Council of 27 April 2016 on the protection of natural persons with regard to the processing of personal data and on the free movement of such data, and repealing Directive 95/46/EC (General Data Protection Regulation) OJ EU L 119/1.

[30] STEP, 'About us' <http://www.step.org/about-us> last accessed 1 August 2021.

[31] See STEP, 'Digital assets: Practitioner's guide, England and Wales' (2020) <https://www.step.org/system/files/media/files/2020-03/Digital%20Assets%20Practitioner%20Guide%20-%20England%20&%20Wales.pdf> last accessed 1 August 2021. For a useful guide by a legal professional, see L Sagar, *The Digital Estate (Wills and Probate)* (Sweet & Maxwell 2018). For very helpful practical guidance with tips and advice, see S Hartung, *Digital Executor(R): Unraveling the New Path for Estate Planning* (FriesenPress 2021).

The book develops the concept of post-mortem (later, postmortal) privacy, that is, privacy of deceased individuals, which I pioneered conceptually in my previous work with Edwards, and later further developed in my research. It offers suggestions for law reform, useful for legislators and policymakers. It also provides answers of interest for the academic community, the technology industry and the legal profession. Finally, the book provides some practical considerations and advice beneficial for all Internet users in the UK, EU, US and more broadly.

Bibliography

Abram C, 'Welcome to Facebook, everyone' *Facebook Blog* (26 September 2006) <http://blog.facebook.com/blog.php?blog_id=company&m=9&y=2006> last accessed 1 August 2021.

Abramovitch SH, 'Virtual property in virtual worlds' *Gowlings.com* (2009) <http://www.gowlings.com/knowledgecentre/publicationPDFs/TLI-2009-Susan-Abramovitch-Virtual-Property-in-Virtual-Worlds.pdf> last accessed 1 August 2021.

Abramovitch SH and DL Cummings, 'Virtual property, real law: The regulation of property in video games' (2007) 6(2) *Canadian Journal of Law and Technology* 73.

Adams R, 'All your Twitter belongs to the Library of Congress' *Guardian* (14 April 2010) <http://www.theguardian.com/world/richard-adams-blog/2010/apr/14/twitter-library-of-congress> last accessed 1 August 2021.

Alexander GS and EM Peñalver, *An Introduction to Property Theory* (Cambridge University Press 2012).

Allen AL, 'Coercing privacy' (1999) 40 *William & Mary Law Review* 723.

Almeling DS, 'Seven reasons why trade secrets are increasingly important' (2012) 27 *Berkeley Technology Law Journal* 1091.

Almeling DS et al., 'A statistical analysis of trade secret litigation in state courts' (2011) 46 *Gonzaga Law Review* 57.

American Law Institute, American Bar Association Continuing Legal Education, 'Representing estate and trust beneficiaries and fiduciaries: Virtual assets' *ALI-ABA Course of Study* (14–15 July 2011) <http://www.cobar.org/repository/Inside_Bar/TrustEstate/SRC/Virtual%20Asset%20Subcommittee%20Research%20%231.pdf> last accessed 1 August 2021.

Arias AV, 'Life, liberty and the pursuit of swords and armor: Regulating the theft of virtual goods' (2008) 57 *Emory Law Journal* 1301.

Aristotle, *The Nicomachean Ethics*, trans. H Rackham (rev. edn, Heinemann 1968).

Associated Press release, *justinellsworth.net* (21 April 2005) <http://www.justinellsworth.net/email/ap-apr05.htm> last accessed 1 August 2021.

Atherton R, 'Expectation without right: Testamentary freedom and the position of women in nineteenth century New South Wales' (1988) 11 *University of New South Wales Law Journal* 133.

Atwater J, 'Who owns email? Do you have the right to decide the disposition of your private digital life?' (2006) *Utah Law Review* 397.

Băbeanu D et al., 'Strategic outlines: Between value and digital assets management' (2009) 11 *Annales Universitatis Apulensis Series Oeconomica* 318.

Baird DG, 'Common law intellectual property and the legacy of International News Service v Associated Press' (1983) 50 *University of Chicago Law Review* 411.

Baldas T, 'Slain soldier's e-mail spurs legal debate: Ownership of deceased's messages at crux of issue' (2005) 27 *National Law Journal* 10.

Balkin JM, 'Virtual liberty: Freedom to design and freedom to play in virtual worlds' (2004) 90(8) *Virginia Law Review* Va. L. Rev. 2043.

Balkin JM and BS Noveck (eds), *The State of Play: Laws, Games, and Virtual Worlds* (NYU Press 2006).

Ball J, 'The boundaries of property rights in English law', Report to the XVIIth International Congress of Comparative Law (2006) 10(3) *Electronic Journal of Comparative Law* 1.

Baron JB, 'Property as control: The case of information' (2012) 18 *Michigan Telecommunications and Technology Law Review* 367.

Bartle R, 'Hearts, clubs, diamonds, spades: Players who suit MUDs' (1996) 1(1) *The Journal of Virtual Environments* <http://mud.co.uk/richard/hcds.htm> last accessed 1 August 2021.

Bartle R, 'Presence and flow: Ill-fitting clothes for virtual world' (2007) 10(3) *Techné: Research in Philosophy and Technology* 39.

Bartle RA, 'Virtual worlds: Why people play' in T Alexander (ed.), *Massively Multiplayer Game Development 2* (Charles River Media 2005) 3–18 <http://www.mud.co.uk/richard/VIRTUALWORLDWPP.pdf> last accessed 1 August 2021.

Barton WB, 'A study in the law of trade secrets' (1939) 13 *University of Cincinnati Law Review* 507.

Baudouin A, 'Fiducie in French law' (2007) 2 *International Business Law Journal* 276.

BBC News, 'Molly Russell: "Why can't I see my daughter's data?"' (6 February 2019) <https://www.bbc.com/news/av/technology-47143315/molly-russell-why-can-t-i-see-my-daughter-s-data> last accessed 1 August 2021.

BBC News, 'Virtual theft leads to arrest' (14 November 2007) <http://news.bbc.co.uk/1/hi/7094764.stm> last accessed 1 August 2021.

BBC News, 'Who owns your e-mails?' (11 January 2005) <http://news.bbc.co.uk/1/hi/magazine/4164669.stm> last accessed 1 August 2021.

BCelebrated <http://www.bcelebrated.com/> last accessed 1 August 2021.

Be RA, 'Dead or alive?: The misappropriation doctrine resurrected in Texas' (1996) 33 *Houston Law Review* 447.

Becker LC, *Property Rights: Philosophic Foundations* (Routledge and Kegan Paul 1977).

Beevolve, 'An exhaustive study of Twitter users across the world' <http://www.beevolve.com/twitter-statistics/#c1> last accessed 1 August 2021.

Bell J et al., *Principles of French Law* (2nd edn, Oxford University Press 2008).

Benkler Y, 'Siren songs and Amish children: Autonomy, information, and law' (2001) 76 *New York University Law Review* 23.

Bennett CJ and CD Raab, *The Governance of Privacy: Policy Instruments in Global Perspective* (MIT Press 2006).

Bentham J, *A Fragment on Government*, ed. W Harrison (Oxford 1948).

Bentham J, *An Introduction to the Principles of Morals and Legislation*, ed. JH Burns and HLA Hart (Athlone Press 1970).
Bernal P, *Internet Privacy Rights: Rights to Protect Autonomy* (Cambridge University Press 2014).
Besen SM and LJ Raskind, 'An introduction to the law and economics of intellectual property' (Winter 1991) 5(1) *Journal of Economic Perspectives* 3.
Beverley-Smith H, *The Commercial Appropriation of Personality* (Cambridge University Press 2002).
Beyer GW and N Cahn, 'Digital planning: The future of elder law' (2013) 9 *NAELA Journal* 135.
Black G, *A Right of Publicity in Scots Law* (PhD thesis, University of Edinburgh 2009).
Black G, *Publicity Rights and Image: Exploitation and Legal Control* (Hart 2011).
Black Mirror, 'Be Right Back', Season 2, Episode 1, 11 February 2013. Series currently available on Netflix and More4.
Blackstone SW, *Commentaries on the Laws of England (1765–1769)* (18th edn, S. Sweet etc. 1829).
Blazer C, 'The five indicia of virtual property' (2006) 5 *Pierce Law Review* 137.
Blizzard, 'World of Warcraft – end user license agreement' <https://www.blizzard.com/en-us/legal/fba4d00f-c7e4-4883-b8b9-1b4500a402ea/blizzard-end-user-license-agreement> last accessed 1 August 2021.
Bosker B and D Grandoni, '9 quirkiest facts about Twitter: Gaze into the soul of the Twittersphere' *Huffington Post* (10 November 2012) <http://www.huffingtonpost.com/2012/10/10/quirkiest-facts-twitter-users_n_1956260.html> last accessed 1 August 2021.
Bouckaert B, 'What is property?' (1990) 13 *Harvard Journal of Law and Public Policy* 775.
Bowman DA and RP McMahan, 'Virtual reality: How much immersion is enough?' (2007) 40(7) *Computer* 36.
boyd d, 'Why youth (heart) social network sites: The role of networked publics in teenage social life' in D Buckingham (ed.), *Youth, Identity, and Digital Media* (MIT Press 2009) 119–29 <http://www.mitpressjournals.org/doi/pdf/10.1162/dmal.9780262524834.119> last accessed 1 August 2021.
boyd d and NB Ellison, 'Social network sites: Definition, history, and scholarship' (2007) 13(1) *Journal of Computer-Mediated Communication* 210.
Boyle J, 'The second enclosure movement and the construction of the public domain' (2003) 66(1) *Law and Contemporary Problems* 33.
Boyle J, *Shamans, Software and Spleens: Law and the Construction of the Information Society* (Harvard University Press 1996).
Bradbury R, 'A proposed UK law would automatically hand loved ones access to your messages, photos, and emails after you die' *Business Insider* (31 January 2022) <https://www.businessinsider.com/uk-law-proposed-for-family-get-devices-deceased-2022-1?utmSource=twitter&utmContent=referral&utmTerm=topbar&referrer=twitter> last accessed 31 January 2022.
Brennan S, 'Crystal Palace space station auction tops 330,000 US dollars' *Joystiq* (2009) <http://massively.joystiq.com/2009/12/29/crystal-palace-space-station-auction-tops-330-000-us-dollars/> last accessed 1 August 2021.
Bridge M, *Personal Property Law* (3rd edn, Oxford University Press 2002).

Buck S, 'How 1 billion people are coping with death and Facebook' *Mashable* (13 February 2013) <http://mashable.com/2013/02/13/facebook-after-death/> last accessed 1 August 2021.

Buckle C, *Natural Law and the Theory of Property: Grotius to Hume* (Clarendon Press 1991).

Buitelaar JC, 'Post-mortem privacy and informational self-determination' (2017) 19(2) *Ethics and Information Technology* 129.

Cahn N, 'Postmortem life on-line' (2011) 25 *Probate & Property* 36.

Cahn N, 'Probate law meets the digital age' (2014) 67 *Vanderbilt Law Review* 1697.

Camp BT, 'The play's the thing: A theory of taxing virtual worlds' (2007) 59(1) *Hastings Law Journal* 69.

Carrier M and G Lastowka, 'Against cyberproperty' (2007) 22 *Berkeley Technology Law Journal* 1485.

Castex L, E Harbinja and J Rossi, 'Défendre les vivants ou les morts? Controverses sous-jacentes au droit des données post-mortem à travers une perspective comparée franco-américaine' (2018) 4(210) *Réseaux* 117.

Castronova E, 'On virtual economies' (2003) 3 *The International Journal of Computer Gaming Research* <http://www.gamestudies.org/0302/castronova/> last accessed 1 August 2021.

Castronova E, 'Real products in imaginary worlds' (2005) 83(5) *Harvard Business Review* 20.

Castronova E, 'The right to play' (2004) 49 *New York Law School Law Review* 185.

Castronova E, 'Virtual world economy: It's Namibia, basically' *Terranova* (3 August 2004) <http://www.terranova.blogs.com/terra_nova/2004/08/virtual_world_e.html> 1 August 2021.

Castronova E, 'Virtual worlds: A first-hand account of market and society on the cyberian frontier' (2001) 618 CESifo Working Papers Series.

Chally J, 'The law of trade secrets: Toward a more efficient approach' (2004) 57 *Vanderbilt Law Review* 1269.

Chan HK, 'Memories of friends departed endure on Facebook' *Facebook* (26 October 2009) <https://www.facebook.com/notes/facebook/memories-of-friends-departed-endure-on-facebook/163091042130> last accessed 1 August 2021.

Chein A, 'A practical look at virtual property' (2006) 80 *St. John's Law Review* 1059.

Chen Y et al., 'An analysis of online gaming crime characteristics' (2005) 15 *Internet Research* 246.

Cheng K and PA Cairns, 'Behaviour, realism and immersion in games' in *Proceedings of the 2005 Conference on Human Factors in Computing Systems*, CHI 2005, Portland, Oregon, 2–7 April 2005 <http://www.uclic.ucl.ac.uk/paul/research/Cheng.pdf> last accessed 1 August 2021.

Cherry MA, 'A taxonomy of virtual work' (2011) 45 *Georgia Law Review* 951.

Chiappetta W, 'Myth, chameleon, or intellectual property Olympian? A normative framework supporting trade secret law' (1999) 8 *George Mason Law Review* 69.

Cifrino C, 'Virtual property, virtual rights: Why contract law, not property law, must be the governing paradigm in the law of virtual worlds' (2014) 55 *Boston College Law Review* 235.

Cirrus Legacy, 'Making it easy for your guardians' <http://www.cirruslegacy.com/139-guardians.html> last accessed 1 August 2021 (no longer available).

Cohn EJ, *Manual of German Law* (British Institute of International and Comparative Law; Oceana Publications 1968).
Cohen JE, *Between Truth and Power: The Legal Constructions of Informational Capitalism* (Oxford University Press 2019).
Cohen JE, *Configuring the Networked Self: Law, Code, and the Play of Everyday Practice* (Yale University Press 2012).
Cohen JE, 'Examined lives: Informational privacy and the subject as object' (2000) 52 *Stanford Law Review* 1373.
Coleman A, *The Legal Protection of Trade Secrets* (Sweet & Maxwell 1992).
Conaglen M, 'Thinking about proprietary remedies for breach of confidence' (2008) 1 *Intellectual Property Quarterly* 82.
Conner J, 'Digital life after death: The issue of planning for a person's digital assets after death' (2010–11) 3 *Estate Planning & Community Property Law Journal* 301.
Cornish W and D Llewelyn, *Intellectual Property: Patents, Copyright, Trade Marks and Allied Rights* (6th edn, Sweet & Maxwell 2007).
Dabbish L et al., 'Understanding email use: Predicting action on a message' in *Proceedings of the 2005 Conference on Human Factors in Computing Systems*, CHI 2005, Portland, Oregon, 2–7 April 2005 <http://www.cs.cmu.edu/~kiesler/publications/2005pdfs/2005-Dabbish-CHI.pdf> last accessed 1 August 2021.
Dale A, 'More estate plans account for "digital assets"' *Wall Street Journal* (13 June 2013) <http://online.wsj.com/article/SB1000142412788732373430457854315 1391292038.html> last accessed 1 August 2021.
Damstedt BG, 'Limiting Locke: A natural law justification for the fair use doctrine' (2003) 112 *Yale Law Journal* 1179.
Darrow J and Ferrera G, 'Who owns a decedent's e-mails: Inheritable probate assets or property of the network?' (2006) 10 *New York University Journal of Legislation and Public Policy* 281.
Davey T, *Until Death Do Us Part: Post-Mortem Privacy Rights for the Ante-Mortem Person* (PhD thesis, University of East Anglia 2020).
Day T, 'Avatar rights in a constitutionless world' (2009–10) 32 *Hastings Communications and Entertainment Law Journal* 137.
DeadSocial <http://www.deadsocial.org/> last accessed 1 August 2021.
Death and Digital Legacy, 'Nebraska is latest state to address digital legacy' (20 February 2012) <http://www.deathanddigitallegacy.com/2012/02/20/nebraska-is-latest-state-to-address-digital-legacy/> last accessed 1 August 2021.
Deenihan KE, 'Leave those orcs alone: Property rights in virtual worlds' (26 March 2008) <http://ssrn.com/abstract=1113402> last accessed 1 August 2021.
Demsetz H, 'Toward a theory of property rights' (1967) 57 *American Economic Review* 347.
Desai DR, 'Property, persona, and preservation' (2008) 81 *Temple Law Review* 67.
de Waal MJ, 'A comparative overview' in KGC Reid, MJ de Waal and R Zimmermann (eds), *Exploring the Law of Succession: Studies National, Historical and Comparative* (Edinburgh University Press 2007).
Dibble J, *My Tiny Life: Crime and Passion in a Virtual World* (Henry Holt 1998).
Dixon M, *Modern Land Law* (7th edn, Routledge 2010).
Dobie WJ, *Manual of the Law of Liferent and Fee in Scotland* (W. Green & Son 1941).

Donner I, 'The copyright clause of the U.S. Constitution: Why did the framers include it with unanimous approval?' (1992) 36(3) *American Journal of Legal History* 361.

Dosch N, 'Overview of digital assets: Defining digital assets for the legal community' *Digital Estate Planning* (14 May 2010) <http://www.digitalestateplanning.com> last accessed 1 August 2021.

Dow EH, *Electronic Records in the Manuscript Repository* (Scarecrow Press 2009).

Duggan M, 'Demographics of key social networking platforms' *Pew Internet* (9 January 2015) <http://www.pewinternet.org/2015/01/09/demographics-of-key-social-networking-platforms-2/> last accessed 1 August 2021.

du Toit F, 'The limits imposed upon freedom of testation by the boni mores: lessons from common law and civil law (continental) legal systems' (2000) *Stellenbosch Law Review* 358.

Dutton WH and G Blank with D Groselj, *Cultures of the Internet: The Internet in Britain. Oxford Internet Survey 2013 Report* (Oxford Internet Institute, University of Oxford 2013).

Dworkin G, *The Theory and Practice of Autonomy* (Cambridge University Press 1988).

Ebke W and MW Finkin, *Introduction to German Law* (Kluwer Law International 1996).

Edwards B, 'The 11 most influential online worlds of all time' *PCWorld* (2011) <http://www.pcworld.com/article/228000/influentialonlineworlds.html> last accessed 1 August 2021.

Edwards L and E Harbinja, '"Be right back": What rights do we have over post-mortem avatars of ourselves?' in L Edwards, B Schafer and E Harbinja (eds), *Future Law: Emerging Technology, Regulation and Ethics* (Edinburgh University Press 2020).

Edwards L and E Harbinja, 'Protecting post-mortem privacy: Reconsidering the privacy interests of the deceased in a digital world' (2013) 32(1) *Cardozo Arts & Entertainment Law Journal* 111.

Edwards L and E Harbinja, 'Written submission', NSW Law Reform Commission: Access to digital assets upon death or incapacity (2019).

Elkin-Koren N and N Netanel, *The Commodification of Information* (Kluwer Law International 2002).

EmailHistory.org, 'Email milestones timeline', ed. dcrocker (6 September 2012) <http://emailhistory.org/Email-Timeline.html> last accessed 1 August 2021.

Eppler MJ and J Mengis, 'The concept of information overload: A review of literature from organization science, accounting, marketing, MIS, and related disciplines' (2004) 20(5) *The Information Society: An International Journal* 325.

Epstein R, 'One step beyond Nozick's minimal state: The role of forced exchanges in political theory' (2005) 22 *Social Philosophy and Policy* 286.

Erdos D, 'Dead ringers? Legal persons and the deceased in European data protection law' (2021) 40 *Computer Law & Security Review* 13.

Erlank W, *Property in Virtual Worlds* (PhD thesis, Stellenbosch University 2012) <http://ssrn.com/abstract=2216481> last accessed 1 August 2021.

Ermi L and F Mayra, 'Fundamental components of the gameplay experience: Analysing immersion' in S de Castell and J Jenson (eds), *Changing Views: Worlds in Play: Selected Papers of the 2005 Digital Games Research Association's Second*

International Conference, 16–20 June 2005, Vancouver (DiGRA 2005) <http://www.uta.fi/~tlilma/gameplay_experience.pdf> last accessed 1 August 2021.

Etzioni A, *The Limits of Privacy* (Basic Books 2000).

European Commission, 'Green paper from the Commission on policy options for progress towards a European Contract Law for consumers and businesses' COM(2010)348 final.

European Commission, 'European Declaration on Digital Rights and Principles for the Digital Decade' Brussels, 26.1.2022 COM(2022) 28 final.

European Commission, 'Proposal for a Regulation of the European Parliament and of the Council on a Common European Sales Law' COM(2011) 635 final.

Everplans, 'State-by-state digital estate planning laws' <https://www.everplans.com/tools-and-resources/state-by-state-digital-estate-planning-laws> last accessed 1 August 2021.

Facebook, 'Accessing your Facebook data; where can I find my Facebook data?' <https://www.facebook.com/help/405183566203254/> last accessed 1 August 2021.

Facebook, 'Adding a legacy contact' *Facebook Newsroom* (12 February 2015) <http://newsroom.fb.com/news/2015/02/adding-a-legacy-contact/> last accessed 1 August 2021.

Facebook, 'Data use policy, some other things to know' <https://m.facebook.com/policy/?page=other> last accessed 1 August 2021.

Facebook, 'Deactivating, deleting & memorializing accounts' <https://www.facebook.com/help/359046244166395/> last accessed 1 August 2021.

Facebook, 'How do I ask a question about a deceased person's account on Facebook?' <https://www.facebook.com/help/265593773453448> last accessed 1 August 2021.

Facebook, 'How do I request content from the account of a deceased person?' <https://www.facebook.com/help/123355624495297> last accessed 1 August 2021.

Facebook, 'How do I request the removal of a deceased family member's Facebook account?' <https://www.facebook.com/help/1518259735093203/?helpref=related> last accessed 1 August 2021.

Facebook, 'How do I submit a special request for a deceased user's account on the site?' <https://www.facebook.com/help/265593773453448> last accessed 1 August 2021.

Facebook, 'How News Feed works' <https://www.facebook.com/help/327131014036297/> last accessed 1 August 2021.

Facebook, 'Memorialization request' <https://www.facebook.com/help/contact/305593649477238> last accessed 1 August 2021.

Facebook, 'Messenger' <https://www.facebook.com/mobile/messenger> last accessed 1 August 2021.

Facebook, 'Making it easier to honor a loved one on Facebook after they pass away' *Facebook Newsroom* (9 April 2019) <https://newsroom.fb.com/news/2019/04/updates-to-memorialization/> last accessed 1 August 2021.

Facebook, 'Privacy checkup is now rolling out' *Facebook Newsroom* (4 September 2014) <http://newsroom.fb.com/news/2014/09/privacy-checkup-is-now-rolling-out/> last accessed 1 August 2021.

Facebook, 'Requesting content from a deceased person's account' <https://www.facebook.com/help/contact/398036060275245> last accessed 1 August 2021.

Facebook, 'Special request for a medically incapacitated or deceased person's account' <https://www.facebook.com/help/contact/228813257197480> last accessed 1 August 2021.

Facebook, 'Terms: Statement of rights and responsibilities' <https://www.facebook.com/legal/terms> last accessed 1 August 2021.

Facebook, 'Terms of use' <http://www.facebook.com/terms.php> last accessed 1 August 2021.

Facebook, 'Timeline' <https://www.facebook.com/about/timeline> last accessed 1 August 2021.

Facebook, 'Uploading photos & profile pictures' <https://www.facebook.com/help/118731871603814/> last accessed 1 August 2021.

Facebook, 'What are tributes on a memorialised Facebook profile?' <https://www.facebook.com/help/745202382483645> last accessed 1 August 2021.

Facebook, 'What data can a legacy contact download from Facebook?' <https://www.facebook.com/help/408044339354739/?helpref=related> last accessed 1 August 2021.

Facebook, 'What happens when a deceased person's account is memorialized?' <https://www.facebook.com/help/103897939701143/> last accessed 1 August 2021.

Facebook Wiki, '*API*, Facebook Developer Wiki' <http://wiki.developers.facebook.com/index.php/> last accessed 1 August 2021.

Facebook Wiki, '*FBML*, Facebook Developer WIKI' <http://wiki.developers.facebook.com/index.php/FBML> last accessed 1 August 2021.

Fairfield J, 'Anti-social contracts: The contractual governance of virtual worlds' (2007) 53 *McGill Law Journal* 427.

Fairfield J, 'The end of the (virtual) world' (2009) 112(1) *West Virginia Law Review* 53.

Fairfield J, 'Virtual property' (2005) 85 *Boston University Law Review* 1047.

Fallon RH Jr., 'Two senses of autonomy' (1994) 46 *Stanford Law Review* 875.

Favro J, 'A new frontier in electronic discovery: Preserving and obtaining metadata' (2007) 13 *Boston University Journal of Science and Technology Law* 1.

Feinberg J, 'Autonomy, sovereignty, and privacy: Moral ideals in the Constitution?' (1983) 58 *Notre Dame Law Review* 445.

Fennell LA, 'Adjusting alienability' (2009) 122 *Harvard Law Review* 1403.

Fields L, 'Facebook changes access to profiles of deceased' *ABC News* (22 February 2014) <http://abcnews.go.com/Technology/facebook-access-profiles-deceased/story?id=22632425> last accessed 1 August 2021.

Final Fling <http://blog.finalfling.com/> last accessed 1 August 2021.

Floridi L, 'Distributed morality in an information society' (2013) 19(3) *Science and Engineering Ethics* 727.

Floridi L, 'On human dignity as a foundation for the right to privacy' (2016) 29 *Philosophy and Technology* 307.

Floridi L, *The Ethics of Information* (Oxford University Press 2013).

Floridi L, *The Fourth Revolution: How the Infosphere Is Reshaping Human Reality* (Oxford University Press 2014).

Fox Z, '10 online activities that dominate Americans' days' *Mashable* (15 August 2013) <http://mashable.com/2013/08/15/popular-online-activities/> last accessed 1 August 2021.

Freeman SR, *Collected Papers* (Harvard University Press 1999).

Friedman DD et al., 'Some economics of trade secret law' (1991) 5 *Journal of Economic Perspectives* 61.

Friedman LM, 'The law of the living, the law of the dead: Property, succession and society' (1966) *Wisconsin Law Review* 340.

Friedmann WG, *Law in a Changing Society* (2nd edn, Penguin 1972).

Frischmann BM, 'An economic theory of infrastructure and commons management' 89 (2005) *Minnesota Law Review* 917.

Fujichaku RY, 'The misappropriation doctrine in cyberspace: Protecting the commercial value of "hot news" information' (1998) 20 *University of Hawai'i Law Review* 421.

Gambino L, 'In death, Facebook photos could fade away forever' *Associated Press* (1 March 2013) <http://news.yahoo.com/death-facebook-photos-could-fade-away-forever-085129756--finance.html> last accessed 1 August 2021.

Gard ET, 'January 1, 2003: The birth of the unpublished public domain and its international consequences' (2006) 24 *Cardozo Arts & Entertainment Law Journal* 687.

Genders R, 'Fiduciary management of digital assets' (Digital Assets taskforce for STEP (UK) Capacity SIG, Draft 29 April 2013) (on file with the author).

George A, 'The difficulty of defining "property"' (2005) 25(4) *Oxford Journal of Legal Studies* 813.

Gervais DJ, 'Feist goes global: A comparative analysis of the notion of originality in copyright law' (2002) 49 (4) *Journal of the Copyright Society of the U.S.A.* 949.

Gilbert BJ, 'Getting to conscionable: Negotiating virtual worlds' end user license agreements without getting externally regulated' (2009) 4 *Journal of International Commercial Law and Technology* 238.

Gilbert N, 'Number of email users worldwide 2021/2022: Demographics & predictions' *FinancesOnline* <https://financesonline.com/number-of-email-users/> last accessed 1 August 2021.

Glushko B, 'Tales of the (virtual) city: Governing property disputes in virtual worlds' (2007) 22 *Berkeley Technology Law Journal* 507.

Gong J, 'Defining and addressing virtual property in international treaties' (2011) 17 *Boston University Journal of Science and Technology Law* 101.

González LH, 'Trade secret protection . . . in the cloud' (2013) 24(7) *Entertainment Law Review* 245.

Google, 'Inactive Account Manager for trusted contacts' <https://support.google.com/accounts/answer/3036514?hl=en> last accessed 1 August 2021.

Google, 'Submit a request regarding a deceased user's account' <https://support.google.com/accounts/contact/deceased?hl=en&ref_topic=3075532&rd=1> last accessed 1 August 2021.

Google, 'Terms of service' (effective 31 March 2020) <http://www.google.com/intl/en-GB/policies/terms/> last accessed 1 August 2021.

Gordon WJ, 'A property right in self-expression: Equality and individualism in the natural law of intellectual property' (1993) 102 *Yale Law Journal* 1533.

Graves CT, 'Trade secrets as property: Theory and consequences' (2007) 15 *Journal of Intellectual Property Law* 39.

Gray K, *Elements of Land Law* (Butterworths 1987).

Greenberg J and J Arndt, 'Terror management theory' in PAM Van Lange, AW Kruglanski and ET Higgins (eds), *Handbook of Theories of Social Psychology: Volume One* (SAGE 2011).

Greenberg L, 'Metadata and the world wide web' (2003) *Encyclopedia of Library and Information Science* 1876.

Gretton GL and AJM Steven, *Property, Trusts and Succession* (2nd edn, Bloomsbury Professional 2013).

Grimmelmann JTL, 'Saving Facebook' (2009) 94 *Iowa Law Review* 1137.

Grimmelmann JTL, 'Virtual worlds as comparative law' (2004) 49 *New York Law School Law Review* 147.

Guest AG (ed.), *Oxford Essays in Jurisprudence: A Collaborative Work* (Oxford University Press 1961).

Guibault L and PB Hugenholtz (eds), *The Future of the Public Domain* (Kluwer Law International 2006).

Gutwirth S et al. (eds), *Computers, Privacy and Data Protection: An Element of Choice* (Springer Science Business Media 2011).

Hammond RG, 'Quantum physics, econometric models and property rights to information' (1981) 27 *McGill Law Journal* 47.

Hansen D, B Shneiderman and M Smith, *Analyzing Social Media Networks with NodeXL: Insights from a Connected World* (Morgan Kaufmann 2010).

Hansmann H and U Mattei, 'The functions of trust law: A comparative legal and economic analysis' (1998) 73 *New York University Law Review* 434.

Harbinja E, 'Does the EU data protection regime protect post-mortem privacy and what could be the potential alternatives?' (2013) 10:1 *SCRIPTed* 19.

Harbinja E, 'Emails and death: Legal issues surrounding post-mortem transmission of emails' (2019) 43(7) *Death Studies* 435.

Harbinja E, *Legal Aspects of Transmission of Digital Assets on Death* (PhD thesis, University of Strathclyde 2017).

Harbinja E, 'Legal nature of emails: A comparative perspective' (2016) 14 *Duke Law and Technology Review* 227.

Harbinja E, 'The "new(ish)" property, informational bodies, and postmortality' in M Savin-Baden and V Mason-Robbie (eds), *Digital Afterlife: Death Matters in a Digital Age* (Taylor & Francis 2020) 89–106.

Harbinja E, 'Posthumous medical data donation: The case for a legal framework' in J Krutzinna and L Floridi (eds), *The Ethics of Medical Data Donation*, Philosophical Studies Series, vol 137 (Springer 2019) 97–113.

Harbinja E, 'Post-mortem privacy 2.0: Theory, law and technology' (2017) 31 *International Review of Law, Computers & Technology* 26.

Harbinja E, 'Social media and death' in L Gillies and D Mangan (eds), *The Legal Challenges of Social Media* (Edward Elgar 2017).

Harbinja E, 'Virtual worlds – a legal post-mortem account' (2014) 11:3 *SCRIPTed* 273 <http://script-ed.org/?p=1669> last accessed 1 August 2021.

Harbinja E, 'Virtual worlds players – consumers or citizens?' (2014) 3(4) *Internet Policy Review* <http://policyreview.info/articles/analysis/virtual-worlds-players-consumers-or-citizens> last accessed 1 August 2021.

Harbinja E, L Edwards and M McVey, 'Chatbots that resurrect the dead: Legal experts weigh in on "disturbing" technology' *The Conversation* (1 March 2021) <https://www.theconversation.com/chatbots-that-resurrect-the-dead-legal-experts-weigh-in-on-disturbing-technology-155436> last accessed 1 August 2021.

Harbinja E, L Edwards and M McVey, 'Governing ghostbots' (2022) *Computer Law and Security Review* (forthcoming).

Harbinja E and H Pearce, 'Your data will never die, but you will: A comparative analysis of US and UK post-mortem data donation frameworks' (2020) *Computer Law and Security Review* 36.

Hardin G, 'The tragedy of the commons' (1968) 162 *Science* 1243.

Harris GJ, 'Metadata: High-tech invisible ink legal considerations' (2009) 78 *Mississippi Law Journal* 939.

Harris JW, *Property and Justice* (Clarendon Press 1996).

Hartung S, *Digital Executor(R): Unraveling the New Path for Estate Planning* (FriesenPress 2021).

Hasanović J and E Adilović, 'The double life of virtual: Emancipation as immobilization in an isolated age' in ŞŞ Erçetin, ŞN Açıkalın and E Vajzović (eds), *Chaos, Complexity and Leadership* (Springer Proceedings in Complexity 2020).

Haworth S, 'Laying your online self to rest: Evaluating the Uniform Fiduciary Access to Digital Assets Act' (2014) 68 *University of Miami Law Review* 535.

Hayton DJ (ed.), *European Succession Laws* (2nd edn, Jordans 2002).

Heeks R, 'Understanding "gold farming" and real-money trading as the intersection of real and virtual economies' (2010) 2(4) *Virtual Economies, Virtual Goods and Service Delivery in Virtual Worlds* 1.

Hegel GWF, *The Philosophy of Right*, trans. TM Knox (Oxford University Press 1967).

Heller MA, 'The tragedy of the anticommons: Property in the transition from Marx to markets reviewed' (1998) 111(3) *Harvard Law Review* 621.

Heller MA and R Eisenberg, 'Can patents deter innovation? The anticommons in biomedical research' (1998) 280 *Science* 698.

Henkin L, 'Privacy and autonomy' (1974) 74 *Columbia Law Review* 1410.

Hess C and E Ostrom, *Understanding Knowledge as a Commons from Theory to Practice* (MIT Press 2007).

Hetcher S, 'User-generated content and the future of copyright: Part two – agreements between users and mega-sites' (2008) 24 *Santa Clara Computer & High Technology Law Journal* 829.

Hill JW, 'Trade secrets, unjust enrichment, and the classification of obligations' (1999) 4 *Virginia Journal of Law and Technology* 2.

Hof R, 'Second Life's first millionaire' *Businessweek Online* (2006) <https://www.bloomberg.com/news/articles/2006-11-25/second-lifes-first-millionaire> last accessed 1 August 2021.

Hogan Lovells International LLP, 'Study on trade secrets and parasitic copying (look-alikes) ("2012 study")' MARKT/2010/20/D (13 January 2012) <http://ec.europa.eu/internal_market/iprenforcement/docs/trade/Study_Trade_Secrets_en.pdf> last accessed 1 August 2021.

Hohfeld WN, 'Some fundamental legal conceptions as applied in judicial reasoning' (1913) 23 *Yale Law Journal* 16.

Holloway D, 'Hillary Clinton flirts with Second Life' *Crikey* (11 July 2007) <http://www.crikey.com.au/2007/07/11/hillary-clinton-flirts-with-second-life/> last accessed 1 August 2021.

Holm J and E Mäkinen, 'The value of currency in World of Warcraft' (2018) *Journal of Internet Social Networking & Virtual Communities* article 672253.

Honoré AM, 'Ownership' in AG Guest (ed.), *Oxford Essays in Jurisprudence: A Collaborative Work* (Oxford University Press 1961).

Hopkins JP, 'Aferlife in the cloud: Managing a digital estate' (2013) 5 *Hastings Science and Technology Law Journal* 210.

Horn N et al., *German Private and Commercial Law: An Introduction* (Clarendon Press 1982).

Horowitz SJ, 'Competing Lockean claims to virtual property' (2007) 20(2) *Harvard Journal of Law and Technology* 443.

House of Lords Select Committee on the European Communities, *Report on the Protection of Personal Data* (HMSO 1993).

Hudson A (ed.), *New Perspectives on Property Law, Obligations and Restitution* (Cavendish 2004).

Huff Post Tech, 'Karen Williams' Facebook saga raises question of whether users' profiles are part of "digital estates"' *Huffington Post* (15 March 2012) <http://www.huffingtonpost.com/2012/03/15/karen-williams-face book_n_1349128.html> last accessed 1 August 2021.

Hughes J, 'Copyright and incomplete historiographies: Of piracy, propertisation, and Thomas Jefferson' (2005–6) 79 *Southern California Law Review* 993.

Hughes J, 'The philosophy of intellectual property' (1988) 77 *Georgetown Law Journal* 287.

ifidie, 'What happens to your Facebook profile if you die?' <http://ifidie.net> last accessed 1 August 2021.

International Legal Practitioner, 'Restrictions on testamentary freedom: A comparative study and transnational implications' (1990) 15 *International Legal Practitioner* 14.

Jacobsen MH (ed.), *Postmortal Society: Towards a Sociology of Immortality* (Routledge 2017).

Jankowich AE, 'The complex web of corporate rule-making in virtual worlds' (2006) 8 *Tulane Journal of Technology and Intellectual Property* 1.

Jankowich AE, 'Property and democracy in virtual worlds' (2005) 11 *Boston University Journal of Science and Technology Law* 173.

Juul J, 'A history of the computer game' *Blog* (2001) <http://www.jesperjuul.net/thesis/2-historyofthecomputergame.html> last accessed 1 August 2021.

Kant I, *The Metaphysics of Morals*, trans. M Gregor (Cambridge 1991).

Kant I, *Observations on the Feeling of the Beautiful and the Sublime*, trans. JT Goldthwait (2nd edn, University of California Press 2003).

Kasket E, 'Access to the digital self in life and death: Privacy in the context of posthumously persistent Facebook profiles' (2013) 10:1 *SCRIPTed* 7.

Kasket E, *All the Ghosts in the Machine* (Robinson 2019).

Kastenbaum R, *On Our Way: The Final Passage through Life and Death (Life Passages)* (University of California Press 2004).

Kelly M, 'Memories of friends departed endure on Facebook' *Facebook Blog* (26 October 2009) <https://www.facebook.com/blog/blog.php?post=163091042130> last accessed 1 August 2021.

Kerr OS, 'Criminal law in virtual worlds' 2008 *University of Chicago Legal Forum* 415.

Kieff S, 'Property rights and property rules for commercializing inventions' (2001) 85 *Minnesota Law Review* 697.

Kitch EW, 'The law and economics of rights in valuable information' (1980) 9 *Journal of Legal Studies* 683.

Knight W, 'Gamer wins back virtual booty in court battle' *New Scientist* (23 December 2003) <http://www.newscientist.com/article/dn4510-gamer-wins-back-virtual-booty-in-courtbattle.Html> last accessed 1 August 2021.

Korolov M, 'Outrage grows over new Second Life terms' *Hypergrid Business* (30 September 2013) <http://www.hypergridbusiness.com/2013/09/outrage-grows-over-new-second-life-terms/> last accessed 1 August 2021.

Koops BJ, 'Forgetting footprints, shunning shadows: A critical analysis of the "right to be forgotten" in big data practice' (2011) 8:3 *SCRIPTed* 256.

Kraut R et al., 'Internet paradox revisited' (2002) 58(1) *Journal of Social Issues* 49.

Krebs on Security, 'How much is your Gmail worth?' (June 2013) <http://krebsonsecurity.com/2013/06/how-much-is-your-gmail-worth/> last accessed 1 August 2021.

Kretschmer M, L Bently and R Deazley, 'The history of copyright history (revisited)' (2013) 5(1) *WIPO Journal* 35.

Kulesza A, 'What happens to your Facebook account when you die?' *Blog* (3 February 2012) <http://blogs.lawyers.com/2012/02/what-happens-to-facebook-account-when-you-die/> last accessed 1 August 2021.

Kutler N, 'Protecting your online you: A new approach to handling your online persona after death' (2011) 26 *Berkeley Technology Law Journal* 1641.

KZero Worldswide, 'Consumer virtual reality: State of the market report' *KZero* (2014) <http://www.kzero.co.uk/blog/category/education-and-academia> last accessed 1 August 2021.

KZero Worldswide, 'Radar charts Q2 2014 VWs and MMOs shown by genre, average user age and status' *KZero* (2004) <http://www.kzero.co.uk/blog/category/education-and-academia> last accessed 1 August 2021.

Lamm J, 'Defending your ownership and privacy in Twitter (and other online accounts)' *Digital Passing Blog* (25 July 2012) <http://www.digitalpassing.com/2012/07/25/defending-ownership-privacy-twitter-online-accounts/> last accessed 1 August 2021.

Lamm J, 'Digital property created on the Internet every 60 seconds' *Digital Passing Blog* (20 June 2011) <http://www.digitalpassing.com/2011/06/20/digital-property-created-internet-every-60-seconds/> last accessed 1 August 2021.

Lamm J, 'Facebook blocks demand for contents of deceased user's account' *Digital Passing Blog* (11 October 2012) <http://www.digitalpassing.com/2012/10/11/facebook-blocks-demand-contentsdeceased-users-account/> last accessed 1 August 2021.

Lamm J, 'February 2013 list of state laws and proposals regarding fiduciary access to digital property during incapacity or after death' *Digital Passing Blog* (13 February 2013) <http://www.digitalpassing.com/2013/02/13/list-state-laws-proposals-fiduciary-access-digital-property-incapacity-death/> last accessed 1 August 2021.

Lamm J, 'Planning ahead for access to contents of a decedent's online accounts' *Digital Passing Blog* (9 February 2012) <http://www.digitalpassing.com/2012/02/09/planning-ahead-access-contents-decedent-online-accounts/> last accessed 1 August 2021.

Lamm J, 'To my son, I leave all my passwords' *Trusts and Estate Magazine* (July 2009) <http://www.gpmlaw.com/portalresource/lookup/wosid/cp-base-4-5968/media.name=/To_My_Son_I_Leave_All_My_Passwords.pdf> last accessed 1 August 2021.

Lamm J, 'What is digital property?' *Digital Passing Blog* (21 June 2010) <http://www.digitalpassing.com/2010/06/> last accessed 1 August 2021.

Lamm J et al., 'The digital death conundrum: How federal and state laws prevent fiduciaries from managing digital property' (2014) 68 *University of Miami Law Review* 385.

Landes WM, 'Copyright protection of letters, diaries and other unpublished works: An economic approach' (1992) 21 *Journal of Legal Studies* 79.

Landes WM and RA Posner, 'An economic analysis of copyright law' (1989) 18 *Journal of Legal Studies* 325.

Landes WM and RA Posner, *The Economic Structure of Intellectual Property Law* (Harvard University Press 2003).

Lasar M, 'Most Internet time now spent with social networks, games' *Arstechnica* (2010) <http://arstechnica.com/business/2010/08/nielsen-social-networking-and-gaming-up-email-uncertain/> last accessed 1 August 2021.

Lastowka FG, 'The Player-Authors Project' (30 November 2013) <http://ssrn.com/abstract=2361758> or <http://dx.doi.org/10.2139/ssrn.2361758> last accessed 1 August 2021.

Lastowka FG, *Virtual Justice: The New Laws of Online Worlds* (Yale University Press 2010).

Lastowka FG and D Hunter, 'The laws of the virtual worlds' (2004) 92 *California Law Review* 1.

Law Commission, 'Digital assets: Call for evidence' (April 2021) <https://www.lawcom.gov.uk/project/digital-assets/> last accessed 1 August 2021.

Law Commission, 'Making a will' (consultation paper 231, 2017) <https://www.s3-eu-west-2.amazonaws.com/lawcom-prod-storage-11jsxou24uy7q/uploads/2017/07/Making-a-will-consultation.pdf> last accessed 1 August 2021.

Law Commission, *Working Paper No. 110: Computer Misuse* (Her Majesty's Stationery Office 1988).

Lawson FH and B Rudden, *The Law of Property* (Oxford University Press 2002).

Lee D, 'Facebook reviews family memorials after dad's plea' *BBC* (6 February 2014) <http://www.bbc.co.uk/news/technology-26066688> last accessed 1 August 2021.

Lee Y and A Chen, 'Usability design and psychological ownership of a virtual world' (2011) 28(3) *Journal of Management Information Systems* 269.

Lemley MA, 'Property, intellectual property, and free riding' (2005) 83 *Texas Law Review* 1031.

Lemley MA, 'Terms of use' (2006) 91 *Minnesota Law Review* 459.

Lemley MA and PJ Weiser, 'Should property or liability rules govern information?' (2007) 85 *Texas Law Review* 783.

Lenhart A, S Jones and A Macgill, 'Adults and video games' *Pew Internet* (2008) <http://www.pewinternet.org/Reports/2008/Adults-and-Video-Games/1-Data-

Memo/07-Virtual-worlds-and-MMOGs-have-yet-to-catch-on.aspx> last accessed 1 August 2021.

Lessig L, *Code: Version 2.0* (Basic Books 2006).

Lessig L, *Free Culture: How Big Media Uses Technology and the Law to Lock Down Culture and Control Creativity* (Penguin 2004).

Leung S, 'The commons and anticommons in intellectual property' (2010) *UCL Journal of Law and Jurisprudence* 16.

Li v *Beijing Arctic Ice Tech Dev Co* (Beijing Chaoyang Dist People's Ct 18 December 2003) <http://www.chinacourt.org/public/detail.php?id=143455> last accessed 1 August 2021.

Linden Lab, 'Second Life affiliate program' <http://secondlife.com/corporate/affiliate/?lang=it-IT> last accessed 1 August 2021.

Linden Lab, 'Second Life residents to own digital creations' *Press Release* (2003) <http://creativecommons.org/press-releases/entry/3906> last accessed 1 August 2021.

Litman J, 'Information privacy/information property' (2000) *Stanford Law Review* 1283.

Locke J, *An Essay Concerning Human Understanding*, ed. P Nidditch (Oxford 1979).

Locke J, *Second Treatise of Government: Essay Concerning the True Original Extent and End of Civil Government*, ed. with an intro. CB Macpherson (Hackett 1980).

Lodder AD, 'Dutch Supreme Court 2012: Virtual theft ruling a one-off or first in a series?' (2013) 6(3) *Journal of Virtual Worlds Research* 1.

Lombard M and T Ditton, 'At the heart of it all: The concept of presence' (2004) 3(2) *Journal of Computer-Mediated Communication* <http://onlinelibrary.wiley.com/doi/10.1111/j.1083-6101.1997.tb00072.x/full> last accessed 1 August 2021.

Lopez AB, 'Posthumous privacy, decedent intent, and post-mortem access to digital assets' (2016) 24(1) *George Mason Law Review* 183.

Lyman J, 'Gamer wins lawsuit in Chinese court over stolen virtual winnings' *TECHNEWSWORLD* (19 December 2003) <http://www.technewsworld.comystory/3244Lhtml> last accessed 1 August 2021.

McAfee, 'McAfee reveals average Internet user has more than $37,000 in under-protected "digital assets"' (27 September 2011) <http://www.mcafee.com/hk/about/news/2011/q3/20110927-01.aspx> last accessed 1 August 2021.

McCallig D, 'Data protection and the deceased in the EU' Presentation at the Computer Privacy and Data Protection 2014 Panel: Exploring post-mortem privacy in a digital world, 21–23 January 2014) (on file with the author).

McCallig D, 'Facebook after death: An evolving policy in a social network' (2014) 22(2) *International Journal of Law and Information Technology* 107.

McCallig D, 'Private but eventually public: Why copyright in unpublished works matters in the digital age' (2013) 10:1 *SCRIPTed* 39.

McClean J, 'The common law life estate and the civil law usufruct: A comparative study' (1963) 12(2) *International & Comparative Law Quarterly* 649.

McClurg AJ, 'A thousand words are worth a picture: A privacy tort response to consumer data profiling' (2003) 98 *Northwestern University Law Review*.

McGhee JA (gen. ed.), *Snell's Equity* (31st edn, Sweet & Maxwell 2004).

Maciel C and V Pereira (eds), *Digital Legacy and Interaction: Post-Mortem Issues* (Springer 2013).

McKinnon L, 'Planning for the succession of digital assets' (2011) 27(4) *Computer Law and Security Review* 362.

McNealy J, 'Who owns your friends?: Phonedog v Kravitz and business claims of trade secret in social media information' (2013) 39 *Rutgers Computer and Technology Law Journal* 30.

Macpherson CB, *The Political Theory of Possessive Individualism: Hobbes to Locke* (Wynford edn, new edn, Oxford University Press 2011).

MacQueen HL, 'Ae fond kiss: A private matter?' in A Burrows, D Johnston and R Zimmermann (eds), *Judge and Jurist: Essays in Memory of Lord Rodger of Earlsferry* (Oxford University Press 2013).

MacQueen HL, 'Intellectual property and the common law in Scotland c1700–c1850' in CW Ng, L Bently and GD Agostino (eds), *The Common Law of Intellectual Property: Essays in Honour of Professor David Vaver* (Hart 2010).

MacQueen HL, '"My tongue is mine ain": Copyright, the spoken word and privacy' (2005) 68 *Modern Law Review* 349.

MacQueen HL, 'The war of the booksellers: Natural law, equity, and literary property in eighteenth-century Scotland' (2014) 35(3) *Journal of Legal History* 23.

Mahmassani H et al., 'Time to play? Activity engagement in multiplayer online role-playing games' (2010) *Journal of the Transportation Research Board* 129.

Makuch E, 'Activision Blizzard profits hit $1.1 billion in 2012' *Gamespot* (2013) <http://www.gamespot.com/articles/activision-blizzard-profits-hit-11-billion-in-2012/1100-6403613/> last accessed 1 August 2021.

Malgieri G, 'R.I.P: Rest in privacy or rest in (quasi-)property? Personal data protection of deceased data subjects between theoretical scenarios and national solutions' in R Leenes, R van Brakel, S Gutwirth and P de Hert (eds), *Data Protection and Privacy: The Internet of Bodies* (Hart 2018).

Mann A, 'Comments from Facebook on the European Commission's proposal for a Regulation' *Github* (25 April 2012) <https://github.com/lobbyplag/lobbyplag-data/raw/master/raw/lobby-documents/Facebook.pdf> last accessed 1 August 2021.

Martin JC, 'Have you ever wondered what happens to your Facebook account after you have passed away?' *Silicon Valley Estate Planning Journal* (27 February 2015) <http://johncmartinlaw.com/ever-wondered-happens-facebook-account-pass-away/> last accessed 1 August 2021.

Matthews P, 'The French fiducie: And now for something completely different?' (2007) 21(1) *Trust Law International* 17.

May C, 'Between commodification and "openness": The information society and the ownership of knowledge' 2005 (2) *Journal of Information Law & Technology* <http://www2.warwick.ac.uk/fac/soc/law/elj/jilt/2005_2/may/> last accessed 1 August 2021.

Mayer-Schoenberger V and JR Crowley, 'Napster's second life? – The regulatory challenges of virtual worlds' (2006) 100 *Northwestern University Law Review* 1775.

Mazzone J, 'Facebook's afterlife' (2012) 90 *North Carolina Law Review* 67.

Meehan M, 'Virtual property: Protecting bits in context' (2006) 13 *Richmond Journal of Law and Technology* 1.

Mellows AR, *The Law of Succession* (4th edn, Butterworths 1983).

Merges RP, *Justifying Intellectual Property* (Harvard University Press 2011).

Merrill TW and HE Smith, 'The property/contract interface' (2001) 101(4) *Columbia Law Review* 773.
Microsoft, 'Accessing Outlook.com, OneDrive and other Microsoft services when someone has died' <https://support.microsoft.com/en-us/office/accessing-outlook-com-onedrive-and-other-microsoft-services-when-someone-has-died-ebbd2860-917e-4b39-9913-212362da6b2f?ui=en-us&rs=en-us&ad=us> last accessed 1 August 2021.
Microsoft, 'My family member died recently/is in coma, what do I need to do to access their Microsoft account?' (Ael_G. asked 15 March 2012) <http://answers.microsoft.com/en-us/outlook_com/forum/oaccount-omyinfo/my-family-member-died-recently-is-in-coma-what-do/308cedce-5444-4185-82e8-0623ecc1d3d6> last accessed 1 August 2021.
Microsoft, 'Services agreement, Outlook 3.1' <http://windows.microsoft.com/en-gb/windows-live/microsoft-services-agreement> last accessed 1 August 2021.
Mill JS, *On Liberty*, ed. G Himmelfarb (Penguin 1984).
Mill JS, *Principles of Political Economy* (8th edn, Longmans, Green, Reader and Dyer 1878).
Mill, JS and J Bentham, *Utilitarianism and Other Essays*, ed. A Ryan (Penguin Books 1987).
Miller D, 'Determining ownership in virtual worlds: Copyright and license agreements' (2003) 22 *Review of Litigation* 435.
Montville C, 'Reforming the law of proprietary information' (2007) 56 *Duke Law Journal* 1159.
Moon K, 'The nature of computer programs: tangible? Goods? Personal property? Intellectual property?' (2009) *European Intellectual Property Review* 396.
Moringiello JM, 'Towards a system of estates in virtual property' (2008) 1 *International Journal of Private Law* 3.
Morse T and M Birnhack, 'The posthumous privacy paradox: Privacy preferences and behavior regarding digital remains' (2020) *New Media and Society* 1.
Mossoff A, 'What is property? Putting the pieces back together' (2003) 45 *Arizona Law Review* 371.
Munzer SR (ed.), *New Essays in the Legal and Political Theory of Property* (Cambridge University Press 2001).
My Digital Executor <http://www.mydigitalexecutor.co.uk/the-solution-2/> last accessed 1 August 2021.
MyHeritage <https://www.myheritage.com/deep-nostalgia> last accessed 1 August 2021.
Nadkarni A and SG Hofmann, 'Why do people use Facebook?' (2012) 52 *Personality and Individual Differences* 243.
Naffine N, 'When does the legal person die? Jeremy Bentham and the "auto-icon"' (2000) *Australian Journal of Legal Philosophy* 25.
National Conference of Commissioners on Uniform State Laws, Drafting Committee on Fiduciary Access to Digital Assets, 'Fiduciary Access to Digital Assets Act' (15–16 February 2013 Drafting Committee Meeting) <http://www.uniformlaws.org/shared/docs/Fiduciary%20Access%20to%20Digital%20Assets/2013feb7_FADA_MtgDraft_Styled.pdf> last accessed 1 August 2021.
National Conference of Commissioners on Uniform State Laws, Drafting Committee on Fiduciary Access to Digital Assets, 'Fiduciary Access to Digital Assets Act' (22 October 2013) <http://www.uniformlaws.org/shared/docs/Fiduciary%20

Access%20to%20Digital%20Assets/2013nov_FADA_Mtg_Draft.pdf> last accessed 1 August 2021.

National Conference of Commissioners on Uniform State Laws, Drafting Committee on Fiduciary Access to Digital Assets, 'Fiduciary Access to Digital Assets Act' (July 2014) <http://www.uniformlaws.org/shared/docs/Fiduciary%20Access%20to%20Digital%20Assets/2014_UFADAA_Final.pdf> last accessed 1 August 2021.

Nelson JW, 'Fiber optic foxes: Virtual objects and virtual worlds through the lens of Pierson v Post and the law of capture' (2009) 14 *Journal of Technology Law & Policy* 5.

Nelson JW, 'The virtual property problem: What property rights in virtual resources might look like, how they might work, and why they are a bad idea' (2010) 41 *McGeorge Law Review* 281.

Nelson JW, 'A virtual property solution: How privacy law can protect the citizens of virtual worlds' (2011) 36 *Oklahoma City University Law Review* 395.

Netanel NW, 'Copyright alienability restrictions and the enhancement of author autonomy: A normative evaluation' (1993) 24 *Rutgers Law Journal* 347.

Nichol GR, 'Children of distant fathers: Sketching an ethos of constitutional liberty' (1985) *Wisconsin Law Review* 1305.

Nicholas B, *The French Law of Contract* (2nd edn, Clarendon Press; Oxford University Press 1992).

Nicholas K, 'Welfare propositions in economics and interpersonal comparisons of utility' (1939) *Economic Journal* 49.

Nimmer RT and PA Krauthaus, 'Information as a commodity: New imperatives of commercial law' (1992) 55 *Law and Contemporary Problems* 103.

Norberg PA and DR Horne, 'The privacy paradox: Personal information disclosure intentions versus behaviors' 41(1) (2007) *Journal of Consumer Affairs* 100.

Notopoulos K, 'How almost anyone can take you off Facebook (and lock you out)' *BuzzFeed* (4 January 2014) <http://www.buzzfeed.com/katienotopoulos/how-to-murder-your-friends-on-facebook-in-2-easy-s#.xbLyLygo2> last accessed 1 August 2021.

Nozick R, *Anarchy, State and Utopia* (Basil Blackwell 1974).

OECD, 'Participative web: User-generated-content' DSTI/ICCP/IE(2006)7/FINAL (12 April 2007) <http://www.oecd.org/sti/38393115.pdf> last accessed 1 August 2021.

Office for National Statistics, 'Internet access – households and individuals, Great Britain: 2020' (7 August 2020) <https://www.ons.gov.uk/peoplepopulationandcommunity/householdcharacteristics/homeinternetandsocialmediausage/bulletins/internetaccesshouseholdsandindividuals/2020> last accessed 1 August 2021.

Office of the Canadian Privacy Commissioner, *Report of Findings into the Complaint Filed by the Canadian Internet Policy and Public Interest Clinic (CIPPIC) against Facebook Inc., under the Personal Information Protection and Electronic Documents Act* (16 July 2009) <https://www.priv.gc.ca/cf-dc/2009/2009_008_0716_e.asp> last accessed 1 August 2021.

Öhman C and L Floridi, 'The political economy of death in the age of information: A critical approach to the digital afterlife industry' (2017) 27 *Minds & Machines* 639.

Öhman C and L Watson, 'Are the dead taking over Facebook? A big data approach to the future of death online' (2019) *Big Data & Society* 1.
Oppenheimer MS, 'Cybertrash' (2011–12) 90 *Oregon Law Review* 1.
Ortiz DR, 'Privacy, autonomy, and consent' (1988) 12 *Harvard Journal of Law and Public Policy* 21.
Oxford English Dictionary (*OED*) (online edn, Oxford University Press 2013) <http://www.oed.com/>.
Pace CJR, 'The case for a federal Trade Secrets Act' (1995) 8 *Harvard Journal of Law and Technology* 427.
Palmer N and E McKendrick (eds), *Interests in Goods* (Lloyd's of London Press 1993).
Password Box, 'Legacy Locker' (now True Key) <https://www.passwordbox.com/legacylocker> last accessed 1 August 2021.
Penner JE, 'The "bundle of rights" picture of property' (1996) 43 *UCLA Law Review* 711.
Penner JE, *The Idea of Property in Law* (Oxford University Press 1997).
Pennington N, 'You don't de-friend the dead: An analysis of grief communication by college students through Facebook profiles' (2013) 37 *Death Studies* 617.
Pennock JR and JW Chapman (eds), *Property* (New York University Press 1980).
Peredes TA, 'Blinded by the light: Information overload and its consequences for securities regulation' (2003) 81(25) *Washington University Law Quarterly* 417.
Perrone M, 'What happens when we die: Estate planning of digital assets' (2012/13) 21 *CommLaw Conspectus* 185.
Peterson GR, 'Trade secrets in an information age' (1995) 32 *Houston Law Review* 385.
Peterson J, 'Lockean property and literary works' (2008) 14(4) *Legal Theory* 257.
Pew Research Center, 'Social media use by age group over time' <http://www.pewinternet.org/data-trend/social-media/social-media-use-by-age-group/> last accessed 1 August 2021.
Pew Research Center, 'Social media use over time' <http://www.pewinternet.org/data-trend/social-media/social-media-use-all-users/> last accessed 1 August 2021.
Pew Research Center, 'Social networking fact sheet' <http://www.pewinternet.org/fact-sheets/social-networking-fact-sheet/> last accessed 1 August 2021.
Pistorius T, 'Click-wrap and web-wrap agreements' (2004) 16 *SA Mercantile Law Journal* 568.
Pollitzer B, 'Serious business: When virtual items gain real world value' (10 October 2009) <http://ssrn.com/abstract=1090048> last accessed 1 August 2021.
Posner RA, 'Privacy, surveillance, and law' (2008) 75 *University of Chicago Law Review* 245.
Post RC, 'The social foundations of privacy: Community and self in the common law tort' (1989) 77 *California Law Review* 957.
Pound R, 'The law of property and recent juristic thought' (1939) 25 *ABA Journal* 993.
Price C and A DiSclafani, 'Remembering our loved ones' *Facebook Newsroom* (21 February 2014) <http://newsroom.fb.com/news/2014/02/remembering-our-loved-ones/> last accessed 1 August 2021.
Purcell K, 'Search and email still top the list of most popular online activities' *Pew Research Internet Project* (9 August 2011) <http://www.pewinternet.

org/2011/08/09/search-and-email-still-top-the-list-of-most-popular-online-activities/> last accessed 1 August 2021.
Quach K, 'A developer built an AI chatbot using GPT-3 that helped a man speak again to his late fiancée. OpenAI shut it down' *The Register* (8 September 2021) <https://www.theregister.com/2021/09/08/project_december_openai_gpt_3/> last accessed 8 September 2021.
Quinn PJ, 'A click too far: The difficulty in using adhesive American law license agreements to govern global virtual worlds' (2010) 27 *Wisconsin International Law Journal* 757.
Rackspace Hosting, 'Generation cloud: A social study into the impact of cloud-based services on everyday UK life' (16 November 2011) <http://www.rackspace.co.uk/sites/default/files/whitepapers/generation_cloud.pdf> last accessed 1 August 2021.
Radicati S and J Levenstein, 'Email market, 20, 2013–2017' *The Radicati Group* (November 2013) <http://www.radicati.com/wp/wp-content/uploads/2013/11/Email-Market-2013-2017-Executive-Summary.pdf> last accessed 1 August 2021.
Radin MJ, 'Property and personhood' (1982) 34 *Stanford Law Review* 957.
Raff MJ, *Private Property and Environmental Responsibility: A Comparative Study of German Real Property Law* (Kluwer Law International 2003).
Rahmatian A, 'Copyright and commodification' (2005) 27(10) *European Intellectual Property Review* 371.
Rahmatian A, 'Originality in UK copyright law: The old "skill and labour" doctrine under pressure' (2013) 44(4) *International Review of Intellectual Property and Competition Law* 4.
Randall S, 'Judicial attitudes toward arbitration and the resurgence of unconscionability' (2004) 52 *Buffalo Law Review* 185.
Rao R, 'Property, privacy, and the human body' (2000) 80 *Boston University Law Review* 359.
Rappaport AJ, 'Beyond personhood and autonomy: Moral theory and the premises of privacy' (2001) *Utah Law Review* 441.
Ratiu F, 'People you may know' *Facebook Blog* (2 May 2008) <http://blog.facebook.com/blog.php?post=15610312130> last accessed 1 August 2021.
Raz J, *The Morality of Freedom* (Clarendon Press 1986).
Reahard J, 'Linden Lab's Second Life "extremely profitable" company looking to expand' *Massively by Joystiq* (2012) <http://massively.joystiq.com/2012/03/15/linden-labs-second-life-extremely-profitable-company-looking/> last accessed 1 August 2021.
Regan P, *Legislating Privacy: Technology, Social Values, and Public Policy* (University of North Carolina Press 1995).
Reich C, 'The new property' (1964) 73 *Yale Law Journal* 733.
Reid KGC, 'Obligations and property: Exploring the border' (1997) *Acta Juridica* 225.
Reid KGC, MJ de Waal and R Zimmermann (eds), *Exploring the Law of Succession: Studies National, Historical and Comparative* (Edinburgh University Press 2007).
Reimann M and R Zimmermann (eds), *The Oxford Handbook of Comparative Law* (Oxford University Press 2006).

Reuters, 'Sweden first to open embassy in Second Life' (2007) <http://www.reuters.com/article/2007/05/30/us-sweden-secondlife-idUSL3034889320070530> last accessed 1 August 2021.
Reverte M, 'QG Second Life d' Hillary Clinton' *YouTube* (5 June 2008) <http://www.youtube.com/watch?v=_iCyRL1Bp-Y> last accessed 1 August 2021.
Rex F, 'LambdaMOO: An introduction' *LambdaMOO* <http://www.lambdamoo.info> last accessed 1 August 2021.
Rigamonti P, 'The conceptual transformation of moral rights' (2007) 55 *American Journal of Comparative Law* 67.
Riley P, 'Litigating Second Life land disputes: A consumer protection approach' (2009) 19(3) *Fordham Intellectual Property, Media and Entertainment Law Journal* 877.
Risch M, 'Why do we have trade secrets?' (2007) 11 *Marquette Intellectual Property Law Review* 1.
Rogers J, 'A passive approach to regulation of virtual worlds' (2008) 76 *George Washington Law Review* 405.
Roncallo-Dow S et al., 'Authorship in virtual worlds: Author's death to rights revival?' (2013) 6(3) *Journal of Virtual Worlds Research* 1.
Rose M, 'Nine-tenths of the law: The English copyright debates and the rhetoric of the public domain' (2003) 66 *Law and Contemporary Problems* 75.
Rose-Ackerman S, 'Inalienability and the theory of property rights' (1985) 85 *Columbia Law Review* 931.
Rosen J, *The Unwanted Gaze: The Destruction of Privacy in America* (Vintage 2001).
Rosler H, 'Dignitarian posthumous personality rights – an analysis of US and German constitutional and tort law' (2008) 26 *Berkeley Journal of International Law* 153.
Ryan A, *Property* (Open University Press 1987).
Ryan ML, 'Immersion vs. interactivity: Virtual reality and literary theory' (1999) (28)2 *SubStance* 110.
Safranek JP and S Safranek, 'Can the right to autonomy be resuscitated after Glucksberg?' (1998) 69 *University of Colorado Law Review* 737.
Sagar L, *The Digital Estate (Wills and Probate)* (Sweet & Maxwell 2018).
Samuel GH, '"Le droit subjectif" and English law' (1987) 46(2) *Cambridge Law Journal* 264.
Samuel GH, *Understanding Contractual and Tortious Obligations* (Law Matters 2005).
Samuel GH and J Rinkes, *Law of Obligations and Legal Remedies* (2nd edn, Cavendish 2001).
Samuelson P, 'Originality standard for literary works under U.S. copyright law' (2001–2) 42 *American Journal of Comparative Law* Supplement 393.
Samuelson P, 'Privacy as intellectual property?' (1999) 52 *Stanford Law Review* 1125.
Samuelson P, 'Should economics play a role in copyright law and policy?' (2003–4) 1 *University of Ottawa Law & Technology Journal* 1.
Sancya B, 'Yahoo will give family slain Marine's e-mail account' *USA Today* (21 April 2005) <http://usatoday30.usatoday.com/tech/news/2005-04-21-marine-e-mail_x.htm?POE=TECISVA> last accessed 1 August 2021.
Schafer B, 'On living and undead wills: ZombAIs, technology and the future of inheritance law' in L Edwards, B Schafer and E Harbinja (eds), *Future Law: Emerging Technology, Regulation and Ethics* (Edinburgh University Press 2020).

Schlatter R, *Private Property: The History of an Idea* (Allen & Unwin 1951).

Schneewind JB, *The Invention of Autonomy: A History of Modern Moral Philosophy* (Cambridge University Press 1998).

Schofield J, 'What happens to your Facebook account when you die?' *Guardian* (30 October 2014) <http://www.theguardian.com/technology/askjack/2014/oct/30/what-happens-to-your-facebook-account-when-you-or-a-loved-one-dies> last accessed 1 August 2021.

Schramm M, 'Man buys virtual space station for 330k real dollars' *Joystiq* (2010) <http://www.joystiq.com/2010/01/02/man-buys-virtual-space-station-for-330k-real-dollars/> last accessed 1 August 2021.

Schwartz PM, 'Privacy and democracy in cyberspace' (1999) 52 *Vanderbilt Law Review* 1609.

Schwartz PM, 'Property, privacy, and personal data' (2003) 117 *Harvard Law Review* 2056.

Sease EJ, 'Misappropriation is seventy-five years old; should we bury it or revive it?' (1994) 70 *North Dakota Law Review* 781.

SecureSafe, 'Questions about data inheritance' <http://www.securesafe.com/en/faq/inheritance/> last accessed 1 August 2021.

Shen C, P Monge and D Williams, 'The evolving virtual relationships: A longitudinal analysis of player social networks in a large MMOG' (2011) <http://dx.doi.org/10.2139/ssrn.1929908> last accessed 1 August 2021.

Shen J et al., 'A comparison study of user behavior on Facebook and Gmail' (2013) 29 *Computers in Human Behavior* 2650.

Sherry K, 'What happens to our Facebook accounts when we die?: Probate versus policy and the fate of social-media assets postmortem' (2013) 40(1) *Pepperdine Law Review* 185.

Shiffrin SV, 'The incentives argument for intellectual property protection' (2009) 4 *Journal of Law, Philosophy and Culture* 49.

Shikowitz R, 'License to kill: MDY v Blizzard and the battle over copyright in World of Warcraft' (2009–10) 75 *Brooklyn Law Review* 1015.

Shirky C, 'Social software and the politics of groups' *Networks, Economy, & Culture Mailing List* (9 March 2009) <http://www.shirky.com/writings/group_politics.html> last accessed 1 August 2021.

Simes L, *Public Policy and the Dead Hand* (University of Michigan Law School 1955).

Simpson MP, 'Trade secrets, property rights, and protectionism – an age-old tale' (2005) 70 *Brooklyn Law Review* 1121.

Slaughter J, 'Virtual worlds: Between contract and property' (2008) 62 *Yale Student Scholarship Papers* <http://digitalcommons.law.yale.edu/student_papers/62> last accessed 1 August 2021.

Smith RM, 'The constitution and autonomy' (1982) 60 *Texas Law Review* 175.

Sofka C, A Gibson and D Silberman 'Digital immortality or digital death? Contemplating digital end of life planning' in MH Jacobsen (ed.), Postmortal Society: Towards a Sociology of Immortality (Routledge 2017).

Solove DJ, '"I've got nothing to hide" and other misunderstandings of privacy' (2007) *San Diego Law Review* 744.

Solove DJ, *Understanding Privacy* (Harvard University Press 2008).

Spiekermann S, J Grossklags and B Berendt, 'E-privacy in 2nd generation e-commerce: Privacy preferences versus actual behavior' in *Proceedings of the 3rd ACM*

Conference on Electronic Commerce, Tampa Bay, Florida, 14–17 October 2001 <https://www.dl.acm.org/doi/10.1145/501158.501163> last accessed 1 August 2021.

Statista, 'Experience of and interest in online content creation in the United Kingdom (UK) in 2012' <http://www.statista.com/statistics/271826/online-content-creation-experience-and-interest-of-respondents-in-the-uk/> last accessed 1 August 2021.

Statista, 'Most popular social networks worldwide as of April 2021, ranked by number of active users' <https://www.statista.com/statistics/272014/global-social-networks-ranked-by-number-of-users/> last accessed 1 August 2021.

Statista, 'Number of peak concurrent Steam users 2013–2021' <https://www.statista.com/statistics/308330/number-stream-users/#:~:text=Steam%20had%20approximately%20120%20million,monthly%20active%20users%20in%202019> last accessed 1 August 2021.

Statista, 'Popular digital activities among Internet users in the United States 2019' <https://www.statista.com/statistics/184559/typical-daily-online-activities-of-adult-internet-users-in-the-us/> last accessed 1 August 2021.

Statista, 'Social media in Asia Pacific – statistics & facts' (8 June 2021) <https://www.statista.com/topics/6606/social-media-in-asia-pacific/#:~:text=The%20favored%20social%20media%20app,prominent%20mark%20on%20the%20industry> last accessed 1 August 2021.

Statista, 'World of Warcraft estimated subscribers from 2015 to 2030' <https://www.statista.com/statistics/276601/number-of-world-of-warcraft-subscribers-by-quarter/> last accessed 1 August 2021.

Steam, 'Steam & game stats' (2014) <http://store.steampowered.com/stats/> last accessed 1 August 2021.

Steam, 'Subscriber agreement' <http://store.steampowered.com/subscriber_agreement/> last accessed 1 August 2021.

Steinberg AB, 'For sale – one level 5 barbarian for 94,800 won: The international effects of virtual property and the legality of its ownership' (2009) 37 *Georgia Journal of International and Comparative Law* 381.

Steiner E, *French Law: A Comparative Approach* (Oxford University Press 2010).

STEP, 'About us' <http://www.step.org/about-us> last accessed 1 August 2021.

STEP, Digital assets: Practitioner's guide, England and Wales' (2020) <https://www.step.org/system/files/media/files/2020-03/Digital%20Assets%20Practitioner%20Guide%20-%20England%20&%20Wales.pdf> last accessed 1 August 2021.

Strahilievitz LJ, 'The right to destroy' (2005) 114 *Yale Law Journal* 781.

Suzor N, 'The role of the rule of law in virtual communities' (2010) 25 *Berkeley Technology Law Journal* 1817.

Sweetser P and P Wyeth, 'GameFlow: A model for evaluating player enjoyment in games' (2005) 3(3) *ACM Computers in Entertainment* article 3A <http://www.itee.uq.edu.au/~penny/_papers/Sweetser-CIE.pdf> last accessed 1 August 2021.

Tarney TG, 'A call for legislation to permit the transfer of digital assets at death' (2012) 40 *Capital University Law Review* 773.

Terdiman D, 'Curious case of lawsuit over value of Twitter is settled' *CNET News* (3 December 2012) <http://news.cnet.com/8301-1023_3-57556918-93/

curious-case-of-lawsuit-over-value-of-twitter-followers-is-settled/> last accessed 1 August 2021.

Terdiman D, 'Tech titans seek virtual-world interoperability' *CNET News* (15 October 2007) <http://news.cnet.com/Tech-titans-seek-virtual-world-interoperability/2100-1043_3-6213148.html> last accessed 1 August 2021.

Thomas DA, 'Anglo-American land law: Diverging developments from a shared history – part III: British and American real property law and practice – a contemporary comparison' (1999–2000) 34 *Real Property, Probate and Trust Journal* 443.

TotalSubs, MMOData.net <http://users.telenet.be/mmodata/Charts/TotalSubs.png> last accessed 1 August 2021.

Troy D, 'The truth about email: What's a normal inbox?' *Pando Daily* (5 April 2013) <http://pando.com/2013/04/05/the-truth-about-email-whats-a-normal-inbox/> last accessed 1 August 2021.

Truong OY, 'Virtual inheritance: Assigning more virtual property rights' (2009) 21(3) *Syracuse Science and Technology Law Reporter* 57.

Tully J, *A Discourse on Property: John Locke and His Adversaries* (Cambridge University Press 1980).

Tur R, 'The "person" in law' in A Peacocke and G Gillett (eds), *Persons and Personality: A Contemporary Inquiry* (Basil Blackwell 1987).

Turner AE, *The Law of Trade Secrets* (Sweet & Maxwell 1962).

Turner AE, 'Nature of trade secrets and their protection' (1928) 42 *Harvard Law Review* 254.

Turner Hopkins, 'Report for Ofcom: The value of user-generated content' *OFCOM* (21 June 2012) <http://stakeholders.ofcom.org.uk/binaries/research/research-publications/content.pdf> last accessed 1 August 2021.

Twitter, 'About public and protected Tweets' <https://support.twitter.com/articles/14016> last accessed 1 August 2021.

Twitter, 'About Twitter' <https://about.twitter.com/company> last accessed 1 August 2021.

Twitter, 'Contacting Twitter about a deceased user or media concerning a deceased family member' <https://support.twitter.com/groups/56-policies-violations/topics/238-report-a-violation/articles/87894-contacting-twitter-about-a-deceased-user-or-media-concerning-a-deceased-family-member> last accessed 1 August 2021.

Twitter, 'Impersonation policy' <https://help.twitter.com/en/rules-and-policies/twitter-impersonation-policy> last accessed 1 August 2021.

Twitter, 'Inactive account policy' <https://support.twitter.com/groups/56-policies-violations/topics/236-twitter-rules-policies/articles/15362-inactive-account-policy> last accessed 1 August 2021.

Twitter, 'Policies and violations' <https://support.twitter.com/groups/56-policies-violations#topic_237> last accessed 1 August 2021.

Twitter, 'Privacy policy' <https://twitter.com/privacy> last accessed 1 August 2021.

Twitter, 'Terms of service' <https://twitter.com/tos> last accessed 1 August 2021.

US Copyright Office, Circular 34, 'Copyright protection not available for names, titles, or short phrases' (reviewed January 2012) <http://copyright.gov/circs/circ34.pdf> last accessed 1 August 2021.

Vacca R, 'Viewing virtual property ownership through the lens of innovation' (2008) 76 *Tennessee Law Review* 33.

van der Merwe C and AL Verbeke (eds), *Time Limited Interests in Land* (Cambridge University Press 2012).

van der Walt AJ, *Constitutional Property Clauses: A Comparative Analysis* (Kluwer Law International 1999).

Vandevelde KJ, 'The new property of the nineteenth century: The development of the modern concept of property' (1980) *Buffalo Law Review* 29.

Van Vleck T, 'The history of electronic mail' (1 February 2010) <http://www.multicians.org/thvv/mail-history.html> last accessed 1 August 2021.

Veloso III MG, 'Virtual property rights: A modified usufruct of intangibles' (2010) 4 *Philippine Law Journal* 82.

Virtual World Interoperability <http://Virtual Worldinterop.wikidot.com/start> last accessed 1 August 2021.

Wagner J, 'Au to new world the election comes to Second Life! Posting of notes' *Second Life Blog* (2004) <http://secondlife.blogs.com/nwn/2004/04/theelectionco.html> last accessed 1 August 2021.

Wagner K, 'Facebook will make "Look Back" videos for deceased users' *Mashable* (21 February 2014) <http://mashable.com/2014/02/21/facebook-look-back-video-deceased/> last accessed 1 August 2021.

Waisman A, 'Revisiting originality' (2009) 31(7) *European Intellectual Property Review* 370.

Waldron J, *The Right to Private Property* (Clarendon Press 1990).

Ward B et al., 'Electronic discovery: Rules for a digital age' (2012) 18 *Boston University Journal of Science and Technology Law* 150.

Watson A, *Legal Transplants: An Approach to Comparative Law* (Scottish Academic Press 1974).

Wawro A, 'Steam now has over 75 million active accounts' *Gamasutra* (2014) <http://www.gamasutra.com/view/news/208667/Steam_now_has_over_75_million_active_accounts.php> last accessed 1 August 2021.

Webpage FX Blog, 'What happens to your online presence when you die? [Infographic]' <http://www.webpagefx.com/blog/internet/happens-online-presence-die-infographic/> last accessed 1 August 2021.

Webster A, 'Steam user violates subscriber agreement, loses $1,800 in games' *Ars Technica* (2011) <http://arstechnica.com/gaming/2011/03/steam-user-violates-subscriber-agreement-loses-1800-in-games/> last accessed 1 August 2021.

Weimer DL and AR Vining, *Policy Analysis* (5th edn, Longman 2011).

Weinreb N, 'Copyright for functional expression' (1998) 111 *Harvard Law Review* 1149.

Welch C, 'Twitter halts plan to remove inactive accounts until it can memorialize dead users' *The Verge* (27 November 2019) <https://www.theverge.com/2019/11/27/20986084/twitter-inactive-accounts-usernames-memorialize-deceased-users-not-removing> last accessed 1 August 2021.

Welch C, 'Twitter will remove inactive accounts and free up usernames in December' *The Verge* (26 November 2019) <https://www.theverge.com/2019/11/26/20984328/twitter-removing-inactive-accounts-usernames-available-date> last accessed 1 August 2021.

Wellman B et al., 'Does the Internet increase, decrease, or supplement social capital? Social networks, participation, and community commitment' (2001) 45(3) *American Behavioral Scientist* 436.

Wertheim M, 'Virtual camp trains soldiers in Arabic, and more' *New York Times* (6 July 2004) <http://www.nytimes.com/2004/07/06/science/virtual-camp-trains-soldiers-in-arabic-and-more.html?pagewanted=all&src=pm> last accessed 1 August 2021.

Westbrook TJ, 'Owned: Finding a place for virtual world property rights' (2006) *Michigan State Law Review* 779.

White E, 'The Berne Convention's flexible fixation requirement: A problematic provision for user-generated content' (2012–13) 13 *Chicago Journal of International Law* 685.

Whittaker S, 'Personal information management: From information consumption to curation' (2011) 45(1) *Annual Review of Information Science and Technology* 1.

Williams D, T Kennedy and R Moore, 'Behind the avatar: The patterns, practices and functions of role playing in MMOs' (2011) *Games & Culture* 171.

Williams TC, 'Property, things in action and copyright' (1895) 11 *Law Quarterly Review* 223.

Wood O and GL Certoma, *Hutley, Woodman and Wood Succession: Commentary and Materials* (4th edn, Law Book Co 1990).

Wu S, 'Digital afterlife: What happens to your data when you die?' (2013) <http://dataedge.ischool.berkeley.edu/2013/pdf/digital-afterlife-white-paper.pdf> last accessed 1 August 2021.

Yahoo!, 'Options available when a Yahoo account owner passes away' <https://help.yahoo.com/kb/mobile/SLN9112.html?impressions=true> last accessed 1 August 2021.

Yahoo!, 'Terms of service' <https://info.yahoo.com/legal/eu/yahoo/utos/en-gb/> last accessed 1 August 2021.

Yoon U, 'South Korea and indirect reliance on IP law: Real money trading in MMORPG items' (2008) 3(3) *Journal of Intellectual Property Law and Practice* 174.

Zemer L, 'On the value of copyright theory' (2006) *Intellectual Property Quarterly* 1.

Zimmermann R, D Visser and K Reid (eds), *Mixed Systems in Comparative Perspective* (Oxford 2004).

Zuckerberg M, Facebook post, *Facebook* (25 March at 22:30) <https://www.facebook.com/zuck/posts/10101319050523971> last accessed 1 August 2021.

Index